WHAT YOUR COLLEAGUES ARE SAYING . . .

If I were in charge of the world, every school would have a required media studies course, and every faculty would do a book study around *Fighting Fake News*. This book is an essential tool in helping students to be more consciously aware, reflective, and rational about the waves of news and other forms of "angertainment." I lost count of how many times I said, "Yes!" while reading this book.

—Kelly Gallagher
Teacher, Author, and Consultant

Fighting Fake News is a must-read for every teacher. I plan to read it and reread it because I know each time, I will be able to glean better information. I would love to have the opportunity to see this kind of instruction put into place.

—Lydia Bagley
Instructional Support Specialist, Cobb County School District

Talk about timely! *Fighting Fake News* begins by describing the cognitive short-cuts we all (not just the fringe) are prone to—how we so easily fit information to pre-existing biases. The authors show how digital media exploit this tendency by directing us to sources that feed these prejudices. And they provide carefully crafted lessons to promote critical analysis and thoughtful citizenship. It's the book we need now.

—Thomas Newkirk
Professor Emeritus at the University of New Hampshire

The authors have provided a timely and important analysis of the problem of fake news and how teachers can help students become more critical readers in a digital world. Drawing from their years of research into teaching reading and argument, the authors make the turn to digital texts with the same passion and commitment to developing students' literacies that they bring to all their work. *Fighting Fake News* is clearly organized, providing a wealth of practical lessons for teachers to adapt.

—Kristen Turner
Professor of Teacher Education and Program Director, Drew University

Fighting Fake News

For our students and our students' students, living in tumultuous times.
We wrote this book for you.

Fighting Fake News

Teaching Students to Identify and Interrogate Information Pollution

Jeffrey D. Wilhelm

Michael W. Smith

Hugh Kesson

Deborah Appleman

CORWIN Literacy

FOR INFORMATION:

Corwin

A SAGE Company

2455 Teller Road

Thousand Oaks, California 91320

(800) 233-9936

www.corwin.com

SAGE Publications Ltd.

1 Oliver's Yard

55 City Road

London EC1Y 1SP

United Kingdom

SAGE Publications India Pvt. Ltd.

B 1/I 1 Mohan Cooperative Industrial Area

Mathura Road, New Delhi 110 044

India

SAGE Publications Asia-Pacific Pte. Ltd.

18 Cross Street #10-10/11/12

China Square Central

Singapore 048423

Printed in the United States of America

ISBN 9781071854655

President: Mike Soules

Vice President and
   Editorial Director: Monica Eckman

Director and Publisher,
   Corwin Classroom: Lisa Luedeke

Associate Content
   Development Editor: Sarah Ross

Production Editor: Melanie Birdsall

Copy Editor: Deanna Noga

Typesetter: C&M Digitals (P) Ltd.

Proofreader: Chris Dahlin

Indexer: Sheila Hill

Cover Designer: Candice Harman

Marketing Manager: Megan Naidl

This book is printed on acid-free paper.

23 24 25 26 27 10 9 8 7 6 5 4 3 2 1

Contents

Visit the companion website at
resources.corwin.com/fightingfakenews
for downloadable resources.

Guide to Lessons

CHAPTER 3: LESSONS FOR GETTING STARTED: KNOWING YOUR OWN MIND

Lesson 3.1: Finding Good Information, Evaluating It, and Verifying It. This lesson is designed to build habits for finding good information, verifying strong and safe evidence through lateral reading, evaluating data patterns, and mindfully justifying interpretations of these patterns. (p. 46)

Lesson 3.2: Ranking and Evaluating Evidence. This lesson provides deliberate practice with evidentiary reasoning because students must explain how any example fits the criteria better or (not) and asks them to consciously "choose to believe or disbelieve." (p. 50)

Lesson 3.3: Learning With a Beginner's Mind. In this lesson, students learn how to open their minds and actively seek out different perspectives while confirming and disconfirming information so that we openly see the breadth of reasonable alternate positions in conversations about different topics. (p. 57)

Lesson 3.4: Actively Seeking Out Alternative Positions. By developing understanding of the Default Mode System of the brain, this lesson helps students look for counterclaims, new perspectives, and disconfirming evidence relative to their own usual viewpoints. (p. 60)

Lesson 3.5: Trigger Tracking and Fever Charts. This lesson utilizes Fever Charts as a tool for us to become aware of, and then control, our cognitive biases. (p. 63)

Lesson 3.6: Monitoring Mind Misdirection. This lesson examines optical illusions and misdirection texts to help us see how our brain can misperceive due to cognitive biases like confirmation or availability bias. It helps learners understand what happens when they read and how to promote more mindful and powerful reading.

Lesson 3.7: "Noticing and Naming" Practice for Controlling Cognitive Biases. This lesson concentrates on understanding and recognizing three of the most common cognitive biases: availability, confirmation, and overdramatization biases. (p. 71)

Lesson 3.8: Self-Study of Social Media Use. In this lesson, learners monitor their own social media use and explore how we are all being manipulated through cognitive bias. (p. 83)

CHAPTER 4: LESSONS USING RULES OF NOTICE IN ONLINE READING

CHAPTER 5: LESSONS FOR TEACHING POINT OF VIEW IN DIGITAL MEDIA

Social Media Extension: The social media extension asks students develop criteria for the reliability of posts on issues that matter to them. (p. 163)

CHAPTER 6: LESSONS FOR EXAMINING NEWS, NONFICTION, AND DIGITAL TEXTS THROUGH LITERARY LENSES

Lesson 6.1: Fake News and Fairy Tales. This lesson uses *The True Story of the Three Little Pigs* to illustrate how the teller of the tale determines what the "true" story is. (p. 173)

Lesson 6.2: A Not-So-Modest Proposal. This lesson uses the classic text by Jonathan Swift, "A Modest Proposal," to demonstrate how to look at a text from a variety of critical perspectives, each yielding a different reading. (p. 176)

Lesson 6.3: Barack Obama: In the Running? This lesson centers on a real fake news article that claimed Barack Obama was running for president of Kenya. Students will use a variety of lenses to excavate the ideology behind the fake claims. (p. 178)

Lesson 6.4: A Theory Relay. In small groups, students will encounter five different fake news websites. Armed with theory cards, they will use different theoretical perspectives to consider the motivations behind each of the websites. (p. 181)

Lesson 6.5: How to Tell a True War Story: Tim O'Brien and Ukraine. This lesson begins with a discussion of the difference between fact and fiction as animated in Tim O'Brien's classic story, "How to Tell a True War Story" from *The Things They Carried*. We then look at news dispatches from different sources covering the war in Ukraine and discuss the degree to which fact and fiction are intermingled. (p. 185)

CHAPTER 7: LESSONS FOR TEACHING STUDENTS TO EVALUATE EVIDENCE AND RESEARCH

Lesson 7.1: Thinking About Evidence in Text-Based Arguments. This lesson focuses on having students write about the extent to which Atticus Finch is a role model and in doing so evaluating evidence from both within and outside the text. (p. 203)

Social Media Extension: This asks students to examine and evaluate responses to *To Kill a Mockingbird* on Twitter and Facebook. (p. 206)

Lesson 7.2: Thinking About Evidence in Topical Issues. This lesson focuses on preparing students to write an argument about the impact of social media on youth by evaluating the way that research is presented in digital sources. (p. 212)

Social Media Extension: This asks students to evaluate the research presented on a tweet endorsing a personal care product. (p. 221)

Acknowledgments

We'd like to thank all the folks at Corwin who helped in the production of the book and who will help in its marketing: Deanna Noga, Melanie Birdsall, and Megan Naidl. A special shout-out to our friend and editor Lisa Luedeke for her encouragement and unwavering support.

Jeff wants to thank his daughter Jasmine Wilhelm for trying out many of the ideas in this book and for providing helpful insights based on units of study she created on dealing with information pollution (you can see one of these units in our online resources for this book). Jeff also thanks the many Boise State Writing Project fellows who helped him think about many of the ideas explored here and for implementing many of the assignments, reflecting, and reporting back. Special thanks to Jamie Nolevanko and Jackie Miller in this regard. Thanks, too, to Ben Brunwin and Bob Moy for their guidance in our thinking about how to experience and understand what happens when we read and when we are misdirected by text. Thanks and a twenty-one gun salute to all the Boise State Writing Project fellows with whom Jeff has had the pleasure to teach, learn, and engage in thinking partnerships over the past 20 years.

Michael and Hugh thank the late Jay Imbrenda for all he taught us about teaching, Kristen Turner for her insightful suggestions, and the teachers and students of the Pathway Project, whom we cannot identify by name because of confidentiality agreements but who contributed so much to the work we report here. We'd also like to thank Chris Bruner, Dave Burkavage, Devin Cahill, Darin Hardy, Mike Shields, and all their colleagues at Ernst & Young for the financial support that made that work possible.

Michael also would like to thank his research assistant Jessica Hadid for helping him clarify his ideas on teaching argument and his colleagues Tim Patterson, Janelle Bailey, and Doug Lombardi for their help in thinking about how academic argument plays out across disciplines. As always, Michael thanks his wife, Karen Flynn, for her support. His granddaughter Gabrielle White and his daughter Rachel Smith have served as patient ambassadors to the digital world. Thanks to both.

In addition to his coauthors, especially Michael who also served as his dissertation advisor, Hugh would like to thank Katherine Fry and everyone in Brooklyn College's Media Studies program, as well as the late DC Vito and everyone at

TheLAMPNYC. He could not have written this book without the support of Anna, Augie, Ren, and his mum and dad, who always encouraged him to write.

Deborah would like first and foremost to thank her coauthors—Jeff, Michael, and Hugh—who were unfailingly patient with her multitasking during the writing of this book. She'd also like to acknowledge Dr. Sam Wineburg for his groundbreaking work on adolescents and fake news. His work inspired us. Finally, she thanks her husband, John Schmit, for his support and for all the ongoing conversations about teaching and learning.

Corwin gratefully acknowledges the contributions of the following reviewers:

Lynn M. Angus Ramos
Curriculum Coordinator, DeKalb County School District
Decatur, GA

Lydia Bagley
Instructional Support Specialist, Cobb County School District
Marietta, GA

Melissa Black
Teacher, District of Columbia Public Schools
Washington, DC

Lydia Bowden
Assistant Principal, Berkmar High School
Lilburn, GA

Tiffany Coleman
Literacy Professor, Gwinnett County
Loganville, GA

Carmen Gordillo
Language Arts Teacher and Part-Time Lecturer, Rutgers University
Toms River, NJ

Christina Nosek
Teacher and Consultant, Lucille Nixon School
Mountain View, CA

iStock.com/Arkadiusz Warguła

PART I

So Much at Stake

NOTES

CHAPTER 1

The Case for Teaching Critical Reading and Fighting Fake News

"If people don't have the facts, democracy doesn't work."

—Federal Judge Amy Berman Jackson

"It is always easy to question the judgment of others in matters of which we may be imperfectly informed."

—P. D. James

"Anyone who can make you believe absurdities can make you commit atrocities."

—Voltaire

Recent events and their aftermaths have made us even more committed and devoted to the project of this book. As we prepare it now for publication, we are roiled by the wake of the 2020 election and the Capitol riot on January 6, 2021, the Congressional investigation into it, the Facebook files and whistleblower, the continuing misinformation of various kinds about vaccinations and public health policy as COVID and its variants evolve, fake Twitter accounts, mal-information from Russia regarding the war in Ukraine, and the ongoing use of information pollution by various parties across the political spectrum in relation to issues that profoundly impact American lives, social policy, education, and—we'd contend—the future of democracy.

False and distorted "news" material can't really be said to be anything like a new thing. This kind of subterfuge has been a part of media history long before the advent of social media. It's what makes us pause in the grocery line to look at tabloid headlines from *The National Enquirer, Us, The Sun, In Touch,* and many others. On the internet, headline forms that are called *clickbait* tempt and tease us to read more, yanking our proverbial interest chains through surprise, shock, and awe. From the fake news ("Remember the Maine!") that speciously set off the Spanish-American war to the McCarthy era and the "Red Scare" of the 1950s, the fake WMD in Iraq, to the QAnon of today, the United States has been particularly susceptible to information pollution of all kinds.

The problem at hand: Fostering both open-minded and critical readers in an age of partisanship and rampant information pollution. We argue that *something must be done and done now*, and this book is designed to meet three goals to move us forward:

1. To help learners become highly competent critical readers of all kinds of texts and critical consumers of data who understand how credible and objective fact is reasonably established—and how it can be responsibly used.

2. To help students recognize, interrogate, and responsibly deal with what is often called "fake news," the "New Propaganda," or "information pollution" and help them understand how these kinds of mis-, dis-, and mal-information work and how they are powerfully tailored, curated, and disseminated *to them* in highly targeted and manipulative ways by artificial intelligence (AI) and social media.

3. To help recognize and fight what we'd call *fake skepticism*—or perhaps *ungrounded skepticism*: the ignorance or dismissal of established, credible data from reliable sources, including the pretense that science does not exist or that established scientific findings can be roundly discounted; the suppression of historical understandings based on data and grounded experiences from across different peoples and across time; or the pretense that data about many of the issues facing us are not available or should not be believed.

These three goals are essential to fostering responsible reading, composing, disciplinary engagement, thinking, knowing, and doing. And they are essential to much more: navigating our personal lives and relationships intelligently, creating community and effective social policy, working toward the common good, and robustly engaging in democratic life. The challenges of and the need for critical reading and thinking are not new. It is well known that in ancient Rome, paid political hacks called Panegyrists spread mis-, dis-, and even mal-information, playing the part of influencers in service of various politicians and political interests. What *is* new is the powerful digital technologies that now exist and that can be used by political and business interests to amplify their manipulation by personally targeting us with tweets, short-form videos, and posts that are tailored by AI to our personal psychology and our biases with the purpose of manipulating us to do and think what is in the interest *not of ourselves or our communities, but of some hidden entity.*

> In ancient Rome, paid political hacks called Panegyrists spread mis-, dis-, and even mal-information, playing the part of influencers in service of various politicians and political interests.

Reflection Questions

- What topics do you or your students find particularly captivating or even triggering—topics you just can't help pursuing?

- What topics do you or your students have anxiety about (note well that any form of anxiety makes you particularly susceptible to information pollution—as we will explore)?

Tristan Harris, formerly a design ethicist at Google and now the leader of the Center for Humane Technology, expresses it this way: "News feeds on Facebook or Twitter operate on a business model of commodifying the attention of billions of people per day . . . They have led to narrower and crazier views of the world" (Applebaum & Pomerantsev, 2021, p. 44). In the same article, the authors write:

> The buttons we press and the statements we make online are turned into data, which are then fed back into algorithms that can be used to profile and target us through advertising. Self-expression no longer necessarily leads to emancipation: The more we speak, click, and swipe, the less powerful (and more controlled and manipulated) we are. Shoshana Zuboff, a professor emerita at Harvard Business School, coined the term *surveillance capitalism* to describe this system. (p. 44)

Harris calls social media AI a "race to the bottom of the brain stem" because AI activates our deepest primordial fears and biases to self-select information that will make our views even more entrenched and extreme and that will isolate us over time. (This process works through *confirmation* and then *availability bias*, see Chapters 2 and 3.) Retweeting and "like buttons" create isolated worlds of our own, detached from reality and undermining our capacity to encounter different perspectives and to discern the truth. This undermines common bonds with those even slightly different from us and keeps us from tapping readily available and established sets of knowledge. This process creates an *echo chamber*, and this problem and attendant dangers are exacerbated by other cultural forces of truth suppression and misdirection.

> The more we speak, click, and swipe, the less powerful (and more controlled and manipulated) we are.

This system does not work to the benefit of us, our personhood, or for greater goods like the promotion of democratic culture, the creation of community, or the preservation of the environment. It does not serve a search for truth or work toward positive and transformative ways of engaging, knowing, doing, thinking, and being, which are the pillars of what cognitive scientists now define as *understanding* (Wilhelm, Bear, et al., 2020; Wilhelm, Miller, et al., 2020). As things stand, the system will not help us, but will instead hinder us in addressing the problems that most threaten us, our country, world, and environment.

It's important to understand, as various commentators vigorously argue, that we are losing our freedoms and agency by providing our data to powerful interests; these interests, in turn, use that data to manipulate us to their ends. Experts like Harris have been sounding the alarm for years about how these powerful forms of AI become ever more powerful and manipulative and invisible to us. They change as our behaviors and thinking change, leading us ever deeper down the primrose paths of extremism plotted for us by deeply hidden interests. We are fed ideas that do not test us, dialogue with us, or help us outgrow ourselves, but rather confirm our preexisting cognitive and conceptual biases and intensify them. It's a truism that you can't learn by looking in the mirror or by listening to like-minded dude-bros and bots. AI provides us only with highly personalized lenses and curated posts that submerge us into predispositions and lead to mob-think. These AI platforms are essentially authoritarian, imposing their will on us, demanding compliance, and refusing to show alternatives or enter into open conversation. Suffice it to say that any internet or social media user is now subject to a giant set of social-engineering experiments on their brains.

> These AI platforms are essentially authoritarian, imposing their will on us, demanding compliance, and refusing to show alternatives or enter into open conversation.

In this book, we argue that we must have a clear-eyed view of the current situation and the significant challenges facing us. We also argue for hopefulness and a way forward by cultivating awareness that works toward alternative possibilities—through our own raised consciousness and "wide-awake" activity, our mindful interactions with others both on- and offline, and the conscientiously cultivated ways in which we can teach and learn from others.

TODAY'S NEWS

Though the specific problems of the "New Propaganda" and the instructional tactics and solutions we explore cover all evolving aspects of modern life, for the moment let's focus just on examples that currently dominate the news—though new ones will take their places. What is at stake in the political arena? The historian Snyder (2017) argues that when we give up trying to establish and verify objective facts and be informed by them for political decision making and social policy, tyranny is soon to follow. The future of the democratic project is in peril. If you doubt it, consider "The Big Lie" about electoral fraud in 2020–2021, vis-à-vis Nazi Germany, and their use of propaganda over the Volksradio; or Fascist Italy and their fascist art propaganda projects. Better, read what accomplished historians have to say in "America's Self-Obsession Is Killing Its Democracy" (Klaas, 2022) or in *How Democracies Die* (Levitsky & Ziblatt, 2018).

It's not just politics and elections that are so fraught. If we can't establish, verify, and believe something approaching the "truth"—or at least accept the existence of evidence patterns and objective facts and the reality of basic scientific understandings—then we cannot possibly have informed political decisions, wise and effective public policies for issues like pandemic preparation and vaccinations, or informed ways of moving forward to address education, climate change, food and water safety, or anything else that affects our daily lives and that will determine our future quality of life and even survival.

Let's take the example of public health policy. At the time this chapter was first drafted, according to *The New York Times* (Leonhardt, 2021) there was widespread resistance to the coronavirus vaccines with up to 50% of the American public (including many health workers and teachers) saying they would refuse a vaccination if available on this date. This article appeared 1 year after the onset of the COVID pandemic in the United States. This vaccine resistance was attributed to mistrust and misunderstandings about basic science:

> *"The coronavirus vaccines aren't 100 percent effective. Vaccinated people may still be contagious. And the virus variants may make everything worse. So don't change your behavior even if you get a shot . . ."*

On the day of final edits (August 28, 2022), just as was the case in 2020, "much of this [anti-vaccine] message (like much mis-information and mis-interpretation) has some basis in truth, but it is fundamentally misleading" (Leonhardt, 2021). The evidence so far suggests that full doses of mRNA vaccine effectively eliminate the risk of COVID-19 death from Omicron or any other variant, nearly eliminate the risk of hospitalization, and drastically reduce a person's ability to infect somebody else. Current science indicates that when a vaccinated person is first infected their viral load is equivalent to that of an unvaccinated person. But personal health effects are vastly better, and viral load/infectivity decreases much more rapidly. Although the situation is complicated (as science and life always are) and misinformation about vaccinations (or anything else) often contains some elements of truth, this kind of information pollution and the facile unsubstantiated claims that follow cause great harm.

Takeaway: *Misinformation often grows from a kernel of truth.*

"The alarmism and profound misconceptions continue to exercise a powerful influence on individual behavior and social policy. By now we have seen the real-world costs: Many people don't want to get the vaccine partly because it sounds so ineffectual" (Leonhardt, 2021). And this has a very real effect on the health not just of individuals, but of the community and its interests, for example, on school policy, on responding to new health crises like monkeypox, and on the economy.

Misinformation often grows from a kernel of the truth.

We recount this story in part to illuminate the complexity of scientific understanding: It evolves over time because as data collection methods, resulting data sets, peer review leading to the social construction of knowledge, and other aspects of science are brought to bear, understandings will evolve and become more nuanced. This does not mean that science was initially "wrong," only that scientific understandings develop through a time-tested process for "the constitution of knowledge" (i.e., through agreed-on methods and social networking of a disciplinary "community of practice" [Rauch, 2021]). But this process is generally not understood by the public, and it makes nuanced scientific understanding susceptible to cognitive biases for simplicity and for single causality (Lakoff, 2008).

The problem is widespread. Eric, a graduate student of Jeff's, shared this story:

> During the last presidential election, my mom taught a unit about democracy. She talked to me about having her students find articles and resources about both candidates and their policy plans. She wanted them to be able to identify reliable resources versus bogus resources, such as highly ideological "news sites." She asked her students to compare and contrast the agendas of the candidates, find, and evaluate the evidence supporting their positions, and talked with [her students] about looking at both sides of all issues and digging into actual confirmed evidence before making a decision on who to back. Then a few weeks ago she sent me and some family members a text with the following video link in an effort to warn us about COVID and getting a vaccine: https://bit.ly/3gBKPhE
>
> [When we clicked on the link, we found that the video had been removed from YouTube "for violating community guidelines"!] One of her friends had found this video on Facebook and forwarded it. I talked to my mom about how this New American organization is an extreme non-mainstream media company proceeding from extreme ideological positions, that they are not journalists using accepted methods and evidence of the kind she demanded of her students!

We are all susceptible to fake news.

Yet Eric's mother, the history teacher, was not persuaded—in large part, Eric thought, *because she agreed with the position being promoted.*

Takeaway: *We are all susceptible.*

The costs of this susceptibility are profound in any area of democratic life and every subject area in school. If we do not know what news sources to trust, or what kinds of research are authoritative, then we will be subject to the whims of anyone who wants to influence us. In public policy, we are guided by preexisting beliefs and loyalties instead of current data patterns. We become subject to intense emotional manipulations and may think and then act irresponsibly. If we do not understand how research works and are not persuaded by confirmed findings accepted across a discipline, then we will make personally and culturally destructive decisions. And on it goes, with no end in sight. For these reasons, we think that it is critical to learn to consciously recognize and deal with (1) our own cognitive biases and (2) information pollution and data manipulation.

We also believe it is our responsibility to critically read—and to access and interrogate and justify evidence and then make use of evidentiary reasoning. This is the bailiwick of every teacher (and every citizen!) of every subject, K–college.

This critical reading project can easily be incorporated and should be included in units of study across all subject areas and at all grade levels. And it must be: because we are all so vulnerable—and because the stakes are so high for all of us personally and collectively.

Critical reading is a kind of "threshold knowledge" (Meyer & Land, 2003)—even an anchor form of threshold knowledge—that is, knowledge that transforms our lives by taking us through gateways to new, more responsible, and expert ways of engaging, knowing, thinking, and doing—now and forevermore. It is important to understand that only when we teach deliberately and systemically, again and again, can we overcome deeply embedded cognitive biases. We need repeated deliberate practice with this skill set over time (Ericsson & Pool, 2016). If even just a few K–12 teachers in every school take this project on, the mindsets and capacities of our students can and will be transformed.

For example, what if every one of us and every one of our students learned to silently ask this question: "Am I truly seeking the truth right now, or am I just trying to justify something preexisting within myself?" Such a question can raise conscious awareness of the aim and contents of thinking, and reasons for our feelings during a disagreement, a critique, when confronting claims or data patterns that conflict with our perspective, or when something turns out differently than hoped or desired. In such scenarios we are all tested to move from the pursuit of self-justification to the pursuit of truth. What if we continuously reminded ourselves that learning and improvement always involve change, often include discomfort, and nearly always include profound changes in outlook, understanding, and action?

REMAINING CURIOUS

Let's be clear: We are not against differences of opinion and honest debate. We argue here that our default position should always be curiosity, before evaluating and perhaps dismissing or revising a point of view. But we do want curiosity to be followed by a demand for evidence from credible sources and across sources. Fabricated data and faulty reasoning harm others, oneself, and the social fabric. We need what Michael (Smith et al., 2012), following Toulmin's call for the kind of evidence that is adequate and satisfactory to our audience (1958), calls "safe" evidence (that which can be accepted on its face by all reasonable parties), and the kinds of reasoning and thinking about evidence that are used in the ways of disciplinary experts. And we need self-awareness about our trust in or doubt of the sources we find and even more so of those that find us.

> Our default position should always be curiosity.

Curiosity and openness are essential to learning. Part of maturity is not only knowing how and why your own positions have value but also understanding that other positions—many at odds with your own and the justifications for them—also have value. But it doesn't end there. Our own positions are always limited, and many cannot be justified; the same is true of the positions of others.

After asking for evidence with an open mind, confirming it, and evaluating the reasoning about the evidence (or the lack of it), we must be prepared to accept, revise, or discount certain positions—even long-standing ones of our own or our family and friends. We must, in other words, hold all our positions as "categorically tentative," just like a scientist, who always knows that new data collection techniques, new data, and new ways of reasoning are always evolving. (Do you remember when Pluto was still a planet? Well, scientific methods, data, and then understandings changed, and thus Pluto's redesignation!)

> We must hold all our positions as "categorically tentative," just like a scientist.

In Milton's (1644) famous formulation in *Areopagitica*, truth cannot be bested by a bad argument unless all the arguments are not made. If we are right, we should want to correct others. If we are wrong, we should want to be corrected. If, as is most likely, we are partly right and partly wrong, or if there is no absolute right or wrong, or if rightness or wrongness in a specific instance depends on the situation, then the only way to grow and learn is through open and free inquiry, conversation, and the continuous updating of knowledge.

Here's a brief example from Jeff's personal life. His wife, Peggy, has undergone a long and arduous health journey due to blood disease. She has suffered thirty-seven major brain bleeds and two extended comas, and on five occasions she was told that she had fewer than 10 days to live. After 16 years, Peg's condition is still undiagnosed by Western medicine. Jeff and Peggy spent years at various research hospitals like the Mayo Clinic, the National Institute of Health (NIH), the NIH Undiagnosed Disease Program, and others. They were often faced with heart-rending life-and-death decisions. In these cases, they asked for medical articles and studied them, consulted with experts across the world by phone, and made evidence-based decisions about what to do or what not to do. They rejected several experimental therapies as lacking convincing evidence patterns, violating their values, or being too dangerous. After 6 years, and having exhausted Western medicine, they turned to Eastern medicine. Although they had been experimenting with acupuncture, meditation, herbal therapies, diet, and other Eastern medical approaches, turning solely to Eastern medicine was a bold decision, and they received immediate blowback from parents and friends. Peg's parents asked: Don't you want to use research-based treatments? To which Jeff replied: Is 3,500 years of documented research from Traditional Chinese Medicine (TCM) not enough for you? Although TCM operates from a different paradigm than Western medicine (with research based on induction and qualitative methodologies vs. hypothetical deduction and quantitative approaches; a focus on holism and energy vs. a focus on specific symptoms of disease, etc.), it is based on research traditions and evidence consistent with its paradigm.

The bottom line: Peggy and Jeff remained curious. But they did so critically. It was a challenge because cognitive research has demonstrated that the more out of control you feel (and they felt very much out of control and often without a way forward), then the more susceptible you are to fake news and snake oil (Whitson

& Galinsky, 2008). The more anxious you are, the more you will actively seek miracle cures. And there is a lot of snake oil out there for people feeling any kind of desperation, from the political realm to the economic to personal health and beyond. The more desperate you feel, the more you revert to automatic reactions and the more you must consciously assert critical thinking. Here's another thing Jeff and Peggy found out: It's actually quite powerful and even exhilarating to be curious. You are always discovering something new and interesting about the world and how people think, even if you end up discarding it.

The good news: Peggy has been on a mostly consistent trajectory toward greater health since embracing Eastern medicine 10 years ago, and no one talks about her dying from her condition any longer. In retrospect, the two wish they had been more open to TCM earlier, but in desperation (and due to confirmation and availability bias—more on that in a bit) they stuck with what they knew—and what others around them knew and did. They should have been more curious earlier. And they hasten to add that they still go to their Western doctors and embrace Western medicine for parts of Peggy's condition because the evidence supports that move.

To summarize: We want to promote free thinking, open exploration, open debates, and honest exchanges of perspective, *but* we also want to reinforce that you can't have tennis without lines and a net (i.e., without agreed-on rules for engagement). If "anything goes," then you can't have a productive game or any game at all. There are standards for arguments of fact and arguments of judgment, definition, and interpretation. There are established processes and standards for "constituting knowledge" from across different disciplines (Rauch, 2021). We need to adhere to these standards. The same is true when engaged in intellectual debate and policy discussion and personal conversation—all topics we touch on in this book. As Rosling (2018) argues: "A fact-based worldview is more useful for navigating life, just like an accurate GPS is more useful for finding your way in the city" (p. 255). Usually, the most powerful and useful action we can take is to understand existing authoritative data clearly and to discard the positions attempting to manipulate us.

> We need to acknowledge, name, and honor the feelings of others (including our students) so that they will be open to the critical inquiry we're calling for.

That said, there is much social science research about emotion, intuition, bias, and the way these all both guide and misguide us. Decades ago, the poet Muriel Rukeyser (1968) spoke of the "verifiable and the unverifiable fact." Sometimes we know things and navigate from positions that are not strictly fact-based, and these positions can be of value. There is power in different ways of knowing. But it is important to distinguish feelings and intuition from fact. We need to find ways to acknowledge, name, and honor the feelings of others (including our students) so that they will be open to the critical inquiry we're calling for. We need to help our students recognize and privilege the unique powers and susceptibilities of different ways of knowing. Following the example of Peggy and Jeff, we recommend a reworking of Ronald Reagan's famous injunction to "trust (feelings, intuitions, loyalties), but verify" by testing these against the best of what is thought and known out in the world, and against multiple perspectives—truth, after all, cannot be bested unless all the arguments are not made and heard.

We make the case that the most important elements of our approach can and should become throughlines of all teaching in all subject areas and grade levels; namely, by making inquiring into how to understand part of our teaching by exploring

- How to read and respond to various kinds of texts in different contexts

- How to establish the credibility of textual information

- How to responsibly establish and interpret patterns of evidence

- How to mindfully engage in one's own research, myth-busting, and truth-testing

- How to consider the effect of perspective, positionality, and context in all that we read

In this book we therefore

- Suggest ways to use our lessons as a natural part of any unit that involves inquiring, reading, and composing in any curricular area

- Show that success can be achieved by introducing and returning repeatedly to central strategies and expert mental models for critical reading and conscious problem solving—and by structuring learning so that students will get the deliberate practice they need to develop the habits of mind possessed by critical and responsible inquirers, readers, and writers

- Demonstrate the vital importance in all disciplines of discerning the difference between what is real and what is fake or polluted through critical reading, inquiry, and discernment

- Show how such teaching can be naturally integrated into any classroom and into any topic of instruction in ways that will enliven that classroom—and in ways, because it is integrated into ongoing instruction for preexisting goals, that will not cost us extra energy or time

THE COMMITMENTS OF TEACHERS

We are all, first and foremost, teachers. We have all spent substantial parts of our careers as schoolteachers. Although currently working in higher education, we all also continue to work in schools with teachers and with students. Throughout our careers we have certainly been committed to teaching our students how to be better readers, to engage with and be transformed by the unique and powerful ways of knowing offered through literature, and to become competent composers and users of language. But even more than this, in a way that includes and transcends the project of any teacher, we want our students equipped to develop their fullest capacities as human beings, to live healthy and satisfying lives, and to become wide-awake and wide-aware democratic citizens and workers. We work consciously to make our teaching matter beyond reading, writing, and language to the application of these capacities for joy, equity, social justice, civic discourse, democratic work, and personal and social transformation. Therefore, as is obvious to us all at this cultural moment and for the foreseeable future, we must teach our learners to be inquirers, to develop metacognition and mindsight, to become critical readers of the news, critical consumers of online information, and critically aware digital citizens.

> We must teach our learners to be inquirers, to develop metacognition and mindsight, to become critical readers of the news, critical consumers of online information, and critically aware digital citizens.

We see teaching as a way to do what psychologist Gardner and his colleagues (2001) call *good work*. Good work serves compelling personal agendas and larger social purposes (e.g., helping learners be critical readers and thinkers who are involved productively in community issues; participating in promoting deep commitments to equity, social-emotional learning, and mutual respect; proceeding from trust in people's strengths, potential, and possibilities instead of drawing attention to their deficits).

We want our teaching to matter in the here and now—and into the far-off future. We want to nurture lifelong attitudes and habits of mind that lead our students and others around them to thrive. And at this moment we can think of no more powerful way to fulfill these commitments than to teach our students to be critical readers who consciously take on the challenge of social media and the New Propaganda.

We pursue this project with a compelling sense of urgency—but we think this urgency will remain unabated, though the reasons for it might change. As President Biden remarked after Trump's second impeachment acquittal:

> This sad chapter in our history has reminded us that democracy is fragile. That it must always be defended. That we must be ever vigilant . . . And that each of us has a duty and responsibility as Americans, and especially as leaders, *to defend the truth and to defeat the lies* [emphasis added]. (BBC News, 2021)

As many scholars and commentators have made clear: There will *always* be demagogues who manipulate populist sentiment with partial truths and outright propaganda. Even if we navigate this moment, the challenge will reappear (Levitsky & Ziblatt, 2018). Demagoguery has been with us throughout recent U.S. history (Barry Goldwater and Joseph McCarthy) and the histories of other 20th-century democracies. Hitler was legally elected to the German Parliament and was legally appointed Chancellor by President Hindenburg. But this led immediately to the Reichstag fire used as a pretext to suspend all civil liberties. And thus, the Nazi era began. Mussolini was legally elected to the Italian Parliament and was asked to form a government by the Italian King Victor Emmanuel III after thousands of his armed followers marched on Rome and seized control of many local governments (January 6th, anyone?). There will also be new pandemics, new social dilemmas, and compelling—even life-threatening—issues to address. Such is life for human beings on planet Earth. We must prepare ourselves.

Democracies are fragile things, and there will always be threats from inside their workings. So the question becomes: What must be done to strengthen and shore up a commitment to democracy and to democratic ways of thinking, democratic institutions, and values? That is why we take up the call to teach critical reading, thinking, composing, and problem solving in service of democracy and democratic living. The stakes are high. A governor of Virginia, William H. Cabell, asserted in 1808 that education "constitutes one of the great pillars on which the civil liberties of a nation depend" (Albert and Shirley Small Special Collections Library, n.d.). Fake news is now part of the bigger historical family of propaganda.[1] This New Propaganda, its propagation by AI used by business interests, foreign powers, and biased "news" services, and the use by young people of TikTok, Snapchat, Instagram, YouTube, and other ever-evolving platforms to disseminate news to friends and play the role of "influencers" all make the situation even more fragile and fraught and makes us all even more fallible. The current moment (and our future) requires us all, and especially our students, to understand what's at stake, to understand how their minds work and how the mind can be manipulated, and to understand the promises and pitfalls of social media and digital technologies.

> Fake news is now part of the bigger historical family of propaganda.

The good news is while the horse is leaving the barn, it hasn't yet escaped. In an online survey of 853 ten- to eighteen-year-olds (592 of them teens), Robb (2017) found that nearly half of them reported that they value the news. Indeed, 77% of teens reported getting news stories or headlines from social networking sites. Now here's the bad news: McGrew and colleagues (2017) report that their analysis of "thousands of students" responding to "dozens of tasks" found that those students confessed that they were "easily duped" when it came to "evaluating information that flows through social media channels" (p. 5). Something needs to be done. We think that it is every teacher's job to do it. We turn now to some aspects of the challenge facing us as we pursue this project.

DIGITAL READING IS DIFFERENT FROM, THOUGH RELATED TO, LINEAR READING

After reading our call to focus more on digital reading, a teacher might say, "Okay, I'll buy that digital reading is important. But I do teach them to be critical readers. All they need to do is transfer what I taught them to their new digital reading. Isn't that enough?"

Short answer: A Hard No.

Why? In the first place, as Perkins and Salomon (1988) explain, "A great deal of the knowledge students acquire is 'inert'" (p. 23). More recently (2012) they put it this way: "People commonly fail to marshal what they know effectively in situations outside the classroom or in other classes in different disciplines. The

---

[1] Propaganda is meant to PROVOKE not persuade, it promotes a single point of view and uses SEED (simplification, exploitation, exaggeration, divisiveness).

bridge from school to beyond or from this subject to that other is a bridge too far" (p. 248). If students have inert knowledge, then that means they don't apply it in new problem-solving situations. This bridge is just too far.

The reading of digital texts is indeed something new. Turner and Hicks (2015) put it simply: "Digital texts *function differently*" (p. 99). Let's take a moment and think about why.

Perhaps the most influential formulation of reading is Rosenblatt's (1938, 1978) Transactional/Reader Response theory, which frames the reading experience as a unique transaction between a *reader* and a *text* in a given *context*. In digital reading, all three elements of Rosenblatt's formulation are changed in fundamental ways.

Linear Texts vs. Digital Texts

Let's start by thinking about texts. Rosenblatt notes that the decoding done by a listener or speaker creates a new event through a "to-and-fro spiral" between the reader and the "signs on the page" (Rosenblatt, 1938, p. 26). On the one hand, then, with linear texts, all readers engage with the *same text* or set of symbols, though they inevitably create different "poems" (meaning-making responses) from their transactions with those symbols. On the other hand, readers make *unique texts* when they read digital texts by virtue of how they engage with the features of those digital texts.

- Digital texts may have links; linear texts do not.

- Digital texts are likely to have visual elements; many linear texts do not.

- Digital texts may have embedded video; linear texts do not.

- Digital texts will use data from your responses to send you future texts; linear texts cannot do this.

Linear Readers vs. Digital Readers

Now let's turn to readers. As a consequence of the character of digital texts, readers have to play a vastly different role than readers of linear texts. We'd argue that readers of digital texts have a transaction with a text that at least to some extent they author. Do I watch an embedded video? If so, when? Do I click a link? If so, when? When I go to a linked site, how do I engage with that site? And on and on. Coiro (2015) points out that the cognitive demands of online reading differ from those of linear reading as digital readers have to "move between rapid reading-to-locate processes (that occur, for example, when skimming search engine results and navigating through levels of websites) and deeper processes of meaning construction" (p. 56).

In addition, readers of digital texts tend to select the texts they read rather than being given them, as is typically the case in school. Hartman and others (2018) explain: "Online, readers must find and construct their own sets of texts to read closely after searching for and evaluating a potentially infinite set of texts for relevance and trustworthiness" (p. 62).

Linear Contexts vs. Digital Contexts

And now context. Rosenblatt (1938) argues that meaning exists in the transaction between the reader and the text. But that transaction doesn't occur in a vacuum. Readers of linear texts bring what Rosenblatt called a "linguistic-experiential reservoir," organized by schemata (a mental model of how something works and how the various parts relate), to readings of texts. Moreover, the social situations in which transactions occur provide a further variable: Reading for class is surely different from reading on a beach. And reading in science is different than reading like a historian or a literary reader (which is why we all must teach reading and digital reading in our own classrooms and in all subjects). These aspects of context are similar across linear and digital reading experiences. But Rosenblatt doesn't take up the textual context in which reading occurs. The act of selection, which we touch on in the previous paragraph, significantly affects the way that readers, in Turner and Hicks's (2015) words, *encounter* texts. Hartman and colleagues (2018) explain:

> Algorithmic technologies that personalize information serve to create the impression of a vast information landscape when, in truth, every internet reader may be gathering information on a very small information island that is used by, built by, and maintained by people who are just like them (Rainie & Anderson, 2017). When access to ideas, to information, to facts is filtered, synthesized conclusions will reflect those filters too. A necessary part of the critical positioning required for synthesis may be a recognition of how this big-C Context is deliberately designed to predict, to restrict, and to selectively disseminate ideas in ways that further economic, political, or ideological interests. (p. 68)

This process creates what is known as an *echo chamber*. Readers tend to be attracted to texts from perspectives that match their own—and AI makes these kinds of text more available to them. This tendency means that the context of online reading operates in specific ways so that our reading, due to selection algorithms, probably doesn't challenge or test our thinking but rather reinforces it.

THINKING ABOUT TRANSFER OF LEARNING

So what have we established thus far?

- Teaching critical *digital reading* is crucially important.

- We can't count on our students effectively applying what we've taught them about linear texts because their knowledge may well be inert and because digital texts are manifestly different from linear texts.

- If we want transfer to occur, then we have to teach for transfer and provide repeated deliberate practice with it—in this case, we have to teach specifically *how to critically read digital texts*.

Haskell (2000) provides a framework that has long helped us think about how this transfer can be achieved. He presents eleven conditions that foster transfer, which we think can usefully be reduced to four that reflect the notion of what cognitive scientists often call 4D (4-dimensional) teaching and learning for *engaging, knowing, thinking,* and *doing*:

1. **Engaging/Knowing.** Learners must deeply understand the knowledge that is to be transferred and the purposes served by using this knowledge (i.e., the conceptual principles, as well as the purposes and payoffs of using that knowledge must be clear).

2. **Thinking/Doing.** Learners must understand the principles and processes of practice to be transferred (i.e., students must have a mental model and map for applying the principles).

3. **Thinking/Doing and Reflecting.** The classroom (or learning) culture must cultivate a spirit of transfer; learners must be continually considering and rehearsing how the knowledge can be used both immediately and in the future.

4. **Deliberate Practice of Engaging, Knowing, Thinking, and Doing** in actual contexts of use over time. Learners must deliberately and repeatedly practice applying the meaning-making and problem-solving principles to new situations.

To achieve these conditions, we have to address, as a specific focus, critical digital reading, and to do so explicitly and deeply. Quick fixes such as assigning students to use digital sources in one report or another just aren't enough. But in our experience few teachers do any—or at least not much—of the explicit teaching that students need. Our perceptions jibe with those of Turner and Hicks (2015) who explain that "[e]ven our colleagues who use technology regularly and for purposeful learning in their classroom have told us that, sadly, they don't spend much time teaching the skills needed for students to comprehend digital texts" (p. 6). Why? We think the answer is that time is a zero-sum game.

TIME IS A ZERO-SUM GAME

Think of how much we teachers are expected to teach. Just take a look at the ELA Common Core State Standards (CCSS). Our states have each created their own versions of the CCSS (Idaho and Pennsylvania) that are very similar to the CCSS themselves or they are in the process of doing so (Minnesota). ELA teachers are supposed to teach kids to read literature and informative texts; to write arguments, information texts, and narratives; to master the conventions of academic English; to listen open-mindedly and with comprehension; and to speak effectively.

To be sure the CCSS mention digital texts twice. The ninth- and tenth-grade bands call for students to be able to

> Gather relevant information from multiple authoritative print and digital sources, using advanced searches effectively; assess the usefulness of each source in answering the research question; integrate information into the text selectively to maintain the flow of ideas, avoiding plagiarism and following a standard format for citation.

and to be able to

> Make strategic use of digital media (e.g., textual, graphical, audio, visual, and interactive elements) in presentations to enhance understanding of findings, reasoning, and evidence and to add interest.

However, neither standard mentions the explicit addressing of the unique characteristics of digital texts and in any event, the emphasis on digital texts is dwarfed by the attention paid to the other aspects of the ELA curriculum. We have to recognize that already burdened teachers deeply understand that every minute devoted to teaching digital reading is a minute one can't spend teaching the close reading of a complex literary text, having a writing conference, and so on.

So whatever is done in teaching digital reading has to be done with an awareness of a teacher's myriad responsibilities. It has to be integrated into what they already must do, and in ways that serve their deepest hopes, commitments, and desires for their students and our shared future.

THE PLAN FOR THIS BOOK

Our plan for this book is to share strategies, including model lessons, that demonstrate how we can help our students become more critical consumers of their digital reading, and that do so by embedding instruction on digital reading into the instruction we already provide to achieve more long-standing academic aims. The lessons we share are designed both to demonstrate explicit instruction in digital reading and to suggest the extent to which explicit instruction can complement what we already do as well as what we are already deeply devoted and dedicated to. We explore how these lessons are flexible and generative and how they can therefore be adapted for different unit topics, age levels, and subject areas.

In **Chapter 2** we explore the nature of information pollution: what it is in general, its various formulations, how it works, and how it exploits our minds, especially through the manipulation of our cognitive biases. We explore why and how the new digital propaganda/fake news work in the personal and public arenas, and also how these affect disciplinary work and understandings in the social sciences, science, art, STEM, STEAM, and other areas. We focus especially on confirmation, availability, and overdramatization biases, exploring how search algorithms and recommendation protocols leverage our natural vulnerabilities and then deepen these.

Part II of this book, **Lessons for Critical Reading and Fighting Fake News** begins with **Chapter 3.** In this part of the book, we turn to lessons, easily adapted to various situations, for recognizing and working around cognitive biases. These lessons focus on

1. Helping students know their own minds and recognize their areas of susceptibility, especially regarding various cognitive biases

2. Helping learners develop an ethic of responsibility in reading and posting

3. Encouraging lateral reading and the use of mental models for considering textual credibility

Each of these chapters contains two sections. **Part I** lays out the general problem, topic, or focus of the lessons to come, and **Part II** provides adaptable lessons focused on teaching the critical reading of digital texts that can be applied to traditional topics and emphases of instruction. Teachers can embed these in reading and writing lessons across Grades 4 through 12 and in most subject areas.

Chapter 3 provides foundational lessons for getting started with critical reading of media designed to help students recognize and overcome the cognitive biases we all share.

Chapter 4 focuses on transferring understandings about the close reading of linear literary and nonfiction texts to the close reading of digital texts, using *rules of notice* as a mental model of expert reading practice. Rules of notice (Wilhelm & Smith, 2016) are the conventional understandings experienced readers employ as a way to identify what is most important in a text. More specifically, the lessons introduce students to the importance of noticing direct statements of generalization, calls to attention, ruptures, and language and images designed to evoke a reader's response and then engage students in using what they have noticed to develop critical understandings of what they read.

Chapter 5 examines point of view in both literary and nonliterary texts. It explores how to evaluate the reliability of narrators and other information sources, helping students develop a mental model that they can apply to a wide variety of texts. Lessons focus on the criteria that experienced readers apply when they evaluate the reliability of an information source as well as on what to do when the reliability of a source of information is in question.

Chapter 6 focuses on the power of using critical lenses as a tool for understanding literary fiction as well as a wide variety of digital and social media texts. More specifically, the chapter focuses on how the different critical lenses can enliven the teaching of all texts, including digital ones, providing the grounds for rich and varied interpretations and compelling classroom discussions about positioning and credibility. Perhaps even more important, the lessons demonstrate how critical lenses help students detect, critique, and if necessary, resist the biases and ideological positions of authors of nonfiction, news, literary fiction, and digital texts.

Chapter 7 focuses on helping students become more critical readers of both linear and digital arguments as they mine texts in service of the process of reading to write (Greene, 1992). More specifically, the lessons focus on identifying what kind of evidence from within and outside literary texts provide a solid foundation on which to build an argument. Because of the prevalence of references to "research" in support of even the most problematic kinds of information, lessons are also designed to help students develop a mental model for evaluating research.

The book concludes by reprising the importance of addressing the new electronic propaganda and information pollution in classes across the curriculum and at all grade levels and by arguing that doing so can be accomplished in ways that will enrich and not overburden teachers' current practices.

Moving Beyond (available at resources.corwin.com/fightingfakenews) goes from thinking about individual lessons to the planning of a larger unit of study. The online component illustrates how teachers can employ the mental model of EMPOWER (see Wilhelm, Bear, et al., 2020; Wilhelm, Miller, et al., 2020) (Envision, Map, Prime, Orient, Walkthrough, Extend/Explore, Reflect) for planning units that put a variety of nonfiction texts, news items, and literary and digital texts into meaningful conversation in ways that help learners consider issues of positionality evidence, truth value, and cognitive bias.

CHAPTER 2

Fake News: What It Is, Why It Works, and What We Can Start Doing About It

"If you want to teach people a new way of thinking, don't bother trying to teach them. Instead, give them a tool (or tools), the use of which will lead to new ways of thinking."

—R. Buckminster Fuller

"When conventional reality emerges, absolute reality submerges; When absolute reality emerges, conventional reality submerges."

—Buddhist Sage, Mahāsī Sayādaw

After this fall's high school parent night, a father hung around to talk to Jeff. He came up, introduced himself as "Hal's dad," and then launched in:

Dad: I've been wondering what you and this school are doing about all the CRT [critical race theory] and liberal brainwashing that is going on in this school.

Jeff: It sounds to me like you are really concerned about this. Can you tell me more about it?

Dad: I've been reading about all this CRT stuff and how schools are brainwashing kids into thinking that being White* is bad and that American history is bad and how many kids are being humiliated for being White and being made to feel bad.

---

* Note from authors: This text follows the style conventions outlined by the Center for the Study of Social Policy (Nguyễn & Pendleton, 2020; https://cssp.org/2020/03/recognizing-race-in-language-why-we-capitalize-black-and-white).

Jeff:	I hear you saying that you want your son to be valued and respected and for his values to be honored. Am I hearing you correctly?
Dad:	(pause) Well, yeah, but more than that, I don't want him to feel bad about himself. I don't want him learning stuff that just isn't true.
Jeff:	I hear your concern and I share it. I want your son to come as himself, and leave this class as himself, just being a little more educated and informed as a reader, writer, and thinker. I know every teacher in this school is devoted to teaching what counts and can be justified as a form of true expertise. Every student is going to be valued and respected in this school and in my classroom. This is what we do here: We value each other, we value knowledge that counts in the disciplines and world of work, we listen to each other, and value informed opinions of all kinds. We value diversity because that energizes learning. No one is going to be silenced or made to feel bad. But we will work hard to test out our ideas and find evidence that backs them up.
Dad:	I still want to know what you are doing about all this brainwashing!
Jeff:	You are going to have to help me out here. I have never heard of CRT being taught in this school or any other school I know of. I have not heard of students being disrespected by teachers. I just don't know of any evidence that it is happening. Do you know where this is occurring?
Dad:	Well, no, but I know it is happening.
Jeff:	I share your concerns. Here's a tool I use: I look for respected journalists writing on an issue. I've been reading the Idaho newspapers and the *Idaho Education News*, and they have some good stories from reputable journalists who have done a lot of research and investigative reporting. And they conclude that CRT is not taught in Idaho schools or American schools for that matter. I can send you a link if you want. You should read it for yourself! I get daily updates from them, and it keeps me up to date on what is really going on in our schools. Because I'm a concerned dad, just like you!
Dad:	Yeah, okay. But there's a lot of smoke for there not to be a fire!
Jeff:	(laughing) I work with kids so I know there's often a lot of smoke without a fire! But if you read or hear something specific that is concerning, please let me know.
Dad:	And how do you know you are getting your news from a good place?
Jeff:	That's a great question. Here is another tool I use. It's a website called Allsides; it tells you if your source is slanted one way or the other. [Jeff shows him on his phone.] I know that I like to get news from sources that I agree with—which is a basic human tendency—so I use Allsides to monitor myself to make sure I'm getting mainstream views based on real journalism and established facts. There is a lot of misinformation out there so I try to be careful. I'll send you a link and then you'll have my email, too. Let's stay in touch. I know we are on the same team when it comes to Hal's welfare.

Maybe you've had this kind of conversation or one similar to it. In this chapter and Chapter 3 you will learn strategies for helping yourself and others deal with information pollution, including what Jeff did during this conversation:

- Engaging in deep listening and uptake
- Acknowledging there is information pollution and that we are all susceptible to it
- Recognizing our biases and being open to new learning
- Asking respectfully for evidence; expressing respect for evidence-based journalism, science, and disciplinary work; and committing to using facts to inform positions and decisions

Reflection Questions

- From what sources do you—and your students—typically get "news" or other information about specific topics and about the world in general?

- To what degree do you—and your students—seek validation and verification for previously established positions, values, and commitments versus engaging in open exploration and continuing to test what you think and believe?

- What do you do—or could you do—to confirm or disconfirm significant claims about issues that matter as well as the evidence supporting them—and to check the slant of the information sources you use?

In this chapter we also focus on

- What information pollution/fake news is, why we believe and spread it, and how it exploits the basic default functions of our minds
- How being conscious of our cognitive biases and vulnerabilities can help us exercise some level of mindful control that focuses our minds and energy
- How this transformation in consciousness can help us monitor information pollution/fake news and consciously decide what is worth believing or acting on
- How this consciousness will help us deeply listen and productively respond to people influenced by fake news
- How these insights lay the groundwork for the lessons in Chapter 3 that will operationalize them

WHAT IS NEWS?

The issue of "fake news" requires us to consider the nature of "real news." News is generally considered to be an accurate account of a recent, interesting, and significant event (Kershner, 2005) to provide citizens with the information they need "to be free and self-governing" (Kovach & Rosenstiel, 2007, p. 17). It can also be seen as a dramatic account of something novel, and therefore interesting, of an outlier event or phenomenon (Jamieson & Campbell, 1997). News is seen as the professional output of journalism, a field that has established binding standards and processes for providing accurate, objective, and cross-checked reports leading to "independent, reliable, accurate and comprehensive information" (Jamieson & Campbell, 1997, p. 11). Legitimate professional journalism is transparent about its funding, ownership, and professional practices. Professional journalists examine all credible sides of an issue. They make corrections and issue retractions if they make mistakes. Real news informs versus persuades; it presents versus compels. (See the infographic "Is It Legit?," https://newslit.org/educators/resources/is-it-legit/.) This said, "news," like any other kind of understanding or representation of information, is socially constructed and therefore vulnerable not only to journalists' own biases and preferences but also to external entities and forces such as advertisers, paying audiences, government regulators, and so on (Shoemaker & Reese, 2013). News is sold to audiences, and audiences are sold to advertisers (McManus, 1992), a phenomenon that makes news increasingly vulnerable with the rise of digital media and artificial intelligence.

Wardle (2017) of *First Draft News* pointedly rejects the term "fake news." She "censors it in conversation" because it is "woefully inadequate" to describe the issues now at play with social media use (SMU). In part this is because "news" cannot be "fake," or it is not news. She suggests the term "information pollution," which has various forms based on different source problems. In this book, we continue to use the term "fake news" since it is in current use, but also use the terms "new propaganda" and "information pollution."

KNOW YOUR OWN MIND OR BE MANIPULATED!

When Jeff was growing up in rural Ohio there was a county highway near his home with a series of Burma Shave signs that read:

Don't lose your head

To save a minute

You need your head

Your brains are in it!

This is something our students (like any democratic citizen) need to understand—don't lose your head! The consequences are dire—personally and for us all socially. And yet most of the time every one of us has decidedly lost their head—because our minds mostly operate automatically and without our conscious control. This, in short, is what makes us susceptible to information pollution.

Jeff often asks his students what they should do before making a major purchase, one that's going to require a considerable financial sacrifice. They generally say something along the lines of: Do your homework. Check *Consumer Reports*. Talk to friends who are in the know. Read reviews and see what experts have to say. Jeff asks what might happen if we fail to do our homework. Everyone has stories of buyer's remorse, of relatives and their money-pit cars or homes bought without the proper inspections.

Jeff then asks why they would "buy" something as big as their deepest commitments and values, ideas, philosophies, political orientations, hopes, and dreams—which constitute one's identity and way of being in the world—without doing their homework (i.e., reading laterally, checking with experts, and verifying the "influencer's" actual authority and expertise). He demonstrates to his students that everything they have ever heard or read—from an advertisement to a political ad to a tweet to an Instagram post to a poem—is an attempt by somebody with a very specific position on an issue to manipulate you into engaging with, knowing, believing, thinking, or doing something that is in *their* interest. So before we buy or believe anything, we better do our due diligence, or we have unconsciously given the power over our lives, thinking, influence, and our very being to someone else. Yet this is what happens when we are affected by any version of information pollution.

In the last chapter, we took a look at Louise Rosenblatt's (1978) transactional theory of reading, which argues that reading involves the coming together of reader and text in a specific context of use that results in the construction of some kind of meaning. Part of the reader's contribution to this meaning making is their background, personal history, cultural context, experience and facility as a reader, and much else, as well as the purposes of the reader and the reader's life context (both the immediate personal context and purpose, as well as the more general layers like the state of the community or country in which she lives).

The notion of reading as a transaction is consistent with socio-cultural theories of teaching and learning that have held sway in cognitive science and in discussions of effective teaching and learning, communication, and much else over the past 50 years (see Wilhelm, Bear, et al., 2020; Wilhelm, Miller, et al., 2020). These theories hold that all meaning is socially constructed. In other words, we construct our own realities based on our social conditioning, known as *mind conditioning* in Buddhist psychological traditions. To quote Mahāsī Sayādaw, "What and how we understand depends upon how we think." And how we think is deeply influenced by the micro- and meso-cultures we grew up in as well as those we choose to inhabit.

If we want to transform our students and the way they read and understand, if we want to work toward health and productivity, then we must be critical teachers willing to examine and transform ourselves and the way we teach—moving beyond what Zeichner and Tabachnick (1981) call "the salience of the traditional." We must be willing to help learners transform their ways of engaging, thinking, knowing, and doing in school and in their wider lives. Challenges cannot be solved or alleviated by the mindsets that created them. We must constantly ask: *What if it were otherwise?* In

> Although we like to think of ourselves as rational, we are in fact social animals wired for basic survival.

what ways could my practice be improved? How could my teaching be more transformative, powerful, and on-point for my students' current life challenges?

This chapter is about knowing our own minds and understanding how they evolved in ways that mislead us. Throughout this book, we explore how to approach and operate on texts so that we can consider how they are trying to manipulate us, how we can understand those manipulative moves and control them, and then compose a mindfully constructed meaning and a justified position of our own.

But first, a brief introduction to the problem.

WHY DO WE *ALL* BELIEVE AND SPREAD INFORMATION POLLUTION?

It's a big question: *Why are misperceptions about contentious issues in politics, history, and even science seemingly so persistent and difficult to correct?* It's certainly not for want of good information, which is readily available. We know that exposure to good information does not reliably promote accurate and justifiable thinking. Why not? According to a growing body of evidence, the ultimate culprits are

- Cognitive and memory limitations, including deeply embedded cognitive biases
- Preexisting commitments, beliefs, and identities
- Directed motivations to defend or support our identity and group affiliations
- Messages from other people, usually close to us and exercising influence on us, and the views of prominent influencers and political elites (Nyhan & Reiflet, 2010)

A summary of the evidence shows that people become even more prone to information pollution when these factors are in play (e.g., from Allport & Postman, 1947, all points continue to be supported by current research):

1. There is uncertainty causing fear and anxiety.

2. The information/information pollution is important to the consumer and believable to them. Allport and Postman's (1947) *basic law of rumor* posits that spreading rumors depends on the *ambiguity* of the situation and the *importance* of the misinformation.

3. Believing and spreading the information pollution stakes one's identity by promoting a self-image of "knowing insider"—and it strengthens social connections to one's "tribe."

So, in other words, information pollution is spread and believed when uncertain conditions make people anxious or fearful, creating a greater need for "in-grouping"—a belief that their social identity is a source of superiority, strength, and protection—and that other groups can be blamed and scapegoated for their problems. Although we like to think of ourselves as rational, we are in fact social animals wired for basic survival. In times of perceived uncertainty, danger, conflict, or social change, we seek security by identifying as members of like-minded groups. This situation makes us eager to consume and spread information, both true and false, that puts a lens on the world as a conflict pitting our "righteous" and correctly informed in-group against a threatening out-group. (This is akin to what is known as the *third person bias*—*I* know how to deal with this situation; e.g., fake news, *you* better be careful, *they* are all getting hoodwinked!)

The situation is exacerbated by high-profile political or media figures promoting identity-affirming misinformation. (Intense all-out conflict rallies followers and provides short-term benefits of attention and political clout to these figures.) Another factor is our inherent cognitive biases that short-circuit rational thought. And a final compounder is the use of social media, which exponentially multiplies all previous risk factors. As Fisher (2021) writes, "In an ecosystem where that sense of identity conflict is all-consuming . . . 'belonging is stronger than facts,'" quoting sociologist Zeynep Tufekci.

> As Fisher (2021) writes, "In an ecosystem where that sense of identity conflict is all-consuming . . . 'belonging is stronger than facts,'" quoting sociologist Zeynep Tufekci.

This chapter and the next explore the following:

- What part do we, *we* as human beings, play in this manipulative dance?

- What are the foibles and weaknesses that are hard-wired into *all our* brains that allow us to be so susceptible to the new propaganda and all forms of information pollution?

- How should we operationalize these understandings to study, test, and monitor ourselves and our role as we transact with different kinds of texts?

Next, let's consider the forms of information pollution that we are assailed with.

WHAT ARE THE FORMS OF THE NEW PROPAGANDA AND INFORMATION POLLUTION?

To identify and deal with information pollution, it's useful to have a clear understanding of its different forms and the effects of each. After researching numerous typologies of fake news or information pollution, we offer our own continuum of information pollution/manipulation based on the indices of responsible parties (reader to composer and anyone who reposts), factfulness (fact-based to totally fabricated), and desire to deceive (no intent to deceive to malicious intent) (see Figure 2.1).

The bottom line: Every utterance and every text has been constructed by someone to induce or manipulate us into engaging, knowing, believing, or doing something that fits the composer's purposes. Therefore, we better always ask

- Who constructed this text and why (i.e., what do they want *me* to think, believe or do—and why)?

FIGURE 2.1 Scatter Plot

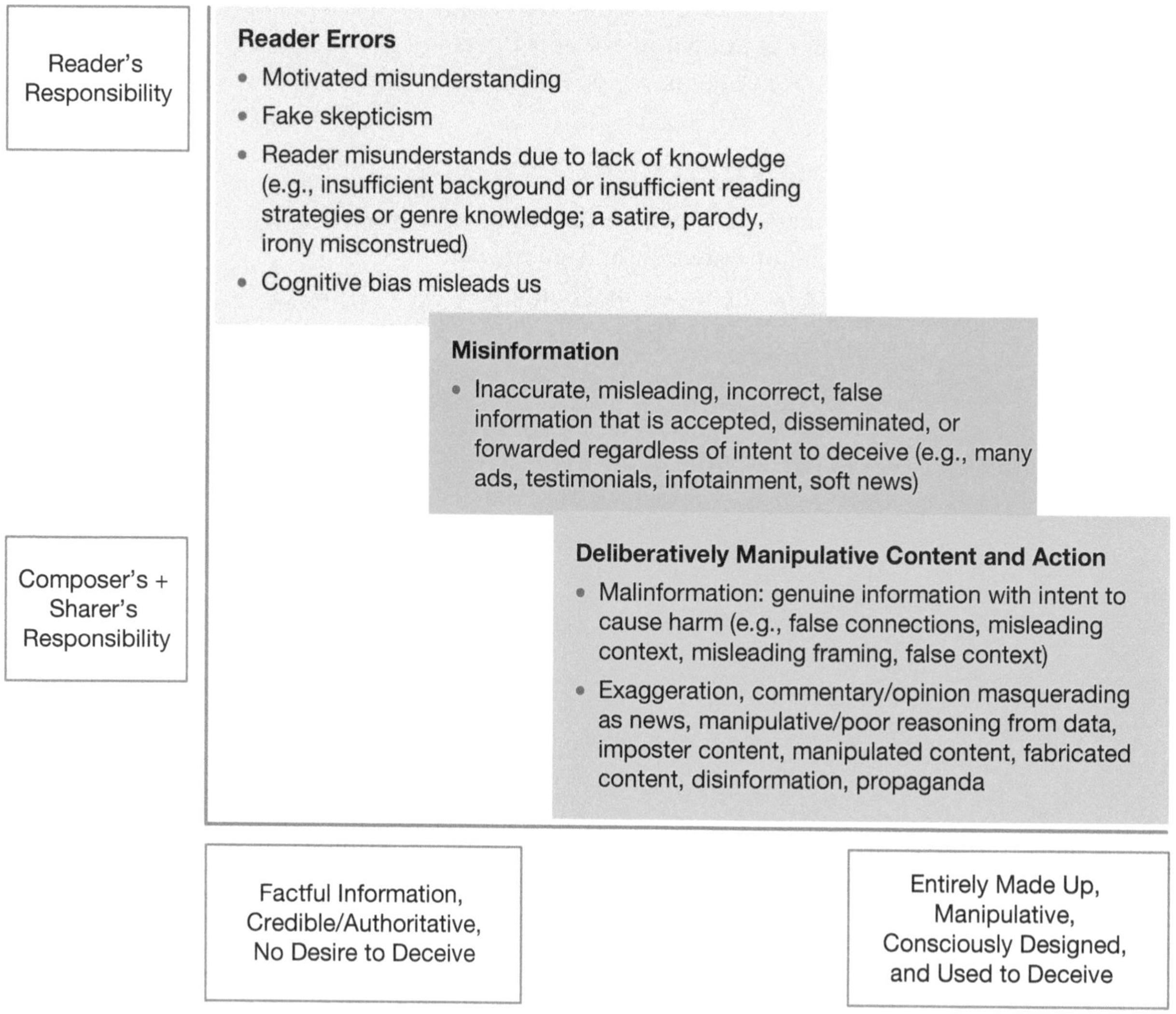

| Reader's Responsibility | **Reader Errors**
• Motivated misunderstanding
• Fake skepticism
• Reader misunderstands due to lack of knowledge (e.g., insufficient background or insufficient reading strategies or genre knowledge; a satire, parody, irony misconstrued)
• Cognitive bias misleads us | |

Misinformation
• Inaccurate, misleading, incorrect, false information that is accepted, disseminated, or forwarded regardless of intent to deceive (e.g., many ads, testimonials, infotainment, soft news)

Deliberatively Manipulative Content and Action
• Malinformation: genuine information with intent to cause harm (e.g., false connections, misleading context, misleading framing, false context)
• Exaggeration, commentary/opinion masquerading as news, manipulative/poor reasoning from data, imposter content, manipulated content, fabricated content, disinformation, propaganda

Composer's + Sharer's Responsibility

| Factful Information, Credible/Authoritative, No Desire to Deceive | Entirely Made Up, Manipulative, Consciously Designed, and Used to Deceive |

• Do I want to go along with them?

• What do I win or lose by going along?

• Who else wins or loses?

> This is what we want our students to be convinced of: *If you don't read critically, then you are being manipulated.*

This is what we want our students to be convinced of: *If you don't read critically, then you are being manipulated.* To be critical, we must become consciously aware and skillful. This is particularly true because social media and information pollution exploit the frailties of our brain evolution and the many cognitive biases that unconsciously control our mental activity.

OVERRIDING THE DEFAULT MODE SYSTEM (SYSTEM 1) WITH CONSCIOUS COMPETENCE (SYSTEM 2)

Are ALL human beings susceptible to fake news/the new propaganda/ information pollution? The answer is an unqualified hard YES. As Nobel Laureate Kahneman (2013) maintains, based on his lifetime of work in human cognition (see *Thinking Fast and Slow*), you are totally deluded or in extreme denial if you choose to believe otherwise. The cognitive science about issues of cognitive bias could not be more clear or convincing. To what degree are we susceptible? Much greater than we would ever suppose.

Are we susceptible to fear, gossip, emotional appeals, identity and group affiliation pressures, and general irrationality in positioning ourselves, making decisions, and deciding what to believe and how to act? YES. YES. YES. And YES!

And further: Are Americans especially susceptible to fake news? We answer yes to this question as well, due to so many factors:

- Our historical divisions since the settlement of North America (e.g., Virginia planters vs. Puritans)

- Our fractured political discourse

- The privileges/oppressions baked into American culture since First Contact

- How we get our news from different and often slanted media/information sources

- A cultivated culture of distrust by politicians and political outlets

- Segregation on many different dimensions of ethnicity, class, culture, and ideology

- Traditions of scapegoating, shaming, and calling out

- The pervasive influence of social media (see, e.g., Anderson, 2017)

As we argued in Chapter 1, this general susceptibility to fake news and information pollution is a great danger to

- Personal and mutual understanding

- Comprehending the world as it is

- Establishing truth, and valuing it

- Developing expertise in any domain

- Wise decision making and accountability

- Productive community and communal life

- Healthy personal and social relationships

- The work of any discipline or profession

- Democratic values and democracy itself

It is our argument that as teachers and responsible citizens we must recognize this problem and directly address it with our students *repeatedly over time* in various contexts and from every possible angle—both direct and indirect—going through the front door, the back door, the side windows, and even the attic and basement!

> Are ALL human beings susceptible to fake news/the new propaganda/information pollution? The answer is an unqualified hard YES.

The problem, in short: Our brains have evolved to operate many basic functions and routines automatically. According to cognitive research, our brains have evolved to use what neuroscientists call the default mode network, and what Kahneman (2013) calls *System 1*.

System 1 uses automatic heuristics (shortcuts) that replace conscious thought. We use this kind of nonthinking in many situations where the risks greatly outweigh the benefits of automaticity. *The most significant issues in life should not be left to mindless defaults.* Kahneman's *System 2*, in contrast, is much slower, more methodical, highly conscious, and thoughtfully process oriented.

Winston Churchill is reputed to have said, "Fear is a reaction. Courage is a decision." Although he wouldn't have known it at the time, Sir Winston was describing the two operating systems of our minds. He was also describing why social media is so powerful (it preys on our fears, prior attachments, and affiliations) as well as what to do about information pollution (proceed deliberately with courage and conscious awareness, mindfully addressing and thinking through the issue at hand).

Over the past 20 years, descriptions of these two systems—Default Mode/System 1 and System 2—and their functions have been widely explored in both scientific and popular publications. This work helps us understand how our basic comprehension, problem, and decision-making processes work—and how they are so often derailed.

The basic problem is this: We are equipped with instincts and thought patterns and biases that were helpful to our ancestors, who lived tribally as hunters and gatherers in a wild natural world. But these instincts make people in the modern world jump to conclusions, react to nonexistent dangers, and make enemies of our potential allies. Instead of mindful attention, we use shortcuts. We stake identity and group affiliation in privileged ways (us vs. them) over thinking hard about what might actually be true, useful, helpful, or functional in any given situation.

The Default Mode System (DMS) and Kahneman's System 1 are essentially the same and reside in the same brain regions. The DMS was discovered when brain researchers were exploring baseline mental activity, which they found to be very fast, highly engaged with emotions, largely self-referential, and highly automatized (see Figure 2.2).

FIGURE 2.2 System 1 vs. System 2

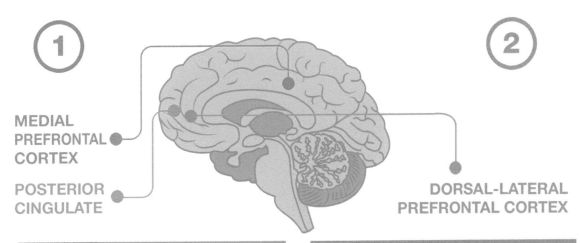

SYSTEM 1	DEFAULT MODE NETWORK	SYSTEM 2

- FAST
- DEFINING CHARACTERISTICS: unconscious, automatic, effortless, irrational and often emotionally involved

- WITHOUT self-awareness, conscious control, or any kind of monitoring or inquiry: "What you see is all there is."

- ROLE: automatic assessment of the situation, takes shortcuts to get through the problem without mindful attention or energy

- Makes up 98% of all our thinking

- SLOW
- DEFINING CHARACTERISTICS: deliberate and conscious, effortful, controlled mental processes, rational thinking and use of mental maps

- WITH self-awareness or control, logic and skepticism, looks at multiple positions and possibilities

- ROLE: seeks new/missing information, asks for justification and verification, makes mindfully considered decisions, uses conscious competence with expert mental maps for solving problems, and revises and improves these maps as needed for new challenges

- Makes up 2% of all our thinking

SOURCE: Illustration by Joel Wilhelm.

System 1 makes us jump to conclusions and respond the same way, no matter the situation. An apt metaphor is how we tend to ski down the same ski tracks (i.e., how we comprehend and address problems repeatedly in the same way) over and over because it's just easier that way—the trail is already cut for us. We engage, know, think, and do the same things in the same ways out of ease and habit. To counter this habit energy, we need to groom the mountain of our mind so we can find new ways to proceed—new ways to frame and interpret problems and to engage with, think about, and address complex issues. This is akin to the Buddhist idea of learning to read the world with a "beginner's mind," that is, an unfettered mind open to all possibilities, not just the ones previously prepared for us—or by us.

System 1 is an evolutionarily ancient, largely primitive, and excessively emotional system. System 1 bypasses all conscious and rational thought and is automatized, mostly subconscious, and immediate. Our fight-or-flight response to perceived danger is an example. Its speed is both its great attribute and its dangerous, delusional downside. The posterior cingulate is the brain part that runs System 1, and interestingly, it is where identity, our sense of self, and ego largely reside.

We operate in System 1 almost all the time.

Takeaway: *Kahneman has famously declared that System 2 is notoriously lazy and prefers to defer all its work to System 1.*

And it turns out that the more fearful or stressed we are, the more this seems to be the case. Interestingly, SMU promotes anxiety, depression, and fear (Taylor-Jackson & Moustafa, 2021), and in an infuriating feedback loop, the more afraid we are and the less control we feel, the more we tend to engage with SMU (Reed, 2020). Just as when you are tired and stressed, simple disagreements can become emotional arguments, when you see an Instagram post of a person with flawless skin you can be moved by the comparative mindset to think, "My skin sucks! I need to find a way to improve my skin!" and start clicking away.

> SMU promotes anxiety, depression, and fear (Taylor-Jackson & Moustafa, 2021), and the more afraid we are and the less control we feel, the more we tend to engage with social media.

Social media uses artificial intelligence (AI) to specifically target the fears, prior attachments, and affiliations that promote more SMU and that deepen commitments to System 1 and our vulnerability to cognitive bias.[1]

There are, in mundane quotidian situations or the rare dangerous ones, advantages in relying on System 1. But System 1 is not the system for navigating the challenges and complexities of the high-stakes issues of modern life. Relying on the creaky old whispers of the evolutionary brain will not help you navigate an argument with your spouse, much less the nonroutine analytical and interactive tasks required by the modern workplace and the challenges of modern cultural life. Neither fighting nor fleeing is an appropriate response here. We must deeply understand our challenges and mindfully address them over time.

As noted earlier in this chapter, Kahneman's System 2, in contrast to System 1, is much slower, more methodical, highly conscious, and thoughtfully process oriented. This fits the theory that early brain regions like the limbic system were built to be reactive and automatic to avoid the serpent in the grass and ensure survival. (Snake! Run! Enemy! Throw spears!) Our capacities to reason and consciously override instinct are due to the increasingly complex world and the evolution of our brains

---

[1] Kahnemann does assert that System 2—for all its deliberation—can be based on intuited flaws (e.g., some of our most treasured political beliefs are, he argues, profoundly rooted in personal history). So a political affiliation that I might make quickly, intuitively, with the gut of me, is something that's been so ingrained in me that it's as easy as $2 + 2 = 4$ for me, built on a pattern of selected and trusted narratives on which I've placed authority. And any deliberation I do based on this history will necessarily be flawed.

over time. But these System 2 capacities take tremendous energy and willpower to use, and they are undermined by the attractive ease offered by System 1—and by SMU and information pollution, which bids to do our thinking for us. If we do not mindfully and consciously read, write, and act, then we are quite literally using *the bottom of our brainstem*. And we do this instead of using the most recently evolved and powerful parts of our brain—including the mindful tools of cognition these new brain parts afford us. (When we ask what a teen could have possibly been thinking after they have done something stupid or harmful, the answer is always: They weren't! They weren't thinking, that is! They were using System 1.)

COGNITIVE BIAS RULES THE DAY

Bottom line: We are far less rational and far less correct in our thinking than we'd like to give ourselves credit for. The side effect of System 1 is that we all suffer from *cognitive bias*. A cognitive bias refers to a systematic pattern of deviation away from justified and mindful reason—a lapse of rationality in judgment or problem solving.

Kahneman (2013) discovered not only the two operating systems of our brain. His discovery of the bandwidth of each system and the different results produced by each made his research even more significant. These were breakthrough insights into the typical lack of reasoning in human decision making. He showed how the two thought systems arrive at different results even given the same inputs. His work foregrounds the power of the subconscious mind and automatic nonthinking in our daily lives. We tend to consider ourselves rational human beings who carefully consider our decisions and actions. Kahneman proved this wrong and showed that our mental activity is almost entirely irrational.

> We tend to consider ourselves rational human beings who carefully consider our decisions and actions. Kahneman proved this wrong and showed that our mental activity is almost entirely irrational.

AVAILABILITY, CONFIRMATION, AND OVERDRAMATIZATION BIASES

Two of the most prevalent shortcut biases are *availability bias* and *confirmation bias*. These come into play when we are making judgments and decisions.

Availability Bias

- This bias provides us with a mental shortcut that relies on the immediate cases that come most easily to our minds.

- We value information that springs to mind quickly as being more significant.

- When making decisions, we automatically think about related events or situations from our own limited immediate experience.

- We judge those events to be more frequent and probable in all cases.

- We overestimate the probability and likelihood of similar things happening in the future.

My neighbor's chihuahua bit me, so all small dogs are dangerous! I know someone who won a big prize in the lottery, so I can win, too!

Availability cascades

When a story about any topic, like "the election was stolen," goes viral, which triggers further posts, stories, and discussions making the information pollution (or justified news in some cases) more "available" and therefore influential on us and others.

Availability bias takeaways

When images are placed side-by-side or in a collage, it's nearly impossible not to draw connections between them—because possible connections (which are likely nonexistent) have been invited and made available to us.

Presenting genuine photos or videos in false contexts is one of the most common tactics used to spread misinformation online—because it exploits availability bias.

Confirmation Bias

- This is our bias to adhere to preconceptions and to attend only to information that confirms these preconceptions, leading us to ignore, immediately dismiss, or reshape any information that does not confirm our a priori positions and commitments.

- We interpret situations and information in ways that confirm preexisting beliefs.

- The bigger the emotional charge related to the preconception, the more System 1 is engaged and the worse the bias.

This is a reason why it is difficult to have a serious conversation about abortion, climate change, political alliances, gun control, race relations, vaccinations, and many other issues to which we have deeply committed and emotionally charged positions.

Confirmation bias examples

I am committed to the idea that chihuahuas are dangerous, and I saw one barking at my neighbor and I can see that he is dangerous and will viciously bite!

or

I think chihuahuas are lovable and loyal, and I see the barking as protective of the household.

Types of confirmation bias

Biased information searches, biased interpretations of information, and biased information recall

If it feels TOTALLY AND UNDENIABLY true to you, then confirmation bias certainly has you!

If it strongly confirms what you think, then your enthusiastic interpretation probably stinks!

OVERDRAMATIZATION BIASES

The famous public health policy expert Hans Rosling (2018) poses a scheme of cognitive biases that he maintains are hard-wired into our brains, all centered on what he calls the *overdramatization bias*—that we evolved to notice and focus on what is most dramatic. (The stock market is going down so it is going to continue to go down and will crash! Sell! Sell! Sell!) This is System 1 survival thinking. Rosling's antidote, proposed in his book *Factfulness: Ten Reasons We're Wrong About the World—and Why Things Are Better Than You Think*, is to monitor ten aspects of this bias and to test them against the facts that are available (see the lessons in Chapter 3).

Again, we see that what is necessary to fight cognitive bias is

- The ability to access, evaluate, and value good information

- The ability to monitor our cognitive biases as we consider, interpret, and make use of this information

We repeat: *Everyone* is affected by cognitive bias. *Literally everyone.* It's part of our humanity and our evolution. But who is most susceptible? It turns out that the people who are especially anxious, fearful, emotionally charged, or who are feeling out of control of their lives are most prone to manipulation (e.g., Our elections are rigged! There is no coronavirus!). Writing in the journal *Science*, researchers Whitson and Galinsky (2008) found that people who lack a sense of control are more likely to perceive conspiracies, develop superstitions, and see images that don't exist. "When individuals are unable to gain a sense of control objectively, they will try to gain it perceptually" (2008). We seek and make up patterns to simplify the reasons for our lack of control, they write, creating "distortions of objective reality" (2008).

> Everyone is affected by cognitive bias. Literally everyone. It's part of our humanity and our evolution.

Many historians and psychologists also make the case that Americans are particularly susceptible to conspiracy theories.[2] Anderson (2022) argues that the capacity

---

[2] Anderson (2022) argues that "[t]here is an American instinct to believe in make-believe, from the Pilgrims to P. T. Barnum to Disneyland to zealots and fantasists of every stripe . . . to Donald Trump." "America was founded by wishful dreamers, magical thinkers, and true believers, by impresarios and their audiences, by hucksters and their suckers. Believe-whatever-you-want fantasy is deeply embedded in our DNA" (Anderson, 2022).

for blurring delusion and verifiable reality is a deeply held American predilection. (Tupac is alive! Vaping is safe if it's not nicotine!) Much psychological and psychiatric research (e.g., Friedman, 2020) agrees, though the problem is seen as a generalized human failing, with Americans being perhaps especially susceptible—and these psychological researchers see education as the remedy:

> We are cognitively hard-wired for plausibility, not for truth or accuracy. Thus, conspiracy theories and misinformation will always have a receptive audience. We can help our patients to counter this all-too-human tendency by encouraging their capacity for critical thinking and skepticism. As a society, our survival depends on it. (Friedman, 2020, n.p.)

For some, according to historian Richard Hofstadter writing in the 1960s, susceptibility to information pollution and the "paranoid style" of American culture is due to anti-intellectualism and an associated distrust of experts that he thought was due in part to an American "passion for equality." Because we believe that knowledge should be accessible and understandable by all, if we do not understand something then it is suspect, and we think it is probably being used for perverse purposes. (Don't get vaxxed! Bill Gates is putting computer chips into your body! "Climate scientists" are corrupt and can't clearly explain climate change so it must be a hoax!)

> The strongest indicators of conspiratorial belief aren't ignorance or political leaning, they found, but a belief in the struggle between good and evil.

We also become more susceptible the more we segregate ourselves physically and intellectually. In *The Big Sort: Why the Clustering of Like-Minded America Is Tearing Us Apart,* Bishop (2009) demonstrates how Americans are segregating not just by social class, but by belief and ideology. He shows how this segregation leads to increased availability and confirmation bias.

Intellectual laziness is another culprit. University of Chicago researchers Oliver and Wood (2014) found the belief in conspiracy theories is commonplace in America (52% of Americans "consistently endorse some kind of conspiratorial narrative" in surveys conducted from 2006 to 2011). The strongest indicators of conspiratorial belief aren't ignorance or political leaning, they found, but a belief in the struggle between good and evil. American culture simply leans into that sort of thinking. "For many Americans, complicated or nuanced explanations for political events are both cognitively taxing and have limited appeal," they write, so we believe conspiracies because they are easier to grasp, "more accessible and convincing." System 1, anyone? (For other factors, see 10 Factors That Shape a Rumor's Capacity for Online Virality: https://bit.ly/3TP8A3R.)

And then there is social media. Because they are advertisement driven, social media platforms will use any means necessary to keep users engaged, making great use of cognitive bias to manipulate us. In an op-ed, researcher Zeynep Tufecki (2018) described YouTube as "the great radicalizer." After viewing Trump rallies on YouTube as part of her research, she found that White supremacist videos began auto-playing for her. Inquiring into this phenomenon she found that viewing Bernie Sanders videos led to feeds of anti-Bush 9/11 conspiracy videos, vegetarianism to veganism, jogging to ultramarathons—every new feed confirmed what was assumed to be her bias and made more extreme views of it available. YouTube, she concludes, "promotes, recommends and disseminates videos in a manner that appears to constantly up the stakes," Tufecki writes. "Given its billion or so users, YouTube may be one of the most powerful radicalizing instruments of the twenty-first century" (Tufecki, 2018).

> Because they are advertisement driven, social media platforms will use any means necessary to keep users engaged, making great use of cognitive bias to manipulate us.

There are surprises in the research about those who are especially susceptible. Research indicates that people will go to great lengths to

> use their intellectual abilities to persuade themselves to believe what they *want* to be true rather than attempting to actually discover the truth. According to this view, political passions essentially make people unreasonable, even—indeed, especially—if they tend to be good at reasoning in other contexts. (Roughly: The smarter you are, the better you are at rationalizing.) (Kahan et al., 2012)

Some of the most striking evidence used to support this position comes from an influential 2012 study in which Kahan and colleagues "found that the degree of political polarization on the issue of climate change was greater among people who scored higher on measures of science literacy and numerical ability than it was among those who scored lower on these tests" (see also Kahan, 2013, 2021; Kahan et al., 2012). In other words, the more adept you were at scientific reasoning, the better you were at offering different interpretations of the data to serve your own a priori position.

The implications here are as profound as they are astonishing: Intelligence, the capacity to analyze and reason, can—when combined with prior partisan commitments and/or passions tinged with emotional charge—worsen the problem of cognitive bias and disputes over facts and their meaning. No one is immune. We must take on, as Alastor "Mad-Eye" Moody (Professor of Defense Against the Dark Arts in the Harry Potter series) urges his students: "Constant vigilance!" (Jeff has only read the books in German, where Moody yells "Sei Wachsam!" or "Be awake!") *We are all susceptible!*

In Buddhist psychology, much is made of skillful means, skillful knowing, and skillful response. These terms are synonymous with *mindfulness* or *conscious awareness*. Karma means you can't get away with doing nothing because doing nothing or not deciding is also an action and decision. So we must exercise agency, skillfully come to know our own mind, and move forward toward an aspirational future. Skillful effort is activating System 2 and exerting conscious competence. This resonates with Ericsson and Pool's (2016) (Ericsson is the world's expert on expertise, a title we'd like to have!) notion of deliberate practice. Expertise is developed through skillful effort to develop the mental models and maps of expert activity. Deliberate practice must be System 2 because it consciously works to always correspond more closely to more expert and comprehensive ways of engaging, knowing, doing, thinking, and being—aka 3D/4D teaching and learning (Wilhelm, Bear, et al., 2020; Wilhelm, Miller, et al., 2020). Jeff's friend, Tom Facziewicz, is a Buddhist teacher, and he is fond of saying that social media preys on the unaware mind. "Everything is fake until you're awake —awake to how your mind works and doesn't work!"

To move forward, we must

1. Acknowledge our situation, including the ways the sections of our primitive brains work and the ways social media works on our primitive brains

2. Set an aspiration to do better and to become more conscious, aware, and skillful

3. Use the tools and practices that will lead us toward that aspiration. That is, know how to access good information and have ways to verify it and be internally persuaded through openness (beginner's mind), lateral reading, and other processes

The lessons in our next chapter seek to achieve these goals.

Reflection Questions

- In what situations and conditions have you been especially susceptible to confirmation, availability, or overdramatization bias? Why do you think this is the case?

- In what situations and conditions have your students been especially susceptible to confirmation, availability, or overdramatization bias? Why do you think this is the case?

iStock.com/Kar-Tr

PART II

Lessons for Critical Reading and Fighting Fake News

NOTES

CHAPTER 3

Lessons for Getting Started: Knowing Your Own Mind

"Be curious; not judgmental."

—Attributed to Walt Whitman, used in the *Ted Lasso* TV series

"The ultimate, hidden truth of the world is that it is something that we make, and could just as easily make differently."

—David Graeber

Jazzy, Jeff's daughter, is teaching a lesson to her high schoolers on evaluating evidence and then responsibly reasoning from that evidence. She is using a lesson from Stanford's Civic Online Reasoning project (see Lesson 3.1 in the lessons section of this chapter).

Jazzy projects the following two questions:

- What is the source of the evidence?

- Is that source trustworthy?

These questions deal with the reliability of the evidence.

Then this:

- Does the evidence directly relate to and support the claim being made?

This is about the evidence's relevance to the claim—in this case, that there has been a prodemocracy protest in Iran.

When we analyze evidence, we need to pay attention to both whether it is reliable and whether it is relevant to the claim.

She then projects a Twitter feed of a "democracy protest." The Twitter bio identifies the person posting as Kambree Kawahine Koa, a "journalist" and "political news contributor" who is a verified Twitter user (since the lesson, Kambree has changed her bio). The tweet reads: "WOW! 300,000 March for democracy in Iran!" Before watching, Jazzy asks the class what they think so far.

Keenan:	Well, she's a journalist, so it must be real.
Jazzy:	How do we know she is a journalist?
Awa:	She says so, right there in the bio!
Jazzy:	But who wrote the bio?
	(Silence)
Jazzy:	Do people always tell the truth about who they are?
Sheffia:	Well, most of the time.
Jazzy:	Even online? How could we check to see if she is really a journalist?
Timor:	And she's a verified user.
Jazzy:	What does that mean? Does it mean we know that she is a journalist? Or just that she's not a bot?

> Despite the immensely powerful manipulations of artificial intelligence (AI) and social media, and the cognitive biases embedded in our minds, research does show that we can be more consciously aware, reflective, and rational about news and other forms of information.

After a short discussion and some cross-checking and lateral reading, which throws Kambree's designation as a journalist in some doubt, Jazzy shows the video (https://twitter.com/KamVTV/status/947539441878368256).

The video shows masses of people moving along a major highway, chanting, and waving flags.

So far the kids seem impressed and murmur things like: "Major protest!" "Those people are fired up!" "Looks like it could be from Iran."

Manar, a student who recently arrived from Iraq, cuts in.

Manar:	That's not true! This is totally NOT from Iran! They are not chanting in Farsi—they are speaking Arabic—they are speaking the wrong language for Iran! And the flags are not from Iran!
	There is silence, then Timor yells: "Fake news!" And many conversations break out. Jazzy quiets the class.
Arale:	Wow—your background knowledge helps you smell out the crap, but if you don't have any background, you can really get fooled!
Jazzy:	If you don't have the background, and you know that can make you vulnerable, then what do you have to do?

Awa:	You have to build some background!
Sahra:	Yeah, if you are super into soccer, there is way less chance to be duped about misinformation about soccer. But if you don't know about politics you will have to work at it!
Jazzy:	Okay, team, this kind of work is what we call *lateral reading*, and *you have to do it* to evaluate the reliability of evidence—especially, like Awa and Sahra tell us, if you don't have a lot of background.

Reflection Questions

- When *should* we engage in lateral reading to check the reliability of sources and of evidence?

- When *must* we do lateral reading in order to be responsible readers and people?

- How can we motivate ourselves and our students to engage in this work?

KNOWING YOUR OWN MIND

Here is the good news. Despite the immensely powerful manipulations of artificial intelligence (AI) and social media, and the cognitive biases embedded in our minds, research does show that we *can* be more consciously aware, reflective, and rational about news and other forms of information; that we can be critical of sources, that we *can* control for bias, and that we *can* teach in ways that help meet these goals. Based on that research, Pennycook and Rand (2019) argue that

> We believe everything we see and hear. This is why availability bias is so powerful.

"[i]n many and perhaps most cases, it seems, reason does promote the formation of accurate beliefs." And we would add: *IF we can consciously activate reason and control for cognitive bias*, reason, in this sense, being the System 2 thinking we discussed in the last chapter. Likewise, Wood and Porter (2019) have shown that kindly and respectfully correcting someone else's misconceptions with data and clear reasoning—and doing so with good will—typically does not backfire and can lead to developing a liminal space for questioning and then for deepened and more accurate understanding.

In the neuroscience around gullibility, it's established *that we are doomed to believe whatever we see or hear.* As we discussed in Chapter 2, the limbic system and its attendant System 1 "mental moves" developed to promote survival: "That is food, run toward it and grab it! That is danger, flee ASAP!" In survival situations, there is no time for questioning or reflection—it's all about automatic response: sense it and act! System 1 is our Default Mode System of nonthinking, and we know it is triggered and compounded by attractive possibility, anxiety, or fear. Conscious effort must be exerted to activate and employ System 2 because it moves beyond the automatic and involves questioning, evaluation of data, analysis, and reflective open-minded interpretation, all necessary for more long-term and complex challenges. It's a truism of neuroscience that *we do not decide what to believe*. We believe everything we see and hear (System 1). So we need to consciously activate System 2 and deliberately make use of it. We *must decide what to disbelieve.*

Bottom line: We are all immensely susceptible to System 1 response, and to cognitive biases of all kinds, known as *legacy cognitive blindness*. We are much more susceptible to these frailties than we believe even when we are aware of them.

> Changing your mind is the surest sign to show that you have one!

That's in part because the psyche wants to keep us in a dense fog of mutually reinforced legacy hardware that assumes those near us and most like us are most powerful, right, and safe. In our primordial past, this promoted survival because it maintained social affiliation and unity with one's tribe. This is no longer the way to survival and success. This is also the premise behind the necessity of cultivating Beginner's Mind, employed in the lessons that follow.

These lessons engage learners with the twin goals of becoming both more curious and open while simultaneously becoming more self-aware and critical of oneself and of information and its sources.

We remind our students what the slam poet Taylor Mali relays in his poem "Like Lily Like Wilson": Changing your mind is the surest sign to show that you have one!

We use Walt Whitman's injunction as a mantra, too; Jeff has this on a poster behind his desk:

"Be curious; not judgmental!"

Followed by:

"Refrain from statements: first listen and ask questions!"

As with all lessons in this book, we are providing model lessons that express and develop important mental models of instruction that will help students internalize powerful maps for navigating the wild world of information pollution. But these are general and very generative models, and you should absolutely adapt the materials, the lessons, the instructional support, the time frames, and all else to meet the needs of your particular students and situation.

We also always advise teachers to DO the lessons they assign—either beforehand as a dry run and rehearsal or along with students to provide a model for what they are doing, along with all the fits and starts. Doing so will help you see how the assignment works, what challenges are offered, and also how you might adapt the assignment for your students and situation. We have also found it immensely useful to invite students to provide feedback for adapting and revising the lesson for future students.

LESSON SUMMARIES

Lesson 3.1: Finding Good Information, Evaluating It, and Verifying It. This lesson is designed to build habits for finding good information, verifying strong and safe evidence through lateral reading, evaluating data patterns, and mindfully justifying interpretations of these patterns.

Lesson 3.2: Ranking and Evaluating Evidence. This lesson provides deliberate practice with evidentiary reasoning because students must explain how any example fits the criteria better (or not) and asks them to consciously "choose to believe or disbelieve."

Lesson 3.3: Learning With a Beginner's Mind. In this lesson, students learn how to open their minds and actively seek out different perspectives while confirming and disconfirming information so that we openly see the breadth of reasonable alternate positions in conversations about different topics.

Lesson 3.4: Actively Seeking Out Alternative Positions. By developing understanding of the Default Mode System of the brain, this lesson helps students look for counterclaims, new perspectives, and disconfirming evidence relative to their own usual viewpoints.

Lesson 3.5: Trigger Tracking and Fever Charts. This lesson utilizes Fever Charts as a tool for us to become aware of, and then control, our cognitive biases.

Lesson 3.6: Monitoring Mind Misdirection. This lesson examines optical illusions and misdirection texts to help us see how our brain can misperceive due to cognitive biases like confirmation or availability bias. It helps learners understand what happens when they read and how to promote more mindful and powerful reading.

Lesson 3.7: "Noticing and Naming" Practice for Controlling Cognitive Biases. This lesson concentrates on understanding and recognizing three of the most common cognitive biases: availability, confirmation, and overdramatization biases.

Lesson 3.8: Self-Study of Social Media Use. In this lesson, learners monitor their own social media use (SMU) and explore how we are all being manipulated through cognitive bias.

Lesson 3.9: Autobiographical Research: Developing Self-Awareness Through Self-Studies. This lesson asks students to reflect on their day-to-day lives to promote *mindsight*, a kind of focused attention that allows us to see the internal workings of our own minds.

Lesson 3.10: Having Hard Conversations. In this lesson, we brainstorm how we can help ourselves and others to remain open and curious in the face of cognitive biases.

LESSON 3.1
Finding Good Information, Evaluating It, and Verifying It

LESSON BACKGROUND

It's absolutely vital that students cultivate the habits for finding good information and dismissing information pollution, verifying strong and safe evidence through lateral reading, noting and evaluating data patterns, and mindfully justifying their interpretations of these patterns—which is called *evidentiary reasoning*. This lesson is designed to help them develop these habits of mind.

Purpose

- To consciously apply a questioning protocol to test the accuracy and dependability of information provided by any text or utterance

Length

- The initial lesson is 45–90 minutes and then ongoing. Introduce the questioning protocol and then reinforce and use it continuously throughout the school year at every opportunity until it is internalized by learners.

Materials

- Something to read or view, preferably in the context of an inquiry unit, especially texts related to contentious issues that might possibly feature information pollution
- The COR (Civic Online Reasoning) questioning protocol

Resources

- We have found a few very powerful online resources for finding and evaluating good information. Rather than reinventing some very well-crafted wheels, we encourage you to use these resources:
  - One exemplary set of resources is from Sam Wineburg and the Stanford History and Education Group (SHEG) that supports COR. This link allows you to create an account that gives you access to all their materials as well as email updates of their ongoing work: https://cor.stanford.edu/about.
  - Based on their research into professional fact checkers, the COR site also offers a simple **COR questioning model** at https://cor.stanford.edu/curriculum/collections/a-little-of-everything. SHEG provides a sequence of lessons to introduce students to each of these questions, providing deliberate practice with many strategies for answering the COR questions.

LESSON STEPS

Prior to Teaching

Create a SHEG account and familiarize yourself with the SHEG resources.

Step 1

Use the sequence of lessons provided by SHEG to introduce students to each of these COR questions.

1. Who is behind this information?
2. What's the evidence?
3. What do other sources say?

You can dig deeper into Question 1 by asking:

- Is the source(s) authoritative?

And into Questions 2 and 3 by asking:

- Is the evidence credible and safe?
- Is the evidence from an authoritative source?
- Is the evidence repeated across sources? (employ lateral reading!)
- Is the evidence relevant (i.e., on point for our current questions or inquiry)?

Step 2

Model how to use the COR protocol with a text from the unit at hand: You do it *for* the students. Invite students to join in and help out: doing the work *with* you. After some run-throughs students should be able to use the protocol on their own, *by* themselves, or with a peer, and if not, you can do more work with them. (This is the *for-with-by protocol* for gradual release of responsibility.)

Please note: We promote an ethic of teachers doing the work they assign. This provides powerful modeling to students of how to do a task and how to navigate the challenges and then mentoring into the task and monitoring student progress. This kind of modeling, thinking aloud, mentoring and monitoring is a power move of cognitive apprenticeship (Wilhelm, 2013b; Wilhelm, Bear, et al., 2020; Wilhelm, Miller, et al., 2020).

Step 3

After providing deliberate and repeated practice with the questioning protocol, remind students to use COR throughout the year. An anchor chart in the classroom can provide a useful reminder.

NOTES ON THE COR QUESTIONS

The teachers with whom we work have found COR simpler to teach and easier for students to internalize and use than any other questioning protocol that we've tried. We've also found it *internally persuasive* (Bakhtin, 1981) to teachers and students—they understand how COR works and are compelled that these are good questions to ask. COR is useful in its specificity for online content, but it applies to all other texts and conversations. We have found the COR questions easy to transfer to everyday life as well as to academic work—applicable to materials our students encounter on Snapchat, Facebook, Instagram, and other social media applications. We've also found that the COR tools are helpful in making learners aware of AI as a source of information targeted to them, helping them ask: Did I find this meme or did it find me?

ADDITIONAL RESOURCES

- **The SHEG site** offers many great videos, short and longer activities, and other forms of support for deliberately practicing this questioning scheme and for developing other tools such as **lateral reading** (https://cor.stanford.edu/curriculum/collections/teaching-lateral-reading/) that express a powerful mental model of critical reading to evaluate information.

- **OER (Open Educational Resource Project)** is a group that Jeff's National Writing Project site has partnered with on various projects over the years. Access their materials at https://www.oercommons.org/. Searching for fake news on their landing page will lead you to many wonderful resources about helping students find and evaluate data, especially data found online and through SMU. Remixing and sharing of their many great resources are allowed. A search on the site for teaching disinformation leads to many great materials on claim testing, evidence evaluation, and sourcing skill, including many science-oriented resources. They provide many other activities about information pollution (e.g., a game called Factitious that gives students practice in identifying information pollution: https://www.oercommons.org/courseware/lesson/70336).

- **Harmony Square** offers a drama game positioning players in roles (Wilhelm, 2013a) as "disinformation officers" (https://harmonysquare.game).

- **The News Literacy Project** (NLP) is a magnificent online source that we use extensively (https://newslit.org/). The site offers "an online learning platform, a free weekly newsletter, professional development opportunities, a variety of classroom materials and more" including "test yourself" activities for identifying political leanings and biases (all excellent for self-study—see later lessons) and how one's particular leanings will impact your susceptibility. NLP provides periodic news quizzes about issues around which information pollution abounds. Using these keeps learners up to date on current events and misrepresentations about current events and issues, as well as alerting readers to their own biases and susceptibilities.

NLP also provides a newsletter and news quizzes that debunk information pollution and deep fakes called *The Sift*—a kind of rumor roundup, and we recommend subscribing to it. We've found that it keeps us informed about what fake news and information pollution our students are exposed to—things we would otherwise be totally unaware of. We find this kind of work helpful because kids don't typically go to news sources. It's also helpful because we don't necessarily know what internet rumors are out there. The activities here take kids through the process of figuring out whether something is actually a "news item": whether it is credible or information pollution. Their Checkology platform offers standards-aligned news literacy lessons for different subjects and grade levels. We highly recommend subscribing to NLP and continuously using their materials and resources.

- Help students "Google Like a Pro" and post the infographic: https://newslit .org/educators/resources/eight-tips-to-google-like-a-pro.

- Use Google Reverse Image Search (not Google Lens) by right-clicking on an image you want to check the history of, selecting "search for image," reviewing results, and preparing to be amazed by how images are misused, repurposed, and become mis-, dis-, or mal-information.

- Keep up with new developments that you will need to address with students. During our final revisions of this book, several stories came out about DALL-E and other technologies that allow any user, in seconds, to create images from text, manipulate images, and embed images of someone into a video. The opportunities for creating information pollution with these technologies are immense (e.g., https://www.washingtonpost.com/ technology/interactive/2022/artificial-intelligence-images-dall-e).

- There are many other excellent resources. Find and use them!

LESSON 3.2
Ranking and Evaluating Evidence

LESSON BACKGROUND

Ranking is a powerful learning activity because it requires articulating and then applying critical standards. Ranking, therefore, gives students deliberate practice with evidentiary reasoning because they must explain how any example fits the criteria better or not quite as well as another example. This in turn helps students understand mental models for quality evidence (or for anything else that is the basis of a ranking). Here, the resulting criteria for good evidence become the basis of a set of semantic differential scales for evaluating evidence. Learners should employ, reflect on, and improve their scales throughout the school year. This process helps students develop and apply critical standards that express a mental model of good evidence.

Purpose

- To rank examples of evidence based on relative strength and quality. This will help begin a conversation about what makes good, solid, justifiable, and relevant evidence.

- To use the criteria that come up from the ranking to create semantic differential scales for evaluating evidence. The scales will help practice the process of evaluating evidence, a skill that can be applied whenever students encounter information or evaluate what evidence to employ in their own writing, and one that is essential to mining texts and other data sources for evidence to use in support of your own claims in discussion or writing.

Length

- 90–120 minutes

Materials

- Use Handout 3.2A to engage in an "evidence ranking" and/or in the future select any four or five pieces of evidence of varying quality related to a broad claim about the current topic of study. When you select evidence that relates to your current unit, you achieve a *twofer,* making this a priming/orienting activity that also activates and builds student background knowledge about the topic of study.

- Handout 3.2B: Model Semantic Scales for Evaluating Evidence

- Materials to create an anchor chart and a class semantic scale

- Handout 3.2C: Jigsaw Note Catcher

LESSON STEPS

Step 1

Share Handout 3.2A: Model Evidence Rankings (OR share different selections of evidence of varying quality on your chosen topic) with the students and give them time to read/view it.

Step 2

Use Handout 3.2A (or your own version of it) and ask learners to rank each piece of evidence from the item they think is the strongest evidence to the item they think is weakest. Encourage learners to consider WHAT IT IS that makes one piece of evidence stronger than the next piece or makes that second-ranked piece weaker than the first.

Step 3

Students discuss their personal rankings in pairs or small groups, justifying why the top ranking was stronger than the second and third, why the second was weaker than the first, and so on, recording all the criteria that come up for what makes strong evidence. It is not essential to come to an agreement, just to record possible standards for strong and compelling evidence.

Step 4

Students share small group rankings with the whole class, with the purpose of identifying common features and criteria of good evidence that almost everyone can agree on.

Step 5

The agreements about what makes good evidence are put into an anchor chart and converted into semantic scales. (You can use elements of our semantic differential scale model in Handout 3.2B to get started, or you can build a set of scales from the ground up with your students based on their thinking. For the scales, choose qualities that are appropriate to your students' grade level, content area, capacity, assignment at hand, and so on. Semantic scales can be used for any task to articulate mental models for navigating that task and the critical standards that go along with it.)

Step 6

Jigsaw reading of different texts related to the inquiry (for detailed instructions on using the jigsaw strategy in the classroom, see https://www.teachhub.com/teaching-strategies/2016/10/the-jigsaw-method-teaching-strategy).

Note. This jigsaw activity involves learners reading a shared article with a home group and discussing and then recording their use of four key analytic moves (Harris, 2006) using the featured note catcher in Handout 3.2C: (1) supporting a claim about the topic at hand (illustrating); (2) referencing an "expert" in a way that supports a claim (authorizing); (3) putting a new angle, nuance, or spin on the evidence and/or claim (extending); and (4) pushing back—disagree, challenge, interpret in a different way (countering).

They then jigsaw to a group made up of students who have all read different articles. Students use the COR questioning protocol and the semantic scales to find, evaluate, and justify evidence in their home group readings that pertain to the inquiry topic at hand. (We have used short articles offering different perspectives on the pros and cons of allowances, controlling student use of SMU, allowing phones in schools, social media, gun control, and many others that fit a current inquiry unit.) Learners share some strong evidence from their home group's article/source and their thinking about that evidence with their new jigsaw group. They then use the jigsaw note catcher to document the thinking of their group members.

In this way, everyone gets the benefit of knowing the central points and worthwhile evidence from all the articles read in each home group, and everyone gets repeated deliberate practice using the COR protocol and semantic scales to evaluate evidence. Since articles should represent different perspectives, learners also become acquainted with the different viewpoints in the conversation around the topic. All students get to consider how evidence can be used in writing or discussions to support a claim.

Step 7

Discuss the ethics of posting and reposting/sharing; our responsibility to promote good evidence and fight against info pollution.

Step 8

Students use the COR questioning protocol and semantic scales independently when reading, writing, and thinking about potential evidence, evaluating its quality, and considering how the evidence can be responsibly used.

Extension

System 1 leads us to think simplistically: in binaries, dualities, with either/or thinking. The natural and human worlds are more complicated than this. This is one of many reasons why inquiry is a powerful way to teach: Instead of describing issues as black-and-white or about two possible opposing positions, inquiry topics are framed as a dialogue around a complex problem with many possible positions and shades of gray. For example, if inquiring into gun laws or gun rights, one will find that Americans agree on more than they disagree (e.g., banning and buying back assault weapons, age limits for gun purchases, the importance of background checks and mental health screenings). There are multiple positions on these issues, so there are many ways forward for enacting the areas of general agreement. Semantic differential scales can be used by students to apply System 2 to see the various positions and possibilities on any conceptual topic and its policy implications.

For each claim, rank the provided evidence from 1 to 5, with 1 being the *most powerful* evidence to support the claim and 5 being the *least powerful* evidence to support the claim. Be prepared to explain what makes each piece of evidence more or less powerful. Our reasons for justifying what makes the strongest evidence will be put into semantic scales for evaluating evidence that we will use throughout the year.

1. **Claim: The Beatles are the most innovative musical group of all time.**

   Audience: Friendship group

   ___A. At one point, they held the top five spots on the Billboard Top 100 chart—a feat never repeated by anyone else.

   ___B. They originally went by the name of The Quarrymen.

   ___C. Music critic Richie Unterberger writes: "They synthesized all that was good about early rock and roll and changed it into something original and even more exciting—they are the greatest and most influential band of the modern era."

   ___D. *Rolling Stone* magazine lists The Beatles as having the greatest album (*Sgt. Pepper's Lonely Hearts Club Band*) ever and eleven of the top 500 albums—and no other band comes close.

   ___E. They fused rhythm and blues with early rock, wrote in the Mixolydian mode, used orchestral arrangements and unique instruments like the sitar, and generally made innovation part of what they did.

2. **Claim: I need to have an increase in my allowance.**

   Audience: Your parents or caregivers

   ___A. All the kids in my class get more allowance than I do.

   ___B. The prices of the things I buy with my allowance have gone up quite a lot due to inflation.

   ___C. As reported in *US News and World Report*, parenting experts agree that earning allowances in return for chores teaches a strong work ethic, financial literacy, fiscal responsibility, a sense of what it takes to run a household, and a sense of familial belonging.

   ___D. A recent poll of 2,505 teens showed that the average allowance for thirteen- to fifteen-year-olds was over $13, and I only get $5.

   ___E. According to Kaitlyn Laurie, a child and adult psychotherapist in Madison, WI, if kids' allowances aren't enough, it gives kids "the impression things come too hard."

(Continued)

(Continued)

3. **Claim: Our school should allow us to choose what books we want to read for summer reading instead of giving us a required list.**

   Audience: The principal

   ___A.   According to Michael W. Smith and Jeffrey Wilhelm in their award-winning book *"Reading Don't Fix No Chevys": Literacy in the Lives of Young Men*, young people do significantly more reading on their own and enjoy it more when they are allowed to choose what they read.

   ___B.   Adults get to choose what they want to read, and school should be teaching us how to do what adult experts do.

   ___C.   If you read the assigned books too early in the summer, you'll forget them by the time school starts, so athletes who want to do the reading before practice starts during the summer are at a disadvantage.

   ___D.   Most students hate the summer reading books that our school chooses.

   ___E.   On their website, the Waterford Education Group (Waterford .org) reports that allowing learners to choose their own books "improve[s] comprehension, vocabulary, and fluency." Further, they assert that choosing one's own reading promotes decision making, independence, and confidence.

SOURCE: Adapted from Smith et al. (2012).

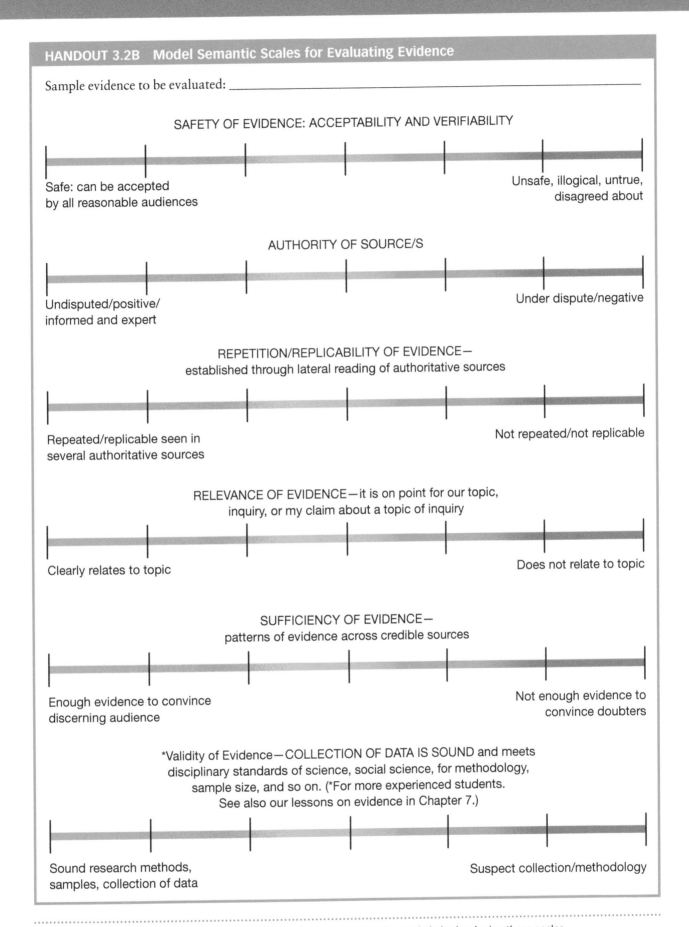

HANDOUT 3.2B Model Semantic Scales for Evaluating Evidence

Sample evidence to be evaluated: _____

SAFETY OF EVIDENCE: ACCEPTABILITY AND VERIFIABILITY

Safe: can be accepted
by all reasonable audiences

Unsafe, illogical, untrue,
disagreed about

AUTHORITY OF SOURCE/S

Undisputed/positive/
informed and expert

Under dispute/negative

REPETITION/REPLICABILITY OF EVIDENCE—
established through lateral reading of authoritative sources

Repeated/replicable seen in
several authoritative sources

Not repeated/not replicable

RELEVANCE OF EVIDENCE—it is on point for our topic,
inquiry, or my claim about a topic of inquiry

Clearly relates to topic

Does not relate to topic

SUFFICIENCY OF EVIDENCE—
patterns of evidence across credible sources

Enough evidence to convince
discerning audience

Not enough evidence to
convince doubters

*Validity of Evidence—COLLECTION OF DATA IS SOUND and meets
disciplinary standards of science, social science, for methodology,
sample size, and so on. (*For more experienced students.
See also our lessons on evidence in Chapter 7.)

Sound research methods,
samples, collection of data

Suspect collection/methodology

SOURCE: Adapted from Smith and Wilhelm (2010). Thanks to Rachel Bear for her help in developing these scales.

ARTICLE TITLE AND STUDENT READERS JIGSAW TEAM EXPERT	PURPOSE IN READING THE TEXT (E.G., POTENTIAL CLAIMS ABOUT OUR INQUIRY TOPIC THAT THE EVIDENCE SUPPORTS, OR A COMMENT THE EVIDENCE MIGHT MAKE ABOUT THE INQUIRY TOPIC)	STRONGEST PIECES OF EVIDENCE BASED ON OUR SEMANTIC DIFFERENTIAL SCALE CRITERIA	POTENTIAL WAYS TO USE THE EVIDENCE: ILLUSTRATING, AUTHORIZING, EXTENDING, COUNTERING	POSSIBLE LIMITATIONS OF EVIDENCE AND/OR SOURCE
Title: Name of Student Expert:				
Title: Name of Student Expert:				
Title: Name of Student Expert:				
Title: Name of Student Expert:				

LESSON 3.3
Learning With a Beginner's Mind

LESSON BACKGROUND

"Clearing the space" and "opening the mind" is akin to what Buddhists call using "the Beginner's Mind." It's the process of dropping all preconceived ideas, expectations, and System 1/Default Mode System ways of thinking about something, to perceive with an open mind as if for the first time, without personal preconceptions or cultural lenses, with fresh eyes and a fresh heart: *just like a beginner*. Steps involve first cultivating Beginner's Mind with our cherished beliefs, ideas, and commitments—to see them objectively, and to consider and interrogate them in new ways using System 2 thinking.

Purpose

- To learn how to set aside, at least temporarily, one's automatic and usual lenses for seeing and thinking so you can see and think in a new way, so you can perceive and entertain new perspectives, and see new possibilities in different viewpoints, stories, evidence, and so on. You will learn how to use the Beginner's Mind so you can outgrow your current self and find new and more powerful ways of engaging, knowing, thinking, doing, and being!

Length

- 60–90 minutes

Materials

- Student journals. Students bring in objects/artifacts with great personal meaning.

LESSON STEPS

Step 1

Ask students to respond in their journals to the following questions. The teacher can model their own responses to get things going:

- Share examples of how you get stuck in a pattern of doing the same things day after day. Ask, What are some mindless habits you just use without much conscious thought? For example:
  - What are some thoughts you find yourself repeating across situations?
  - What stories do you repeatedly tell about yourself, others, particular groups, specific situations, the world and the way it is, and so on?
  - In what situations are you repeatedly indecisive, or do you repeatedly make the same kind of bad decision?

- In what situations do you experience the same kinds of triggers or heightened emotion, the same kinds of resistance to an idea, task, or challenge?

- Ask students to share some of their responses with a trusted peer, if they are willing. What do they notice: Similarities? Contrasts in response? Willing learners can share their responses with the whole class; ask all others to note similarities and differences in their own responses.

Step 2

Tell students: "Because our minds are unconsciously directed by various preconceptions, commitments, values, habits, habit energies, cultural lenses, cognitive biases, limiting belief systems, and repeated stories, our range of possibilities for powerfully and consciously navigating our lives with the greatest awareness, freedom, and power can quickly shrink to a few restricted habits that don't always work very well. How can we break the pattern and access new more powerful ways of seeing and being? Through the practice of Beginner's Mind!"

Step 3

Introduce the **Precious Personal Artifact Activity**. Ask learners to bring in a precious personal artifact (or a photo of one). The meaning should be personal—and not culturally obvious (e.g., an award or a wedding ring have conventional meanings so would be poor choices). The shared artifact should be one with deep and hidden personal meaning and personal history that is not obvious to others (e.g., Jeff often shares a 1940 British farthing that his father carried as a soldier in WWII during the invasion of Normandy and then across France and Germany).

Step 4

Students exchange the object with a partner and record and describe all that they see in that artifact on one half of a sheet of paper—these are observable facts about the object that are "safe"—that all would agree on. On the other half page, they then interpret the possible meanings of each feature recorded. This *reflective* process necessarily depends on applying one's own experience and habitual ways of seeing and interpreting.

Step 5

Students then interview their partners to understand the meaning of the object to its owner. They check and confirm their understanding with mirror statements:

- "What I hear you saying is . . ."

- "This object means X to you because . . ."

- "I hear that this object/feature is significant to you because . . ."

- "The story behind this object is . . ."

This is the process of **reflexivity** because it requires learning to see *from someone else's unique position, experience, and perspective.*

Step 6

Next, learners introduce their partner and share the story and significance of their partner's object to the whole class—or to a small group if time is short. They enter into the perspective of their partner and speak from that perspective.

Step 7

Assign students to small groups for discussions (adapt questions as needed for age and content area):

- What have we learned about inquiry and the process of inquiry?

- What are the shortcomings or even dangers of applying our own experience to that of others? To objects, stories, or other forms of data?

- How can we consciously and reflexively access the perspectives of others?

- How did listing only objective facts before interpreting help cultivate Beginner's Mind?

- How did the interview help cultivate Beginner's Mind and new ways of seeing?

- What have we learned about suspending our own habitual ways of seeing and thinking to make use of Beginner's Mind?

- How can we use what we learned as we move forward to think about information pollution, good evidence, strong reasoning, and seeing from different perspectives? (Based on an activity from Julie Cheville.)

Note: Beginner's Mind is a way to let go of who you think you are and how you unconsciously think, if only for a few precious moments. And this allows for so many new possibilities. Again, this activity can be applied initially to simple objects and processes, and then to more significant ways of thinking, ideas, hopes, commitments, stories, and fears. The activity can achieve twofer status if the object or event that is shared relates to a current reading or inquiry (e.g., if Jeff shared his father's British farthing in the context of a unit on WWII or an inquiry into the experience of warfare for soldiers and their families, or an inquiry into what helps us get through hard times).

LESSON 3.4
Actively Seeking Out Alternative Positions

LESSON BACKGROUND

Human beings default unthinkingly to particular shortcuts for engaging, knowing, thinking, and doing that are often inappropriate or even harmful to oneself, others, deep understanding, and competence. This Default Mode System of the brain is also called System 1, and it promotes lazy nonthinking. We need to mindfully override Default Mode System/System 1 to take more conscious power over our thinking and our lives, particularly in high-stake situations. We need to decide what not to believe since our brains are designed to believe whatever they see, hear, or sense. This makes us vulnerable to manipulation.

Purpose

- To learn how to cultivate a mind-habit of always looking for counterclaims, new perspectives, and disconfirming evidence relative to students' usual viewpoints and habitual positions (i.e., to their own automatic Default Mode System/System 1 thinking)

Length

- 30 minutes if reading is done out of class, 45–60 if reading is pursued in class

Materials

- Articles or excerpts from credible sources that take different points of view on the same issue

You can provide these reading materials in your first pass at this lesson; then, in future iterations of the lesson you can ask students to seek out and find articles with differing points of view and/or a point of view different from their own—making sure these are from credible sources.

LESSON STEPS

Step 1

Provide articles exploring differing positions on a hot topic related to the ongoing inquiry. In subsequent lessons, coach students on how to find texts and perspectives from credible sources presenting differing positions, including a position that the learner strongly disagrees with. This can be a very useful weekly or biweekly activity.

Step 2

Students discuss in dyads or triads how their preexisting viewpoints were challenged.

- What evidence might compel them to consider—even if only in part and tentatively—these alternative points of view?

- What might make them take a revised position that moves closer, even if only somewhat, to points of view that diverge or are oppositional to their own original view?

Step 3

Large group sharing and insights scribed onto an anchor chart around these questions:

- What would or could internally persuade us to revise our thinking on this issue (or other issues) in some way?

- If we are unwilling to be persuaded, what does that indicate about us (our willingness to learn; our commitment to personal growth and improvement; our commitment to truth, justice, competence, informed social policy; our commitment to ideology, tribal affiliations, denial, etc.)?

- How could we open our minds, even tentatively? How might we cultivate Beginner's Mind in such situations to step back and give a different view with some respectful consideration? What benefits might accrue?

Step 4

Activate *counterfactual questioning* when dealing with complex issues by asking students to consider: How might my thinking be different if I was born a different race (it can be helpful to be specific: if I were born Black, Latinx, Native American), in a different country or place (farm vs. inner city), in different circumstances (rich, middle class or poor, with different parents), different eras (the early 1600s or 1960s vs. today), of a different cultural or religious tradition? Explain that this kind of work exercises our social imagination and makes us reflect on the origins of our own thinking and commitments—and to reflect on the thinking and commitments of others. This raises awareness of social context and situation in the development of beliefs, positions, and commitments. This process can make us more open to rethinking our own positions or regarding them as more conditional, situational, and tentative.

Extension

Ask students to choose and read/view their own different oppositional texts. For example, ask them to take the *Diversity Challenge*: If they are a CNN or MSNBC fan, then they need to go to Fox once a week (or vice versa) to make sure they get exposure to diverse sources and positions. If they read the *New York Times*, have them read the *New York Post*. If they get news from social media, have them find an influencer with contrasting views to their usual sources. And if students are unaware of these news and cultural outlets, you have done them a favor in introducing these to them! (*Note.* There are interesting online guides from researchers that rate the political leanings of different news and media sources based on electoral endorsements, op-ed pieces, etc.; e.g., All Sides Media bias chart: https://www.allsides.com/media-bias/media-bias-chart. Have students use these resources to check the bias of any source they use.)

LESSON 3.5
Trigger Tracking and Fever Charts

LESSON BACKGROUND

When we are emotionally triggered, intensely desirous, anxious, or fearful, we revert to System 1/Default Mode nonthinking. This makes us especially susceptible to errors in understanding, judgment, and action—often with harmful effects to ourselves, our relationships, and our community. We therefore need a way to recognize and control such triggers.

Purpose

- To become aware of and track one's emotional triggers, which necessarily moves people into System 1/Default Mode nonthinking

- To engage students in considering how to bracket out, contain, and control these impulses—at least tentatively—so that they can see more objectively and more with a Beginner's Mind

Length

- 90–135 minutes

Materials

- Examples of fever charts like those in Figures 3.1 and 3.2 for characters in a story, historical figures, and evolution of thought about a particular concept. Instructions on how to create a fever chart can be found on the companion website.

Note: The purpose of a fever chart is to track important changes in a character (like their thinking, emotional state, etc.) or culture, situation, force, or concept over the course of time, including over the course of a reading or inquiry. The fever chart tracks the evolution of its focus through a journey over time and helps students identify important moments in the narrative of that focus (person, emotion, etc.). The chart has an x axis for measuring the focus (thinking, emotional state, etc.) and a y axis for influences on that focus, causes of change, and so on. The influences or causes of change, in turn, offer valuable cues to takeaways, generalizations, and themes.

FIGURE 3.1 Fever Chart *Number the Stars*

Here is a basic example of a fever chart tracking Annemarie's courage throughout *Number the Stars*. Students are asked "What makes you say so?" to help them cite data for where they plotted the points on the chart.

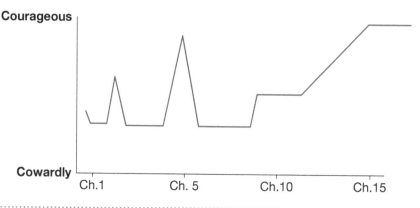

SOURCE: Wilhelm, Bear et al. (2020).

FIGURE 3.2 Fever Chart Example

Mr. Chiu is the protagonist of the story "The Saboteur" by Ha Jin, whose experience with oppressive Chinese bureaucracy leads him to develop a passive but surprisingly powerful way of fighting back. His resistance is charted here.

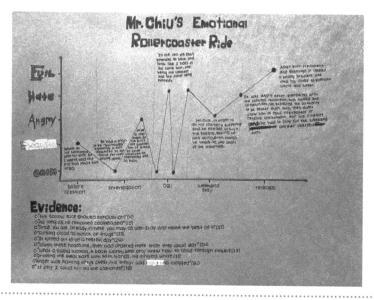

SOURCE: Provided by Jasmine Wilhelm.

LESSON STEPS

Step 1

Tell students that they will chart a character's (or historical figure's or concept's, or force's, etc.) response over time to certain circumstances, demands, ideas, and challenges by using a fever chart. Learners must be able to provide evidence to justify their charting of that response (courage, frustration, resistance) or whatever your focus is by citing evidence (What makes me say so?) and using reasoning (So what?).

Step 2

Share fever chart examples and explore what is revealed about character (or the concept, force) and about what causes characters, ideas, and so on to adapt, learn, deepen commitments, or change. Ask: What are our takeaways?

Step 3

Ask students to create a fever chart for a character, idea, and so on that they have already read about.

Step 4

Next, students will create a fever chart to tell the story of their own evolving understanding, or emotion about, resistance to, and so on, to a topic or idea from the current inquiry unit.

Students read texts exploring different perspectives about the inquiry topic throughout the unit and keep track in their journals of their own strong agreements, disagreements, confusions, and/or their emotional charges to that topic or an aspect of it. Students consider and journal about these questions:

- When am I triggered? What does it reveal about me and my own positions, commitments, hopes, fears, and so on?

- Who does my agreement or disagreement serve? Who wins/who loses?

- Where does my own position fall regarding who/what is served: self-oriented, group/tribe-oriented, world-oriented, or cosmic-oriented (for some higher moral purpose)? How do we feel about that?

Step 5

Students create a personal fever chart (in which they are the character!) of their responses to a focal idea they have encountered throughout a text or an inquiry unit.

Extension

Make a fever chart of a personal position on an issue over time—maybe from throughout one's life about a topic in which understanding has changed—as one learns more from exploring different positions. Then reflect by asking:

- What is compelling to us?

- What do we resist?

- Why?

Share journals and responses at any time and discuss:

- What are we learning about ourselves and the world?

- What triggers us, and how might we control that or bracket/contain it?

LESSON 3.6
Monitoring Mind Misdirection

LESSON BACKGROUND

Optical illusions and misdirection texts can help students see how their brains can misperceive due to cognitive biases like confirmation or availability bias.

Purpose

- To help students see what happens when we read pictures and other texts and how easily we are misdirected and can be misled to misperceive

Length

- 50–75 minutes

Materials

- Optical illusions and misdirection texts
- "What Happens When We Read" PowerPoint (available at the companion website)

LESSON STEPS

Step 1

Tell students that you will be exploring what happens when we *read and interpret* textual information.

Step 2

Project the famous picture titled "My Wife and Her Mother." Don't share the title.

Step 3

Ask students to record—but NOT say aloud—what they see first.

(Almost always this is an old woman in profile, whom they often identify as a witch.)

Step 4

- Ask students, before any sharing is done, if they can see anything else. (Although it may take some prompting, most students will be able to see the young woman who is turned away, with the feather boa coming out from her forehead.)

- Have students share what they saw first and then second. Some students may have difficulty seeing a second image.

Step 5

- Share the title from the original publication of the picture in *Puck* magazine from the 1890s: "My Wife and Her Mother." Ask pairs to discuss what the artist has announced that we as readers/viewers must do through that title. (We have to see two figures, compare them, and make some kind of thematic interpretation like "Watch out! Your wife will someday look like your mother-in-law!" or "Things can really change as we get older!" which they can then choose to accept, adapt, or resist.)

- Share ideas. You can discuss the importance of titles as a *rule of notice* that directs our noticing and interpreting (see Chapter 4).

Step 6

- Ask learners why they saw the old woman first and why they might have had difficulty seeing the young one (or, as will sometimes happen, why some viewers will see the young woman first but not the old one).

- Explain that this is an example of both confirmation and availability bias because when seeing a portrait, the genre expectation (based on prior experience—so availability and confirmation bias are both in play) is to see a person's face or profile. They can see the face of the old woman, which confirms this bias, but it keeps one from seeing the other woman who is turned away because this is a violation of typical genre norms for portraits.

- Also explain that the old woman is more available (her face is bigger), more consistent with their experience (everyone seems old to them!), and the reference to a witch or hag alludes to fairy tales with which they might be familiar (availability bias).

- Ask students if they can see both women at the same time. Explain that they can't (though they might see one and then a nano-second later see the other) because we organize data into meaningful patterns (called *schema*) and once organized in a particular way it is very hard to see the data in a different way (confirmation bias) because we tend to see and think the way we have seen and thought in the past. This is why we can hypertask but not multitask—the brain can only do one thing at a time and perceive data in one schema at a time.

Step 7

Explain that the young woman is a "Gibson Girl" (or "flapper" although they came a bit later) with whom students may be unfamiliar. *Note.* Jeff often has to show his students photos of Gibson Girls (who interestingly influenced modern notions of female beauty), which immediately helps learners see the young woman in this double portrait. They did not yet have the available experience to bring to their transaction with the text to perceive the young woman, and the photo can give them the experience that allows them immediate access for seeing her (availability bias). Explain that this highlights the necessity of background knowledge to comprehension—and the need to build background if you do not have it for a particular topic of text. (In general, the less you know, the more you are susceptible to confirmation and availability bias.) Ask: If you only saw the old or the young woman, are you wrong? Explain that if they only saw one they just did not have the fullest possible interpretation or the one the artist is promoting. In transactional reader response theory, you are not reading well, and not ethically responding to an author, unless you honor *all* the codes of a text—including, in this case, the title. So the picture here and our interpretation of it must be about two women.

Step 8

Show the students the second image and ask them to privately write down what they see. Answers will range from an open doorway (Freudian or Jungian interpretations, anyone?), the back of a moving truck, the top of an empty cereal box, an Abe Lincoln stovepipe hat, a graduated cylinder, two polygons, and so on.

Step 9

Ask learners why they might have seen what they did (perhaps the student who saw the back of a moving van has recently moved, the student who saw an empty cereal box missed breakfast, etc.). This activity can reinforce

- that any object or piece of evidence can be perceived and interpreted in various ways

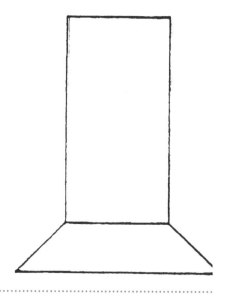

- that reading any kind of text is a transaction that involves the background, lenses, ways of seeing, purposes and needs of the moment, and so on of the reader—as well as the explicit codes of the text (see previous explanation and Chapter 1 on transactional reading). In other words, the meaning does not reside entirely IN a text, or entirely IN a reader, but in the transaction between them. That's why we have to reflectively monitor how we read the word and the world and be curious and reflexive about how others see it and why they might see it that way.

SOURCE: Left illustration created by Joel Wilhelm.

Step 10

Ask students which one is the biggest cat in the image above. They will immediately say that the largest figure is the one furthest to the right.

Have students measure the cats. They will be astounded that the cats are all the same size. Explain that one convention of Western art is to see receding lines as going off into the distance (the technique of the receding line/perspective), and therefore to interpret objects that are in the distance along that receding line as bigger than they appear. Explain that this is an example of how all texts work through conventions, which are just mutual agreements: We agree that two lines that come together on a horizon line mean that we are looking into the distance. This keeps us from seeing actual reality. When Jeff taught aboriginal children in Australia, they saw all the cats as being the same size—because their art does not use this convention; they do not have this agreement about how texts work and must be interpreted. Texts have many such conventions. We have conventional agreements about argument, what counts as evidence, about irony, when you should look for alternate meanings, and so on.

Step 11

- Ask students what the next image (next to the cats) represents and to privately write that down. They will struggle. Then tell them: "Oh no! I showed it to you upside down!" and share this image:

- Ask them to privately write down what they see now. If they have trouble, have them focus on the top left (a horse's head), or center top (the head of the knight). Seeing just one part will immediately lead to perceiving the whole. Explain that this is another example of schema—we organize data into patterns—and if we cannot find a pattern, then data looks confused and meaningless. Availability and confirmation bias can play into our first organization of data.

Note. This activity should reinforce at least two things:

1. Our angle of vision or perspective (and our prior experience and background knowledge) affects what we see (or don't see). If we manipulate the data or see it from a different position, angle, or with a different lens, then it will help us see anew, to see something different, to have an entirely different experience.

2. We are always interpreting and "figuring forth" from data points, filling in what are known as inference gaps. In this picture, we are given less than half the information, but we fill in the gaps to make a complete picture. As Umberto Eco (1978) has famously maintained, reading is the taking of *inferential walks* in which we have "point A and point E and must walk points B, C, and D to connect the two." How we "walk," and what we see, will be influenced by confirmation and availability bias. By controlling for the biases, we can be helped to see new things and in new ways.

Step 14

The sequence continues by exploring sentences and paragraph-length texts (see the online PowerPoint for these additional texts) that reinforce and extend these ideas.

LESSON 3.7
"Noticing and Naming" Practice for Controlling Cognitive Biases

LESSON BACKGROUND

Deliberately practicing more expert and mindful ways of receiving and interpreting information is essential! In this lesson, we concentrate on three of the most common cognitive biases:

1. **Confirmation bias** is simply the tendency to interpret new evidence as confirmation of one's existing beliefs or theories or ways (schema) of seeing and organizing our view of the world (even if this requires quite a stretch!) or to seek only evidence that confirms one's position and to ignore or discount any data that is disconfirming. This leads to fake skepticism.

2. **Availability bias** is the human tendency to think that examples that come readily to mind or that are nearer to our own personal experience are more representative than is actually the case.

3. **Overdramatization bias.** Rosling (2018) proposes that this is the most prevailing human bias. This bias is a cover term for a subset of **ten biases,** which all lead us to overdramatize (i.e., to see things as more extreme and negative than they are) and thus to misunderstand the world. Rosling argues that the cost of this bias is tremendous, in large part because it keeps us from correctly perceiving why and how things are improving and could continue to improve, and therefore hinders our recommitment to the ways social policies and interventions actually work to improve the world and address specific problems like education, poverty, and so on.

These psychological phenomena are just three of a large number of **cognitive biases** that hamper critical thinking and, as a result, our correct understanding of the world and the validity and effectiveness of our positions and decisions. You can also see how media companies or social media platforms that offer political slants (like MSNBC or Fox: see Allsides!) directly and continuously manipulate us through all three of these pervasive biases. (Rosling's [2018] book *Factfulness* is a must-read for all teachers and students!)

Purpose

- To help students recognize common cognitive biases and how they mislead us and others to make snap decisions (System 1/Default Mode System nonthinking) that do not serve our accurate understanding, personal welfare, or the well-being of others and the planet

Length

- The first lesson takes 60–120 minutes; then ongoing as appropriate throughout the year

Materials

- Cognitive bias chart (Handout 3.7A)

- Visual depictions of strategies for fighting overdramatization biases (Handout 3.7B)

- Procedural feedback cue sheets (Handouts 3.7C, 3.7D, and 3.7E)

Resources

- Cognitive bias chart (Handout 3.7A). Charts such as the ones shown are good ones to hang in a classroom and refer to when useful. There are many versions of such charts available online.

LESSON STEPS

Step 1

Provide students with the article: "No, 2016 Wasn't the Worst Year Ever" from the *Valley News* or a similar story about our negativity bias (a kind of over-dramatization bias): http://www.vnews.com/column-worstyear-saturday-vn -123116-7160127.

Step 2

Ask students to discuss their major takeaways from the reading in pairs and then in a larger group. Be sure to highlight how news has a negative and short-term bias that we tend to extrapolate as continuing forever in the same way (the straight-line overdramatization bias), and if we look at *long-term* trends things are improving for humanity so short-term news and news are generally biased mathematically, scientifically, and historically because it rarely considers long-term trends and contexts.

Step 3

Introduce the three major biases (**confirmation, availability,** and **overdramatization/ negativity**) and generate multiple examples of each as a class. Students could find or create a visual image to demonstrate each (like in Handout 3.7A) or students could create visuals or memes demonstrating understanding such as those in Handout 3.7B.

Step 4

Share one of the bias charts featured previously (Handout 3.7A) or another one that you find online or elsewhere.

Step 5

Ask students to read the chart in jigsaw groups, with each individual in groups of four or five to select a different bias and think of examples of it.

Step 6

Share and revise until all agree that each example reflects the selected bias.

Step 7

Share with the class. Post around the classroom.

Step 8

- Ask learners to consider a literary character, TV or movie character, real-life talking head, public figure, or even someone one knows from one's own life. Read about or watch the chosen figure in action, listening carefully to their opinions and justifications.

- Identify a cognitive bias that might be in play for them.

- Use Handouts 3.7C, 3.7D, and 3.7E on giving procedural feedback, aka *causal* or descriptive feedback (Wilhelm, Bear, et al., 2020; Wilhelm, Miller, et al., 2020) to explain how the cognitive bias is working, for example:
  - The way X does/says Y demonstrates cognitive bias A because . . .
  - The bias of X interferes with accurate understanding by A, B, C . . .

- Use procedural feed-forward stems to suggest ways forward for having a more accurate and less biased way of thinking, for example:
  - I wonder what would happen if the character considered/researched/ reframed X by doing Y.
  - I wonder what would happen if the character asked counterfactual questions like Z, because this would control for the bias of A by . . .

Extension

- You also can track characters over time to see the cognitive biases affecting them and the extent of the effect (see the fever chart as a way to track). You can also track your own cognitive biases throughout a unit of study or an event or interaction of some kind.

- Students can also track changes in understanding or thinking for a character or historical figure or one's own understanding over time using something like the chart in Figure 3.3. They can use any change-in-understanding chart, or a fever chart of some kind, showing the effect of cognitive bias on emotions, deeper or more erroneous understanding, and so on.

FIGURE 3.3 Change-in-Understanding Chart

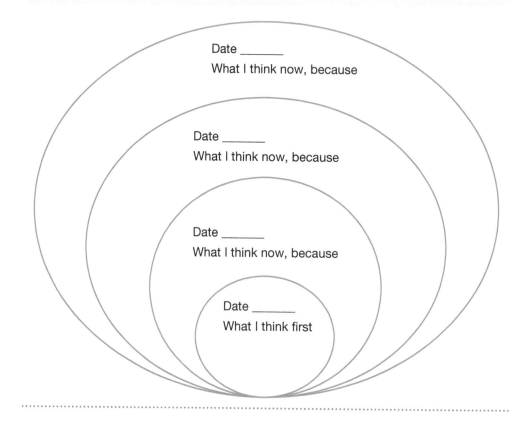

Note: In this activity, it is important to notice and explain changes in understanding and to justify these as moving in the more productive directions toward expert understanding and even ultimate reality. Remember: The surest way to prove you have a mind is to be able to change it. Change in understanding may involve a more justified confirmation of previous views, more nuanced understanding, or fundamental changes and new ways of seeing.

Cognitive Biases that screw up your perception and decision making!

Remix of Major Cognitive Biases: Confirmation Bias, Availability Bias, and related biases

Confirmation Bias/Selective Perception

We only hear information that supports our preconceptions. Information that doesn't fit our prior thinking just doesn't stick—it floats in and out of our brain!

Example: We only see the bad calls made against OUR team!

Reminder: Ask: What other positions are there? What disconfirming information exists?

Availability Bias

We overestimate the importance of information that is most readily available to us—from our life experience media, or in our surroundings—and think that available information is way more the norm than it is.

Example: Climate change can't be true because it's cold today. Smoking must be good for your health because my grandpa smoked and lived to be 100.

Reminder: Under-weigh your own memorable experiences. Look for other positions and possibilities.

Conservatism Bias (related to confirmation bias)

We favor old evidence and old ways of thinking over new possibilities that can be much more correct and powerful.

Example: Humans held on to their prior belief that Earth was flat despite scientific evidence that Earth was round!

Reminder: If you aren't constantly changing your mind, then you are behind the times (i.e., You are not learning or keeping up)!

Bandwagon Effect (related to availability bias)

The more people (especially those near and dear to us) believe something, the more likely we are to climb on the bandwagon! Aka Groupthink.

Example: Everybody has the new app, so you buy it, too! Everybody around you thinks the election was stolen, so you think so, too (without looking at the facts).

Reminder: If it's what everybody around me thinks, then it probably stinks (like a bandwagon).

(Continued)

(Continued)

Blind Spot Bias (related to confirmation bias)

Failing to see our biases and blind spots is a bias in itself! We see other people's biases way better than we see our own!

Example: You know what you know, but not what you don't know. So you see the proofreading errors in your friend's essay, but not your own!

Reminder: The more confident you are, the more your eyes are filled with stars. You don't see things as they are, but *as you are*!

Salience Bias (related to availability bias)

We tend to focus on the most immediate, most charged, and most recognizable features of a person, event, or concept.

Example: We fear airplane crashes although we are thousands if not hundreds of thousands of times more likely to die in a car wreck.

Reminder: Look deeper! Use real-time procedural feedback from a trusted peer!

Overconfidence/Lake Woebegone Effect (related to confirmation bias)

Most of us overestimate our own abilities and capacities. Almost everyone thinks they are above average in most domains!

Example: The more you are interested in or know about something, the more you think your position is the only one. You like to bicycle, so you think you have the corner on the market of knowledge about bicycling.

Reminder: The more confident you are, the more at risk you are. Things are more complex and detailed than we think. Consider how you could be wrong!

Anchoring (related to availability and confirmation bias)

We are all overly influenced and reliant on the very first piece of information that is introduced. It carries more weight and keeps us from straying too far from it—just like an anchor keeping a boat in place!

Example: The first review you read is a bad one, so you won't go to that movie or restaurant even though there are many other reviews that are good. When making an offer to buy, whoever makes the first offer establishes the range of reasonable possibilities.

Reminder: Bracket out first impressions, or you will miss the overall lesson! Look at all the data!

SOURCE: Illustrations by Joel Wilhelm, adapted from student ideas.

1. **The Gap Instinct:** We like to divide all kinds of things into two distinct and often conflicting groups. We tend to see only the extreme ends of data patterns, missing the great middle.

   Look between the extremes!

   Where is most of the data?

   Remember: Reality exists along a wide range!

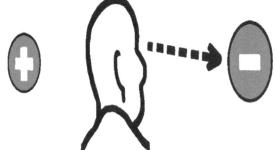

2. **The Negativity Instinct:** We tend to focus on the negative versus the positive.

   Look for improvements and possibilities amidst the challenges!

   Where is the positive news and possibility?

   Remember: Good news and gradual improvements are rarely reported.

3. **The Straightline Instinct:** We falsely think everything will continue at the same pace and same trajectory.

   Consider what and how things might change.

   Imagine how things can change in new ways and what might change them.

   How might the line bend? How might trajectories and pace differ over time?

   Remember: Trend lines are never linear when we look at them over time!

4. **The Fear Instinct:** We tend to overexaggerate risks and focus on information that triggers our fears.

   Consider the real risk. Compare the risk to those of everyday activities.

   How dangerous is this in reality?

   Remember: Never make decisions when you are gripped by fear!

(Continued)

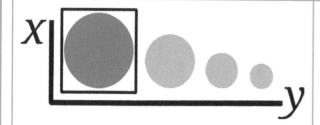

5. **The Size Instinct:** We tend to get things out of proportion, misjudge size, and exaggerate the importance of one data point.

Confirm the actual proportions!

How does this example compare to other examples?

Remember: Rates are more meaningful than amounts, especially when comparing different-sized groups.

6. **The Generalization Instinct:** We often group things together that have significant differences.

Consider how things are actually similar and different in ways that matter.

Are the categories we are using correct and appropriate to the problem at hand?

Remember: "They" are not all the same!

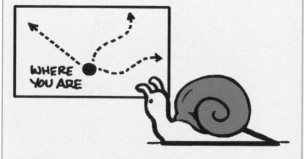

7. **The Destiny Instinct:** The way things are just the way they have to be, because of innate characteristics of people, countries, religions, and cultures.

Consider how most important changes evolve ever so slowly and occur over time, based on multiple causes.

How can you pay attention to and track slow changes and the real multiple causes of situations?

Remember: Things do change, but they often change slowly!

8. **The Single Perspective Instinct:** We see things from one position and fail to even consider that there are other positions to take. We like simplicity! My way or the highway!

Use multiple lenses for seeing and multiple tools for thinking.

What other ways of seeing and thinking are there? What other solutions?

Remember: No tool is good for every job! No lens helps you see everything. Beware of simple ideas and solutions!

9. **The Blame Instinct:** We like to have a simple reason to blame for misfortune. We want to blame individuals or single causes for problems that were created by systems and multiple causes.

Put your pointer finger down!

Think about systems instead of people. What system was designed to make this happen? How could the system be redesigned for different results?

Remember: Look for the multiple causes of problems!

10. **The Urgency Instinct:** It's now or never! We tend to want immediate solutions to problems that were created over time and that will take time to solve.

See what can be done next and do it. Act short term and with short steps. Continuously check progress.

What is the next small step? Take the step, consider, reflect, and then make the next decision.

Remember: Beware drastic actions!

SOURCE: Adapted from Rosling's *Factfulness* Chart. Based on remixes of student work. Illustrations by Joel Wilhelm.

I noticed when Character A did _____ that he was suffering from the cognitive bias of _____ because _____ and then X happened (effect of the bias) _____. I wonder what would happen if Character A tried the correction or monitoring strategy of _____ because then _____.

The way you ___(name effort and strategy used)___ had the effect of ___(describe effect)___ because ___(explain WHY and HOW it worked)___.

I wonder what would happen if you tried _____(define new approach)_____.

Because _____(explain why it might work)_____.

And this could extend learning and effect by _____(potential impact)_____.

LESSON 3.8
Self-Study of Social Media Use

LESSON BACKGROUND

One of many powerful ways to prepare students for success with new challenges is by activating learners' preexisting interests and prior knowledge that relate (conceptually and/or procedurally) to the upcoming learning challenge and to foreground the purpose and payoff of meeting the new challenge. One way to do all this is to frontload instruction by watching videos (or excerpts) that activate background knowledge around an issue that will be studied and build on it in ways that challenge, problematize, or complexify current thinking and behavior.

Purpose

- To become further aware of the ways social media operates to manipulate us, so we can do something about it and take more conscious control over our lives

Length

- 90 minutes if videos are watched outside of class; otherwise, dependent on the video length or the length of excerpts you choose to watch

Materials

- Video(s) of your choice to share with students (examples follow)

Resources

- PBS offers a 7-minute video called "Media*ocracy*" along with a lesson plan on how social media targets you and uses amplification and echo chambers to manipulate your thinking (by exploiting overdramatization bias!), encouraging ever more extreme views and actions. The video also offers agentive alternatives such as curating and monitoring your own news sources. The video foregrounds both the manipulative power of SMU and our own responsibilities as users (https://www.pbs.org/newshour/extra/lessons-plans/decoding-media-bias-lesson-plan).

- We have had great success asking students to watch excerpts from the documentary *The Social Dilemma* (2020) (available through Netflix and other streaming services; YouTube offers many excerpts) and to respond to the issues that come up.

- We have likewise used the film *Coded Bias* (2020) (on Netflix and YouTube) and the Getting Better Foundation's award-winning *Trust Me* (2021) (https://www.trustmedocumentary.com/). These videos explore how we are all being manipulated and controlled when we use social media and what might be done about it.

LESSON STEPS

Step 1

Have students respond to a survey about SMU, stating their level of agreement/disagreement with statements such as

- I am addicted to social media.

- Social media is a safe and reputable place to get news.

- Social media connects you to people with different perspectives.

- Social media often manipulates you into believing things that are for the benefit of political groups or corporations.

- Many of my social media contacts are Russian trolls.

Step 2

Share responses to the survey in pairs, explaining why they responded as they did. Ask students to come up with additional statements to agree/disagree with.

Step 3

Watch video excerpts from the featured videos. Our students responded especially strongly to the teen Russian hacker in *Trust Me*. In this short video he demonstrated how he creates false accounts in less than 3 minutes and uses them to target users.

Step 4

After watching, students record major points of insight, surprise, and resistance and share in dyads or triads.

Step 5

Ask students how what has been learned should inform future engaging, knowing, thinking, doing, and being, especially regarding SMU.

Extension

- Ask students if restrictions could be usefully placed on common human activities because they are dangerous to the self or others. You can likewise ask what current restrictions could be justifiably lifted.

- Propose that one should have to get a license and special training before dating, marriage, or parenting.

- Do a PMI (see https://www.debono.com/de-bono-thinking-lessons-1/1.-PMI-lesson-plan) to discuss plusses, minuses, and points of interest (see Handout 3.8A).

- Next, propose that SMU, given its dangers, the intense responsibility, and System 2 thinking required for mindful use, should be highly restricted by law and require stringent testing and a license to use.

- Ask students to list the plusses, minuses, and points of interest/significance on their own about this statement before turning and talking with a partner and then contributing to a larger discussion. The result is always intense and interesting.

PMI helps promote thinking and discussion by soliciting differing perspectives on an issue. This teaching strategy may be used in a variety of ways: to explore issues for argumentation, promote group discussion, develop thesis statements, and /or activate schema and develop mental models about the conceptual territory of a topic.

Offer a claim

Plus: What positives or pros might follow from the claim?

Minus: What negatives or cons might follow from the claim?

Interesting: What new interesting or significant insights or angles might be revealed through a consideration of the claim? Something you might not have considered previously?

Example: All the seats should be taken out of buses.

P: More people can get into each bus.

It would be easier to get in and out.

Buses would be cheaper to make and repair.

M: Passengers would fall over if the bus stopped suddenly.

Elderly and disabled people would not be able to use buses.

It would be difficult to carry shopping bags or babies.

I: Maybe there should be two types of buses, one with seats and one without seats.

The same bus would do more work and have more flexibility (e.g., one without seats could be used to carry cargo).

Comfort may not be so important in a bus.

Other claim statements we have successfully used:

All cars should be yellow.

All faculty and students should wear mood rings.

Special training and certification from the state should be required prior to dating/marriage/bearing children.

Using social media should require rigorous training, testing, and a license.

PMI EXAMPLE

Article: "Harvesting Danger, Disease, and Disaster: Threats to Our Food Security and Food Supply and What We Can Do About It!"

Genetically Modified Food

PLUS	MINUS	INTERESTING
What are the positive things about GM (genetically modified) foods?	What are the negative things about GM foods?	What are some of the interesting insights about GM food—or any other kinds of human hacks of nature—that came up?

LESSON 3.9
Autobiographical Research: Developing
Self-Awareness Through Self-Studies

LESSON BACKGROUND

When Jeff's daughter Jasmine was a college senior, she had a 10-week assignment to track her use of time and energy through a "time use diary." She had to monitor each segment of the day and how she made use of it. She then rated the quality of that time and described the ways that this time expenditure enriched or impoverished her. The purpose was to become consciously aware of habits and decisions, their causes and impacts, and to be responsible for oneself as a top priority—this included being responsible for how one engages, knows, thinks, and does anything, for every choice you make and action you take (or don't). The process engaged each student in monitoring oneself, one's actions, thinking, consequences, and feelings. Even before she was done with the project, reflected on it, and created an action plan based on her findings, Jazzy had already broken up with her boyfriend, changed how she spent time with friends, began to reconsider some of her beliefs, and suspended her Facebook account, realizing in glaring detail how negative and impoverishing some of these "time sucks" and interactions were—and the alternatives to them.

This activity promotes what Daniel Siegel (2022), a psychologist at UCLA, calls *mindsight*: our human capacity to perceive the mind of the self and others. On his website, he writes:

> It is a powerful lens through which we can understand our inner lives
> with more clarity, integrate the brain, and enhance our relationships
> with others. Mindsight is a kind of focused attention that allows us to
> see the internal workings of our own minds. It helps us get ourselves
> off of the autopilot of ingrained behaviors and habitual responses. It
> lets us "name and tame" the emotions we are experiencing, rather than
> being overwhelmed by them.

Purpose

- To record and analyze students' use of time by keeping a Time/Energy Diary. In this diary students will record each segment of their day and what they do with it, and then rate the quality of each event or segment of time, interpret their findings, and make an action plan for more mindful and productive living based on what they have learned.

Length

- 3–10 days outside of class; 5–10 minutes a day of class time on school days

Materials

- Writing materials

LESSON STEPS

Step 1

For 3 to 10 days, ask students to record each segment of their day, dividing it into events like waking up, preparing for the day, eating breakfast, getting to school, first-period class, and so on.

Step 2

On a scale of 1 to 10, ask students to rate the quality of lived-through experience during that time and the usefulness/productivity of each segment regarding some significant factors such as

- Learning
- Productive struggle (i.e., struggle that leads to learning or progress toward health and happiness, problem solving, meeting an important challenge)
- Social connection
- Personal health
- Pleasure
- Responsibility
- Psychological well-being

Step 3

After a few days, ask students to focus on examining their internet use and SMU and the quality of each segment of this time regarding some significant factors like those listed previously.

Step 4

Ask students to monitor their response on SMU to soapbox topics that trigger them.

- What issues tend to trigger you?
- What rabbit holes or clickbait do you follow?
- What are you likely to share? On what social media platform and why? What are you likely to argue with others about? Comment on? How mindful and responsible are you about these activities?

- Why do you react as you do?
- What alternate positions and reactions are there?

Step 5

Share findings and reflect on the following:

- How often are you connected online?
- For what reasons do you go online?
- How often does going online interrupt or supplant other activities?
- What is the typical result for each reason you go online? Do results differ with intention, situation, platform, or some other factor?
- How could the time have been spent more efficiently? Healthfully? Honestly? Differently?

Step 6

Share the Pearls before Swine cartoon and ask students what point Pastis is trying to make about why we post, and about responsible posting—and whether they agree.

Step 7

Challenge students to go on a short-term social media diet or a complete technology "fast," maybe starting with just a day or two.

Step 8

Ask students to journal about what they notice during an SMU diet or fast. (Jeff's students have reported how difficult this kind of "tech fasting" is at the beginning and how much more productive they are after just a day or two, how much more open they quickly become to new experiences or activities they had given up due to a lack of time.)

LESSON 3.10
Having Hard Conversations

Note: This lesson is based on a BSWP teaching demonstration by teacher Nolevanko (2022), based on the book *How to Have Impossible Conversations* (Boghossian and Lindsay, 2019).

LESSON BACKGROUND

How can we help ourselves and others remain open and curious in the face of cognitive biases?

For one's healthiest and most productive life, it's prerequisite and essential to be awakened to one's own biases and to control for them. This opens up fuller potential and capacity. But we'd also argue, as with any problem facing the world today, that the problems and the solutions are community ones. Dewey (1916) famously asserted that democracy is a conversation and that conversation not only involves speaking but also respectfully listening and responding and then moving forward together in "complementarity." Therefore, what role do we have in helping others be more critical consumers of news, science, social media, and all kinds of other "influencing machines"? The research indicates that we can help those around us be more open-minded if we model critical reading/thinking, proceed with good will, and are willing to stick with the process over the long haul (e.g., Pennycook & Rand, 2019).

Purpose

- To learn ways to engage with others, who may strongly disagree with us, in productive conversations around difficult and challenging topics with big emotional charges

Length

- 75–90 minutes; follow up as desired

Materials

- Handouts 3.10A, 3.10B, 3.10C, 3.10D, and 3.10E
- Writing materials

LESSON STEPS

Step 1

Brainstorm topics that are difficult to discuss with friends, classmates, parents, people from different groups or viewpoints, and so on.

Step 2

Discuss in pairs and then as a class: Why are these kinds of discussions so hard to have?

Step 3

Have students consider, write, and then share responses to these questions:

- How would you describe the most prevalent ways that Americans with different backgrounds/beliefs/ideas engage or talk to each other when they have different viewpoints?

- What do you think is the outcome of different ways of communicating about divisive issues? What are the costs and benefits of these different approaches?

Step 4

Ask students to consider the following quotes, using them as a starting point to explore the purposes and payoffs of being willing to pursue "impossible conversations":

- "We live in a divided, polarized era, and we're not talking with each other. The repercussions of this are vast and deep, including the fear of speaking openly and honestly, an inability to solve shared problems, and lost friendships" (Boghossian & Lindsay, 2019, p. 1).

- "Our main advantage as human beings lies in our ability to think together ... As a society, we have yet to reach our peak in capitalizing on this potential advantage" (Johnston, 2012, p. 93).

- "Diversity brings vitality to any system and to any conversation. If we do not promote diversity in our systems and in our personal relationships, if we do not consider other ways of seeing and knowing—even those with which we deeply disagree—then we are deeply impoverished in our understanding and capacity" (N. Postman, personal communication, November 20, 2002).

Step 5

Consider ways to get started on creating "rules for engagement for impossible conversations" by asking students to do a quick write on each of the following quotes:

- "We can't learn without uncertainty, without error and we shouldn't be threatened by this" (Johnston, 2012).

- "The only way we can get to difficult conversations is to build relationships that can sustain them" (Johnston, 2012).

Step 6

- Watch an episode of "Street Epistemology with Anthony Magnabosco": https://streetepistemology.com/. Warning: The purpose of Magnabosco's videos is to promote better conversations about challenging topics, and Magnabosco typically takes on charged issues of faith, racism, and so on. (Jamie Nolevanko watched the episode "Paul on Faith" with her classes.) If you are uncomfortable with these charged issues, you can choose another video that demonstrates the power moves of deep listening, mirroring, checking understanding, uptake, and so on. (Searching for "Having Hard Conversations + TED talks" brings up several good ones.)

- Inform students that *epistemology* refers to the investigation of what distinguishes justified, evidence-based positions versus personal opinion.

- Ask students to record the moves of using evidence, listening, and response they see (or see promoted) in the video and to consider the effects of each in furthering conversation and making it more (or less) productive. Add positive moves to your "rules of engagement for having hard conversations."

- Have students discuss their video responses in dyads or triads. They then work to create a class anchor chart of "power moves" for making impossible conversations productive.

Step 7

- After your class has constructed its own chart, ask students to choose the one "power move" that they think is most important and write about what makes them say so. As a class identify the top six power moves for productive conversation about difficult topics.

- Do a "6 Corners/Vote with your feet" activity—going to a sign in the classroom designating the one move out of the six that the learner thinks is most important. Students share justifications for their choice with the others at that sign. One person from that "corner" agrees to share the takeaways from the whole group.

Step 9

Get started on a difficult conversation with a less charged point of disagreement. To identify a suitable topic, have students respond individually to the questions on Handout 3.10A.

Step 10

With a partner, ask students to share their answers. Pairs pick a point of disagreement, and, using Handout 3.10B as a guide, attempt to have a productive conversation about your disagreement, making sure to use your "power moves" and "rules of engagement."

Step 11

Check out the following tips. Rewatch "Street Epistemology," or another video of a difficult discussion, and notice which of the tips (see Handout 3.10C) were used and notice how they worked—or might even be able to work better.

Step 12

Try a harder conversation, perhaps about one of the topics in Handout 3.10D, again using the tips from Handout 3.10C.

Step 13

First, work with people you agreed with on a statement of choice. Use Handout 3.10E: Finding Evidence for Beliefs, and begin by finding credible and safe evidence to support your position.

Step 14

Now, ask students to find a partner who disagreed with their statement to discuss the disagreement using all the prior tips, remembering your purpose *is to learn* (not win)!

Step 15

After the discussion, ask students to monitor and reflect on how well they followed the tips and how the tips worked and could work better. What have they learned about the topic at hand and about having difficult conversations? What do they want to remember to try out next time they have a difficult conversation, and how will they remind themselves?

WHAT MY STUDENTS HAD TO SAY!

"People have such different backgrounds, and that does not always represent who they really are."

"I am learning that people have very different views than me about America, but that they can politely disagree. I have also learned that people don't have to agree to get along. We can still be friends and have different views about certain things. People have better intentions than I think it is very possible to talk through a problem to get a solution."

"It's pretty easy to open up to someone once you're forced to do it."

"I'm learning that there are some things you can't agree on at times. I have to try and understand where they are coming from."

"Don't respond in a way where they feel like you are talking down to them. Instead ask them to elaborate or ask them to explain another topic."

ADDITIONAL RESOURCES

- Read De Bono's (2004) *How to Have a Beautiful Mind* as a wonderful book about listening, paying attention to, and respectfully responding to others.

- Read Abrams's (2009) *Having Hard Conversations* with many ideas that can be adapted for discussions with colleagues, friends, parents, and students.

- Discussion structures like Socratic Seminar or British Debate are both ways to organize conversations around careful listening, uptake, and response. These kinds of structures and protocols tend to bracket out emotional responses and promote System 2 thinking. (See Wilhelm, Bear, et al., 2020; Wilhelm, Miller, et al., 2020 for chapter-length treatments about using different kinds of discussion structures.)

- Practice essential practices for listening and responding like **mirroring** and **uptake**. Teach students how to do these things:
  - **Mirroring:** the practice of listening and then repeating back what a person has said and asking for correction.
  - **Uptake:** the process of using the thinking you have heard to extend that thinking and build on it or revise, offer alternatives, or resist the utterance in some way. It is the hallmark of what is called *dialogic discussion.*

CONCLUSION

Let's make no mistake. What we are proposing is a heavy lift. It involves overcoming our own and our students' cognitive biases, habit energy, and deeply entrenched ways of engaging, thinking, believing, knowing, doing, and being that are reinforced by powerful forms of artificial intelligence, and often by friends and family. Engaging more mindfully with the world, social media, news, and data will require constant vigilance and continuous deliberate practice with new habits of mind such as self-reflection, lateral reading, and the use of mental models for verifying data and controlling for cognitive bias. An ethic of responsibility and consciousness in reading and posting can also lead to other forms of cultural responsibility that will be helpful to all.

Every text we read—from a Twitter post to a poem to a political ad to a poster—was written by somebody (or some group) who wants to manipulate us in some way—to encourage or entice us to know, believe, or do something. This means that we always have to ask who this person is or who the people are, what they want from us and why, and whether we want to go along—and how to respond along a continuum of respect and acceptance to justified and reasoned resistance.

It's important to always remember that self-discipline requires a healthy skepticism of your own immediate reactions, thoughts, beliefs, and emotions. These are System 1 responses and are never worth following blindly. We must apply critical literacy (System 2) to these ingrained and automatic ways of reacting and thinking.

Scholar Pedro Noguera (personal communication, 2022) compellingly argues that "[c]ritical literacy is the vaccine for ignorance and delusion." Critical literacy is the way for us to proceed in exercising more conscious, ethical, and mindful control over our own minds, actions, and decisions. It is the way to move beyond being manipulated and toward a healthier worldview and a more compassionate and successful future for ourselves, our community, the world, and the environment. There is much at stake. But it can be done and is well worth doing.

Reflection Questions

- How can we motivate ourselves and our students to engage in this work?

- When could you use one of these assignments—or a part of one of these sequences—in a unit you already plan to teach?

- How would the assignment help students navigate the unit more consciously or powerfully?

- How would the assignment or an adaptation of it help promote learning that you value about the unit topic, as well as other capacities you value?

 Access lesson handouts and more resources at
resources.corwin.com/fightingfakenews.

Check the statements you agree with.

1. __ A hot dog is a sandwich.

2. __ Ghosts are real.

3. __ Playing a game is fun only when you win.

4. __ Summer is the best season of the year.

5. __ The night is better than the day.

6. __ It's sometimes okay to lie.

7. __ Snow is better than sand.

8. __ You have control over whether you experience good luck or bad luck.

9. __ Money can't buy happiness.

10. __ You can't depend on anyone else; you can only depend on yourself.

11. __ Everything happens for a reason.

12. __ In today's world, writers and artists are not as important to society as scientists and engineers.

13. __ Popcorn is a vegetable.

Beginning a Conversation

- Identify your conversational goal(s)—learning from each other

- Build rapport immediately, not with a substantive issue, and find common ground
  - Since we have been building community, just greet your partner

Determine and Discuss Your Topic

- Can you tell me more about . . .?

- Lots of How . . .? And What . . .? Questions

- Other Meaningful Responses
  - Probing for Higher Level Thinking:
    - What examples do you have
    - How does this idea connect to . . . ?
    - What would happen if . . . ?
    - What is another way to look at it?
    - How are _____ and _____ similar?
    - How do you know that? Can you give an example?
  - Reaction/Building on What Others Say
    - I would like to add/disagree/add/connect . . .

Ending a Conversation

- Summary/Synthesize
  - So it sounds like what you are saying is that . . .
  - What I'm getting from this conversation is that we both . . .
  - So what I've learned is that . . .

- Thank you for taking the time to . . .

- I appreciate . . .

HANDOUT 3.10C   Conversation Tips

TIPS
Define important words/concepts upfront
Model the behavior you want to see in your partner
Find a source of information you can both rely on
Ask questions to find understanding and invite conversation
Reveal ignorance of ignorance
Mirror/Synthesize
Avoid certainty, and avoid questions and phrases that imply certainty

Check the statements you agree with.

1. __ America offers opportunity to everyone.

2. __ The American Dream is achievable for everyone.

3. __ You can be whoever you want to be in America.

4. __ Our most inalienable right as Americans is the pursuit of happiness.

5. __ Our most important right as Americans is the freedom of speech.

6. __ Every citizen in America is protected equally under the law.

7. __ People who are poor have just as much of a chance to make it in America as people who are rich.

8. __ America's diversity makes it a better, more vital, and more unique place to live.

9. __ We have more freedom in America than anywhere else in the world.

10. __ America offers you access to more learning and knowledge than other countries.

11. __ America is the world leader in democratic government and life.

12. __ People should be proud to be American.

13. __ People should feel lucky to be American.

14. __ America can be a better place.

15. __ If you do not love America, then you should leave it.

16. __ Loving America means recognizing its faults and shortcomings and working to make America better.

1. In groups, find one belief statement that you all checked and agree with.

2. What do you think?
   - Individually brainstorm specific evidence from reading, observation, and experience that support your point of view. Evaluate the evidence and evidence source. Employ laterality.

BELIEF:		
Evidence from reading with justification of source, evaluation of evidence, how it matches other sources and evidence (lateral reading)	Evidence from observation, how it matches other evidence (laterality)	Evidence from personal, lived-through experience, how it matches others' experience (laterality)

3. Share and vote for the best piece of support within your group.
   - "Bestness" should be measured by direct connection to belief, criteria for strong evidence, for laterality, and should be accepted on these bases without "raised eyebrows."

4. Share with the whole class and they will determine what they think the support is showing.

Extension: Compose a "This I Believe" essay based on your findings.

CHAPTER 4

Lessons Using Rules of Notice in Online Reading

In a school in which Hugh recently worked, students in eleventh and twelfth grade had access to a class set of Chromebooks. Hugh decided to create an online textbook using Google Classroom. The textbook worked well: Hugh had carefully formatted everything so that it was easy to follow and so that there were no messy or unpredictable digital elements. In short, while setting the class up to use their digital devices efficiently, Hugh had cut out all the messiness and distraction we normally encounter online. But then it struck him: By cutting out messiness and distraction, his students weren't able to read in the way we normally read online. Hugh became worried that he'd denied his students opportunities to draw on past reading experiences, and that they were missing chances to hone their online reading practices. He decided to have students work on some texts directly from the internet, with all of their digital features included, and then gauge their reactions.

Things didn't quite go as expected! While some students drew on the wealth of information available to them, many students didn't want to watch embedded videos or click links because they'd been conditioned to understand that schoolwork was based on the written, alphanumeric text. What, they wondered, was the text they were supposed to work on—were advertisements, videos, and font colors things they were supposed to consider? Even when Hugh insisted that students were permitted—and advised—to engage with digital features, some students didn't spot links if they were rendered in an unfamiliar color. To incorporate feature-rich digital material in his class and prepare his students for analytical reading of online texts, Hugh studied the particular demands of reading online. In this chapter, we share what he learned and introduce the teaching tools he developed, including:

- What *born-digital* texts do differently from conventional, linear print texts.

- What reading closely means when reading born-digital texts.

- How we can positively engage with ongoing, society-wide, and contentious conversations in online spaces.
- What sorts of tools we can develop in classrooms to sharpen reading of born-digital texts that transfer to all texts.

CLOSE READING AND DIGITAL TEXTS

In a detective story Hugh read recently, the protagonists were all searching for a red backpack, the contents of which would solve the mystery. Despite a lot of frantic searching, no one was having any luck finding the bag—until, that is, the detective realized she was making some wrong assumptions. She realized the backpack was not human-sized; it belonged to a doll and had been sitting right under everyone's noses. When she knew where to look, she found a USB stick full of incriminating material and solved the case.

The characters in this story didn't know what to look for, and as a result, they didn't know where to look for it. Close reading of texts can be a similarly fruitless task. If students don't know what they're meant to find and where, re-reading and poring over a text looking for elusive details that may unlock meaning is a frustrating exercise. Experienced readers begin to develop instincts for what matters when we read, in effect becoming text detectives. We draw on some pretty complex skills to practice what Wilhelm and Smith (2016) have previously noted as the top-down and bottom-up process of reading. They argue that expert readers are always moving between overarching understandings of the text they're reading to the details they pick up as they read. Experienced readers, for example, recognize that the recipe for ice cubes posted by Chrissy (n.d.) on Food .com is a tongue-in-cheek way to mock overly earnest food sites and chasten those family members who neglect to refill the ice trays. The joke doesn't work as well if you're not familiar with the conventions of recipes, food websites, or satire. Understanding the recipe draws on some quite sophisticated reading skills already, but what might prove even more challenging to the reader is the fact that it appears on Food.com. It is also a genuine recipe, and at point of this writing, it has received over 1,200 reviews and is reviewed at 4 out of 5 stars. We point this out because offline there's little chance that a serious recipe book that appeals to cooks and food writers will scatter in a handful of eccentric or satirical recipes for boiling water or toasting toast. Online it's a different story. Overarching understandings, for example, the expectation that a collection of recipes will be dedicated to food preparation and not comedy, can't guide reading the same way. It's not only recipes that differ in online and traditional print texts; we're increasingly recognizing that online texts differ from offline texts in important ways, and as a result, they make significantly different demands of readers.

BORN-DIGITAL TEXTS

Recognizing that there's something different about texts online and texts in their conventional, linear form is not a new observation. In 2002, the Rand Reading

Study Group concluded that "electronic texts . . . incorporate hyperlinks and hypermedia (and) require skills and abilities beyond those required for the comprehension of conventional, linear print" (Snow, 2002, p. 14). Since then, our understanding of texts online has evolved, just as technology has evolved and scholars have identified some important ways that *born-digital* texts, texts that are "created and managed in digital form" (Turner & Hicks, 2017, p. 13), function.

Three key points we think are important to note:

1. Texts with a range of different digital features (hyperlinks, images, blogrolls, ads, etc.) mean that readers are working to integrate or eliminate multiple sources of information (Cho, 2014; Zhang & Duke, 2008).

2. Online readers are making choices quickly; page elements are appearing simultaneously.

3. Readers can't call up all the same understandings and instincts they rely on in their offline reading. Online texts, created using high-quality graphic design and publishing software, can be distributed worldwide at the click of a button without any of the restrictions, or safeguards, applied to conventional publishing. So while text production has been democratized, it means the internet is an "ill-structured" (Coiro & Dobler, 2007, p. 246) environment where readers have to work hard to judge the value and credibility of what they read.

If you'd like to think about reading processes online, open your preferred web browser and search for "news." Click on any of the stories that appear and then, from first glance, mentally catalog all the things you see (and hear if you have your speakers on). We're guessing it'll be a pretty long list! Now that you've slowed down to consider what you're seeing and perhaps hearing,

- Do some things strike you more than others?

- Do you typically ignore some things you've just cataloged?

- What sorts of mental leaps are you making to make sense of what you see and/or hear (e.g., how do you understand links between images and text)?

- How are you judging the credibility of the news you're reading? If it's a site you're familiar with, then its level of credibility is probably based on past experiences, but if it's a new site to you, what sorts of things are you looking for?

As an experienced reader you no doubt have a pretty keen sense of what's valuable to your reading of linear, print texts, but how far does that translate to your online reading?

The previous reading activity provides practice in gaining overarching understandings that are refined and revised as you notice key details. What we didn't do, though, was provide a system for noticing key details, and we didn't suggest how you could work out a hierarchy of details. Let's turn now to considering how we can do that and how we might teach students to find the key details that will help them become critical readers who evaluate the credibility of what they read. In the following section, we think a bit more about how expert readers dig into texts to find important details, and then we turn to thinking about the specifics of reading born-digital texts.

THE RULES OF NOTICE

If not everything in a text is equally valuable to readers, how might we determine what is valuable? A helpful approach to teaching students to mine texts is developed by Wilhelm and Smith (2016) from Peter Rabinowitz's notion of the rules of notice. Rabinowitz (1987) argued that writers communicate by drawing on shared contexts and shared cultural codes. Readers can explore the ways texts have been constructed if we understand that writers write for the readers they expect, imagine, and invite to the text. Rabinowitz proposed that by following *rules of notice* (p. 43) readers could build an interpretation of texts by looking for the ways authors alert the reader that a detail MUST be noticed, interpreted, and potentially connected to other details.

> By following rules of notice, readers can build an interpretation of texts by looking for the ways authors alert the reader that a detail MUST be noticed.

Wilhelm and Smith's (2016) work focuses on the rules of notice for classroom teaching. If students are trained to look for signaling moves where the author directs reader attention to important details, they can see how authors have deliberately shaped their work. Students also need to be trained to notice genre and text structure to build knowledge about the conventions of different types of texts and how writers rely on or manipulate readers' expectations.

To train students to notice conversations, key details, and genre and text structure, Wilhelm and Smith (2016) condense the rules of notice into four areas that students may be taught:

1. **Direct statements** or generalizations, for example, explicit statements of meaning or principle

2. **Ruptures,** for example, sudden shifts in style or point of view

3. **Calls to attention,** for example, titles or lists

4. **Reader response,** for example, connections to the reader's lived experience, questions, passions, triggers, and so on

Wilhelm and Smith (2016) suggest that these categories should direct classroom approaches, but that they should not be imposed; rather, they should grow from inquiry contexts where students are encouraged to develop and apply new reading capacities that are rewarded and required by the work of inquiry. However, we have already committed to the idea that the born-digital texts operate quite differently from conventional, linear texts, so what do we need to think about before we apply the rules of notice to reading online?

RULES OF NOTICE AND TEXTS BORN DIGITAL

Recognizing Conversations Online

Although Wilhelm and Smith (2016) do not explicitly engage with born-digital texts, we think each of the ways they identify as means for students to be helped become proficient readers can be adapted for these texts. We explain how you might prepare students to notice the conversation, key details, and genre and text structure, then we present three lesson plans that scaffold student learning.

When we read born-digital texts, we can't draw on our mental repository the same way we do when we're reading offline. When we encounter, for example, a traditional feature article, it's usually part of a printed published text, like a newspaper or magazine that has a discrete, stable physical presence. The identity of a publication—its type and purpose—is deliberately established through an aesthetic calculated to attract customers. Tabloids use more pictures and colors than their broadsheet counterparts. The traditional feature article also takes up a place in time and in the case of a newspaper or weekly magazine, the currency of the article is short lived.

Born-digital newspapers and magazines appear on LCD or LED screens rather than paper pages. In the case of pages on websites, each page is a separate HTML object coded to connect with other individual pages, often centered around a landing page, the main point of access. Many pages are dynamic; a page that is "client-side scripted" changes its features each time it is accessed according to information gleaned from the user's browser. A "server-sided page," like a login page, has to reset each time it is accessed. On websites, information may be distributed around the screen and readers may be asked to process multiple sources of information, among them advertising, hyperlinks, brightly colored interactive buttons, sidebars, videos (clickable and auto-play), and images. The same page may be delivered very differently on different devices or browsers because content is optimized for desktop or mobile delivery. Advertising strategies encourage activity and interaction. While the born-digital feature article is published at a date and time, in many cases it will be available indefinitely as part of an accessible digital archive. Individual articles can also be disarticulated from any larger publication online, and the traditional sequencing of the print publication cannot be reproduced. Noting these different features is, however, only a preamble to asking what the significance of change is for teaching and learning in digital environments. That digital environments change the way meaning is made is not a new observation, but it is helpful to recognize how new technologies might make particular demands of literacy educators. We think this quote puts the situation quite well:

> Technologies sometimes change the features of the texts themselves. As a part of comprehension strategy instruction, there are various textual features—tables of contents, headings, figures, captions, glossaries, indexes, keywords, and call-out boxes—of which our students need to be aware. That is, we need to explicitly teach textual features as a way to enhance meaning making. These features are fairly obvious in print texts; reading on a screen, especially a text that is connected to the internet, complicates the issue. (Turner & Hicks, 2015, p. 24)

Deliberate manipulation of the markers we rely on to activate prior knowledge and experience means that our background as readers actually works against us when we try to understand online texts.

In the illustration mentioned before, we noted that Food .com can be both a recipe site and a comedy site, but it's up to the reader to work out when it's meant to be funny and when it's meant to be serious. It's harder to work out which is which because the markers we rely on for conventional texts aren't there in the same way. Complicating matters, the deliberate manipulation of the markers we rely on to activate prior knowledge and experience means that our background as readers actually works against us when we try to understand online texts. Hoax emails, for example, often contain warnings about fraudulent messages, and fake news sites will link to fact-checking sites. Take for example the *Baltimore Gazette*, which is outed as a fake news site in an article in the *Baltimore Sun* (Weigel, 2016). The *Baltimore Gazette* gives every impression of being a genuine newspaper; it has many of the visual features of genuine news sites, and it's accessed on the internet. If all the clues point to the *Gazette* being a newspaper like the *Baltimore Sun* or *Washington Post*, how do we know it's not?

Noticing Details

When many of the ways that we typically judge the credibility and validity of texts are not available to us, it puts more emphasis on the importance of key details. We have to shelve assumptions about what conversations a text is participating in, and what contribution it is making, until we spend more time on the details.

The interaction between elements of a text is so important because so many more media participate in born-digital texts. In online environments images dominate, but words are privileged as the way important information is shared (Kress, 2003). In practice, what this means is that images draw us in, often because of where they appear on pages, but we are still culturally conditioned to look for words to explain what we see. Images can make a claim, the evidence for which is found in the writing, or images can provide the evidence for the text. Readers have to consider what details work together among the different page elements to get our attention, produce emotional responses, and direct our thoughts. As readers we also have to think about how texts are optimized for a range of technologies and platforms that present different key details to be noticed.

A major implication of using the rules of notice with born-digital texts is the demand of critically evaluating online arguments in the context of the commercial internet. We have to think about surrounding data and context within sites; a high ratio of ads to original content on a page might suggest an inclination to commercial rather than informational goals, but we might also ask to what extent might a provocative columnist be employed to drive web traffic, thereby making money rather than to extend journalistic endeavors?

When we worked with high school seniors to apply the rules of notice to born-digital texts, students took over naming of the four categories of the rules of notice:

- Calls to attention became **attention grabbers**

- Ruptures became **twists**

- Direct statements became **statements and demands**

- Reader response became **the vibe**

We used the students' language throughout our teaching, asking, for example, "What grabs your attention here?" and "What vibe are you picking up from what you read?" We saw students

- Astutely link **attention grabbers** to the commercial impetus behind websites

- Recognize that different aspects of texts work to create a **vibe**

- Identify the ways that **twists** operated in written language and in the language of digital coding, for example, when advertisements or auto-play video disrupt linear reading paths

- Grasp quickly how **statements and demands** operate with particular energy in multimedia texts

In sum, using the rules of notice with born-digital texts sensitized students to the techniques writers and designers employ in texts experienced on- and offline. The following lessons introduce students to the importance of noticing direct statements of generalization, calls to attention, ruptures, and language and images designed to evoke a reader's response with the aim of encouraging more incisive critical reading in both academic settings and in the world beyond.

LESSON SUMMARIES

Lesson 4.1: Introducing the Rules of Notice. This lesson asks students to carefully look at texts so that they can begin to consider how the texts are intended to signal and direct the reader to notice particular things. Students will examine the details of print advertisements.

Social Media Extension: Students will consider how stories are at the heart of social media communication. Students will have a creative opportunity to think like designers and apply the rules of notice to reading social media texts.

Lesson 4.2: The Rules of Notice and News Online. In this lesson, we practice looking at how digital texts are constructed to share messages and practice applying the rules of notice to online news.

Social Media Extension: This lesson provides opportunities to practice recognizing the rules of notice and the reading path we take through social media sites.

Lesson 4.3: The Rules of Notice and Social Media. In this lesson, students practice applying the rules of notice to social media texts.

LESSON 4.1, PART I
Introducing the Rules of Notice

LESSON BACKGROUND

This lesson asks students to carefully look at texts so that they can begin to consider how the texts are intended to signal and direct the reader to notice particular things, the details that help refine our understanding of the text.

Purpose

- To introduce and practice applying the rules of notice to texts

- To begin to catalog **calls to attention, reader response, ruptures,** and **direct statements**

- To learn how arguments presented in print advertisements afford opportunities to consider how different media are designed to promote a course of action

Length

- 90–135 minutes (Please note that if you are splitting this lesson across class periods, you may wish to split Step 3 across two class meetings. Alternatively, reviewing Step 3 would be a good springboard into Step 4. You also have a social media extension that you might wish to factor into planning.)

Materials

- Writing materials

- The three advertisements provided in Figures 4.1, 4.2, and 4.3, shared digitally or printed out

- Whiteboard, chart paper, document camera, or other means of recording students' responses. You can prepare a page divided into quadrants, or four blank pages you can attach to the wall.

Resources

- Figures 4.1, 4.2, and 4.3; full-size versions of these ads and their analysis can be found at this book's companion website

LESSON STEPS

Step 1

Introduce the lesson and its purpose. Example: "A vast number of page elements are designed to capture our attention and draw us into reading more deeply. Noticing how our attention is grabbed is part of understanding how all texts function."

Step 2

- Engage students in analysis of an online text rich in calls to attention, reader response, ruptures, and direct statements. We suggest using "Porter Is Not a Bully."

- Divide students into pairs or small groups. Explain that they will see a text that makes a strong, provocative case, and after viewing the text they will have a scale to respond to.

- Students open their online workbook and look at the ad and scale, or project or share printed copies of the advertisement (color is advisable) and the scale.

- Have students make a claim by marking their position on the scale—you may choose if you wish this to be verbal, with a partner, and/or in writing.

The creator of this text expects an audience who will

Want to identify
themselves with it

Want to be won over by
the product and message

Step 3

Call the group together and ask students to back up their claims. Ask them, "What data or evidence has guided your claim?" The following questions can be used to spur conversations. Record their answers in a place where the whole class can see them.

- What do you notice immediately from this ad?

- If you were flicking through a newspaper or magazine, what would jump out at you? Where's your eye drawn?

- Is anything here telling you exactly what to think?

- Is there a good reason for the author to do that?

- When was the last time you watched a movie or TV show or read a book where a good character turned out to be bad and a bad character turned out to be good?

- Was it a shock? Why?

- Why do authors try to create such twists?

- Is there anything that subverts expectations here? Why?

- What do you feel when you look at this ad? Why do you think you felt this way?

Step 4

- Display your page with quadrants (or your four pages of chart paper), while still making the students' analysis of the ad visible.

  Explain, "If we are to be able to transfer our knowledge to other texts, we need to come up with *generalizable rules*. We're going to work with four kinds of rules." You may wish to use this questioning format to help students notice patterns:
  - Authors might choose to speak to us directly to . . .
  - When an author wants to draw our attention to something they might . . .
  - Some ways authors involve us emotionally are . . .
  - Authors sometimes go against our expectations to . . .

You may also wish to check the teachers' guide that follows.

It provides a model for how you might start to build an anchor chart for display in your classroom.

FIGURE 4.1 "Porter Is Not a Bully" Ad

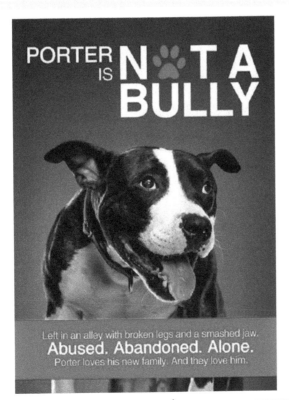

TEACHER GUIDE

Rules of Notice: Porter Is Not a Bully

DIRECT STATEMENTS	RUPTURES
• "NOT a bully": Bullies are bad but so are prejudices • Porter loves and is loved	• Paw replacing the "O" in "NOT" • Periods in Abused. Abandoned. Alone. • Not a cute story; violent and dramatic • Are we the ones bullying Porter because of our preconceptions?

CALLS TO ATTENTION	READER RESPONSE
• Rhythm of Abused. Abandoned. Alone. • Repetition of love • Red paw and white text on a red field (your students may know, or you may want to share, that this was the logo of notabully.org; the organization exists but they've rebranded) • Porter's eyes and friendly loll; he has a halo effect around him • NOT A BULLY in capital letters	• Strong emotive language: bully, left, broken, smashed, loves, love • Left in an alley: no use of the third person • Porter looks gentle and loving and he has a halo effect around him • Guilt about our preconceptions about pit bulls? • Guilt about the strong implication that humans are the real abusers?

POSSIBLE STUDENT RESPONSES

Rules of Notice: Porter Is Not a Bully

STATEMENTS AND DEMANDS	BREAKS AND SHOCKS
• Is NOT a bully • Don't judge this guy; he loves people! They love him!	• Periods make you stop and think: Abused. Abandoned. Alone. • Cute dog, then, boom, horrible story!! • Why the red paw print? • We're not really asked to do or buy anything here. Why?

EYE GRABBERS	HEARTSTRING PULLERS
• The language: "Smashed," "Broken," and "Abandoned" • Repeated words: more means more • Red paw print, white text on red • Porter is super friendly; he's looking up but his head's down like he wants a pat	• Beaten up and then we think he's the bad guy! We're the worst! • He's got a family now, happy ending

- From the student observations you've gathered, begin a class anchor chart where you compile the rules of notice that your class identifies. You need not cover all the items we suggest (see Possible Beginnings), and your students will offer new insights.

POSSIBLE BEGINNINGS TO YOUR CLASS ANCHOR CHART	
Rules of Notice: Porter Is Not a Bully	
STATEMENTS AND DEMANDS	**BREAKS AND SHOCKS**
<ul><li>Statements that tell you what to think, or not to think, about something or someone: "NOT a bully"</li><li>When authors argue against a "straw man" (e.g., all those people who are wrong about pit bulls)</li></ul>	<ul><li>When authors use punctuation to make you stop and think (e.g., periods in Abused. Abandoned. Alone.)</li><li>When you don't get the story you expect to fit with an image (e.g., when you see a sweet picture but you get a violent story)</li><li>When readers are accused (e.g., when it's implied that we victimize someone or something)</li><li>Designs used instead of letters (e.g., a paw replacing the letter a in paws)</li></ul>
EYE GRABBERS	**HEARTSTRING PULLERS**
<ul><li>Violent or scary language, especially when repeated (e.g., "Abandoned. Alone")</li><li>Repeated words: more means more</li><li>Logos and designs (e.g., a red paw print, white text on a red field, highlighted areas of the page)</li><li>Faces and expressions (e.g., friendly faces)</li></ul>	<ul><li>Wanting to get justice (e.g., no one should be bullied)</li><li>Appeals to our sympathy for the weak and small (e.g., making someone or something cute)</li><li>Suggestions that we're guilty (e.g., implying that we're spoiled or judgmental)</li></ul>

Step 5

Engage students in applying what they've learned to two different and more text-heavy ads:

Maxi Milk: Milk for Real Men

Nikewomen.com: My legs . . .

Note: You may, of course, choose alternative texts that fit the kind of unit and inquiry you are doing. The texts we have suggested here are rich in material related to the construction of gender, but they can also lend themselves to discussions of race. The Nike ad we've included here is the least provocative part of a set. Search for nikewomen.com and "my butt" or "I have thunder thighs" for more. We imagine that Old Spice's "Smell Like a Man, Man" campaign would provide opportunities for comparison or further exploration.

If you choose to use these ads, Teacher's Guides are given after the ad.

FIGURE 4.2 "Milk for Real Men" Ad

TEACHER GUIDE	
Rules of Notice: Milk for Real Men	
DIRECT STATEMENTS	**RUPTURES**
• This is "great for doing manly things" • This is a manly man; he looks like one, he does manly things • Muscles are important • Protein is good ("high protein"), but fat is bad ("zero fat")	• The exaggerated scene is tongue in cheek • Milk is for men; we tend to think of it as bland, something for kids • Some nutrition isn't real • Some men aren't actually men
CALLS TO ATTENTION	**READER RESPONSE**
• Text in bold at the right of the image, stylized letter *a* with violent, dynamic symbol • Right: biased design (red colors on right, clouds lightened to highlight slogan and torso of man) • Bottle has been carefully designed; anatomical design suggests scientific research (the bottle literally makes a splash) • Mountaineering gear: enough to be impressive, not enough to obscure the model's physique	• Shirtless man suggests sexualized power; he's meant to be both alluring and intimidating • The metaphor of man conquering nature is repeated in the mountain climber and the scientific development applied to milk • If you're a man, you've got to do manly things like workouts or climbing mountains • The tropes of White, Western fantasies are still (literally) going strong because there are lots of connections between physical fitness and extreme right-wing politics

FIGURE 4.3 "My Legs Were Once Two Hairy Sticks" Ad

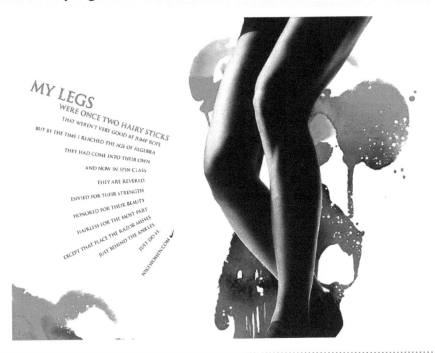

MY LEGS
WERE ONCE TWO HAIRY STICKS
THAT WEREN'T VERY GOOD AT JUMP ROPE
BUT BY THE TIME I REACHED THE AGE OF ALGEBRA
THEY HAD COME INTO THEIR OWN
AND NOW IN SPIN CLASS
THEY ARE REVERED.
ENVIED FOR THEIR STRENGTH
HONORED FOR THEIR BEAUTY
HAIRLESS FOR THE MOST PART
EXCEPT THAT PLACE THE RAZOR MISSES
JUST BEHIND THE ANKLES.
JUST DO IT
NIKEWOMEN.COM

TEACHER GUIDE	
Rules of Notice: My Legs Were Once Two Hairy Sticks	
DIRECT STATEMENTS	**RUPTURES**
• My Legs Were Once Two Hairy Sticks: or my legs are no longer hairy or sticklike • They weren't good at . . . • They've come into their own, revered, honored, hairless . . . • Just do it • Nike recognizes women; go to your own dedicated website at nikewomen .com	• Female body hair is still socially unacceptable so leading with it is odd • Celebrating nascent female sexuality is still taboo • Celebrating yourself as a divine is unseemly • Humor at the end is a sudden twist • No visible branding; selling ideals rather than products functions as a rupture • A critical reader will see that the advertisers' ideas of disruption are problematic because they're selling an idealized female body image and trying to suggest something's lacking in women who don't achieve it

Divide the class into groups or pairs and assign an even number of groups to each of the two ads. For each text, the students respond to the scale:

The audience for this advertisement is expected to

Feel reassured about
who they are

Feel insecure about
who they are

Step 6

- When students have decided on a claim about the text, ask them to add their evidence, or data, into a new table with the rule headings decided on by the class. This table is for their in-class process work—it need not be polished! It might be worth noting that with this ad being reassured or made insecure are both ways the audience has been manipulated.

- Ask groups or pairs to contribute one or two new examples of rules of notice from their work to add to the class anchor chart.

Step 7

- Explain to students that we will transfer the work they've been doing on the messages in ads to literary texts, in this case the poem, *1/11/18 Fake News*.

- Hand out or display the poem and read it aloud and then have students individually mark the scale that follows.

1/11/18

FAKE NEWS

On the bad news station

they're doing interactive

multiple choice questions

such as: "The difference

between fifty and one

hundred dollars is (1) a lot,

(2) an insignificant sum,

(3) fifty per-cent, or

(4) the difference between

fifty and one hundred

dollars." Then the host

introduces a guest

who will, on the basis

of your answer, tell you

how you will vote in

the next election.

....

SOURCE: "1/11/18 Fake News" from *Playlist: Poems* by David Lehman, © 2019. Reprinted by permission of the University of Pittsburgh Press.

The poet suggests his audience is

Too smart to be taken
in by fake news

Vulnerable to
fake news

- When students have decided on a claim about the text, ask them to add their evidence, or data, into another quickly sketched table, or appended to the one created in Step 4.

- Rather than asking students to report back, they'll produce a short, written piece. We recommend having the frame projected and preloaded into digital workbooks if you're using them.

> Readers of the poem [IDENTIFY YOUR POEM] are, we argue, expected to [INCLUDE YOUR RESPONSE TO THE SCALE]. We take this position based on [INCLUDE A RULE OF NOTICE]. We also noticed that [INCLUDE A RULE OF NOTICE]. Additionally, [DESCRIBE HOW A DIFFERENT RULE OF NOTICE IS USED]. Finally, [DESCRIBE HOW A FINAL RULE OF NOTICE IS USED].

Step 8

Conclude the lesson by drawing students' attention to the four categories again. Challenge them to spot the rules of notice in their everyday lives; for example, by simply looking at everyday objects like branding, logos, or wrappers, or by seeking out different text types.

LESSON 4.1, PART II
Social Media Extension

LESSON BACKGROUND

Purpose

- To consider how stories are at the heart of social media communication by highlighting the wider conversations going on around organizations or personalities, and by analyzing how each post or series of posts is a way of intervening in the story to fulfill an objective

- To provide a creative opportunity to think like designers and apply the rules of notice to reading social media text

Length

- 30 minutes

Materials

- Large paper and markers

LESSON STEPS

Step 1

- Organize your class into groups of consultants who are competing for a chance to run a social media campaign for your local school district. We suggest you offer a theme for the post, for example, the value of attendance, the importance of regular exercise, or our students' achievements, and give groups a time limit.

- Explain that to win the opportunity they all have to pitch a post from their campaign.

Step 2

- Explain that businesses and organizations often use agencies to tell stories about their business or organization on social media.

- Ask your class what sort of stories different businesses and organizations tell (e.g., athletic brands, colleges, parks, media personalities).

- Take time to draw out the idea of stories—remind students that there are bigger conversations going on around these organizations or personalities, and each post or series of posts is a way of intervening in the story. You may also unpack the term "campaign" here.

- Explain that each group has to first discuss what conversation they're entering, then what they might do in *one* social media post. They'll briefly note the conversation and what their post will be, but most important, they'll have to identify which rules of notice they'll employ and why.

Step 3

Divide the class into groups and explain that they're going to work on a campaign and that they will begin discussing ideas to make a pitch.

Step 4

Distribute paper, and have students copy the following frame.

- The conversation we're joining is:
- Our post will contribute to the conversation by using
  - Direct statements
  - Calls to attention
  - Ruptures
  - Reader response
- When your time limit runs out, draw the class back together and have them present their ideas.

Exit Ticket

Complete this sentence on a piece of paper, or in an email, and submit it before you leave (we come back to it at the beginning of the next lesson).

The thing that most surprised me about the way the rules of notice are used in social media is _____.

Reflection Questions

- Think about "light bulb" moments you've had when reading texts. Can you think of how to classify these moments of insight under a rule of notice?

- Sometimes students find questioning of dominant discourses and representations needlessly cynical and negative. What's your response to students when students argue that what's normal is simply natural?

LESSON 4.2, PART I
The Rules of Notice and News Online

LESSON BACKGROUND

The conversations we covered in the previous lesson on the rules of notice involved our relationship to animals, our approach to potentially dangerous animals, and if you continued and used all three included images, the construction of gender, body image and ideals, and the health and wellness industry. Moving to online *news*, we recognize that what is relevant, interesting, and age appropriate will mean different things to all our readers, so we offer a lesson plan that can be used with a news site of your choosing.

In Lesson 4.1, your students began to consider how the rules of notice help us read and analyze texts, understanding how they work to create meaning and effect, and manipulate us into knowing, thinking, feeling, or even doing something. In this lesson, we practice looking at how digital texts are constructed to share messages.

Purpose

- To practice applying the rules of notice to online news

- To continue to catalog calls to attention, reader response, ruptures, and direct statements

- To add to our repository of rules of notice

- To start to identify things that we particularly need to notice when reading born-digital texts

Length

- 90–135 minutes

Materials

- A way of projecting images from the internet to a larger screen, or smaller screens for students to work on individually or in groups

- A news site that you have very recently visited—you'll be setting students' work on the site

- Reading Path Activity I (Handout 4.2A), Reading Path Activity II (Handout 4.2B), and the Writing Frame to Reflect on Online Close Reading (Handout 4.2C)

- Writing materials

- Whiteboard, chart paper, or another means of continuing to record students' responses

Some tips for choosing news sites:

- Choose sites that do not use paywalls or email registrations.

- Access the site using a URL rather than saving the site as an image. Having students work with a live site emulates typical online reading patterns and allows you to investigate interactive features as they were intended to be used.

- As far as is possible and appropriate, use material that might pose a distraction; studies have found that students tend to avoid distraction when reading for task completion at school, yet these seemingly frivolous elements are important to the ways that born-digital texts function.

LESSON STEPS

Step 1

Introduce the lesson and its purpose with something like this:

"We've done some surface-level reading and recorded our initial impressions of what we saw and read. Now we have to consider how all the details—the words, images (both moving and still), sound, graphics, sidebars, and so on—and how they contribute to the meaning and effect of that textual conversation."

Step 2

- Ask students what they think a *landing page* is for a website. Explain that it's known as a *lead capture page* or a *destination page* in the industry, but for us it's just that first page we get on a website, and this page is designed to draw us in. Ask the students to think about the connotations of these terms.

- Project the landing page of a newspaper or news site. If you can't project a site, have students look it up on any device available.

- Have students spend 5 minutes individually, or in pairs, looking and noting down everything that their eyes or ears are drawn to without trying to categorize their thoughts. You can either tell students to click through the site on their own, or you can click through for the group.

- Draw the class back together. Ask students for responses and write them up on the board or use a Google Doc. Work as a scribe, or delegate, and ask the class to identify categories from the rules of notice in their answers, challenging students to verbally provide data to support their claims.

- Guide students to select from their responses to add material to your anchor chart. We expect that students will find more calls to attention and direct statements from this initial exercise, something you can highlight for students.

Note: If you are dividing your lesson into (at least) two, this might be a good place to pause. At the end of class meeting one, you may ask students to reflect on their anchor charts, perhaps presenting them to the class group. At the opening of the second class meeting, you may wish to have students note down anonymous observations about the anchor charts made in the previous meeting. You can collect the observations and share select examples.

Step 3

- Remind students that online texts are designed to branch from a landing page to further pages and the readers are expected to engage with different media by saying something like the following:

  "Reading online involves synthesis and sifting—we're going to demonstrate that by reading closely, but not simply from the text on the page we begin with, as we might closely read a conventional book or article."

- Assign students to groups of three or four and assign each group to an interactive feature on the landing page as their starting point.

- Tell them that from that starting point, they are to read and discuss for 15 to 20 minutes moving from the landing page following as many clicks as they wish. As they go, they record their movements and observations using the prompts for the reading path (one student to be the scribe) and Close Reading Activity (the remaining students to take responsibility).

Step 4

Explain that from these notes we will consider some of the conversations present in the initial page. Explain that each group will produce a short reflective piece using the writing frame in Handout 4.2C as a support.

Step 5

- Invite students to consider their reading paths as they read online for their own purposes.

- Lead a whole-class discussion on the rules of notice that most motivated their reading.

Purpose

- To record your movements as you read to recreate the text you have mentally put together as you made sense of all the material you come across

- To be conscious of how rules of notice are used to attract our attention, keep it, and lead it down particular paths

Although you may find this painstaking, it's like an investigator recreating an incident to see it better. Use the writing frame example to get started.

Writing Frame for Recreating Your Reading Journey

We began by reading [DESCRIBE WHAT YOU READ] _____

_____ because [EXPLAIN WHY YOU READ IT: INTEREST/

INTRIGUE/LOOKING FOR FURTHER INFORMATION/ SKEPTICISM—ALL

GREAT REASONS] _____

_____.

Then we clicked [DESCRIBE WHAT YOU CLICKED] _____

_____ because [EXPLAIN WHY YOU CLICKED AND HOW IT

LINKED TO WHAT YOU READ BEFORE] _____

_____.

_____

_____

and we read [DESCRIBE WHAT YOU READ] _____

_____

_____

_____because [EXPLAIN WHY YOU READ IT] _____

_____

_____

_____.

Then we read [CONTINUE WRITING UP YOUR READING PATH USING

THESE PROMPTS].

Purpose

- To continue online reading looking for examples of the rules of notice

- As you continue to read, you'll take in different media (often on the same page) and follow links to further pages and additional sites. You are encouraged to take up the invitations to click, view, and so on offered by authors and designers!

- Note what you're reading/seeing/hearing in the first column, then identify significant rules of notice and why/how they're used in Columns 2 through 5. Don't worry if the table gets quite long.

MEDIA: DESCRIBE THE TEXT OR ITEM	DIRECT STATEMENTS	CALLS TO ATTENTION	RUPTURES	READER RESPONSE

We began our reading from [EXPLAIN WHERE YOU BEGAN ON THE

LANDING PAGE] _____,

noting [EXPLAIN HOW A RULE OF NOTICE OF NOTICE WAS USED

AND WHY] _____

_____.

We understood that [EXPLAIN HOW THIS RULE OF NOTICE WAS

USED TO MAKE A POINT IN AN ARGUMENT] _____

_____. Reading on, we

clicked on [EXPLAIN WHAT YOU CLICKED AND WHY] _____

_____

from which we learned [DESCRIBE WHAT YOU LEARNED] _____

_____

_____. To put forward their argument,

the author/creator of the item [DESCRIBE HOW A RULE OF NOTICE

WAS USED AND WHY] _____

_____

_____. From this point we [EXPLAIN

WHAT YOU CLICKED AND WHY] _____

_____ from which we learned

[DESCRIBE WHAT YOU LEARNED] _____

_____. From our reading activities we learned

[SUM UP WHAT YOU TOOK AWAY FROM YOUR READING—HOW

DID YOU RESPOND TO THE ARGUMENT OR ARGUMENTS YOU

ENCOUNTERED?]

_____

_____

_____

_____

_____

_____

_____

_____.

LESSON 4.2, PART II
Social Media Extension

LESSON BACKGROUND

Purpose

- To provide opportunities to practice recognizing the rules of notice and the reading path you take through social media sites

- To prepare for the next class where we're going to be looking in more depth at interactions between social media and news

Length

- 30 minutes

Materials

- Digital device logged in to social media app of choice

- Something to write or record with (paper and pen or computer)

LESSON STEPS

Step 1

- Explain that they will work in pairs for this activity and that it focuses on their use of social media. Then say something like this:

  "We all make a lot of decisions when we read social media, but we rarely think about those decisions and the ways that they have an impact on what we understand. To highlight those decisions, and the way the rules of notice guide us, one person in each pair will read their favored app for 3 minutes; that means opening Instagram, for example, and clicking and scrolling just as you would normally. This time, however, you have to narrate what you're doing and what rules of notice you see."

- Explain that as the first partner reads and talks, the second partner will jot down what the reader is looking at; while the reader is thinking about the rules of notice, the scribe is recording their actions.

Step 2

- Have students get into pairs and set a timer for between 2 to 5 minutes.

- Wait a couple of minutes and then switch readers and scribes and repeat.

Step 3

After both students have completed the task, give them a few minutes to discuss observations. They can use the following questions as prompts:

- How many pages or sites did you visit?
- Did you notice yourself being pulled in any particular directions?
- Can you use the rules of notice to classify a couple of things that grabbed your attention?
- Can you express in one sentence what you read about or learned?

Step 4

Have students report back with observations to the class group.

Exit Ticket

Think about what social media companies might have accomplished, basing your thinking on your activity in the past few minutes. Did you, for example, add or like content, look at ads, or browse partner sites? Imagine you're a social media CEO and complete this sentence:

"The CEO of [insert company name] would be happy thinking about what I've been doing because every time someone does [describe the activity or activities you and your friends have just completed online] it means that the company [describe how the company benefits]."

Reflection Questions

- Have you paused to consider your own reading path through born-digital texts? What do you notice about the differences between your online and offline reading?

- How did your students respond to being asked to slow down and reflect on their reading of born-digital texts? Did their responses suggest anything about the behaviors and interactions fostered by web content?

LESSON 4.3
The Rules of Notice and Social Media

LESSON BACKGROUND

We have been considering how the rules of notice help us read and analyze texts and how digital texts are constructed to create meanings and effects, and to manipulate us to notice, believe, know, think, and even do things that we might not otherwise do. Our study has moved from stable, print texts, which include different media, to born-digital texts, which include multiple media and require active synthesis of information as readers follow individual paths. In Lesson 4.2, Part II, we turned our attention to social media, a dynamic and highly interactive space where information, and misinformation, is shared almost instantly. Conversations involving social media move quickly; indeed, social media incentivize being topical, provocative, and prolific, often at the expense of reflection and due care. We continue to explore social media in Lesson 4.3.

Studying social media in the classroom is a challenging proposition as we're faced with a difficult contradiction. Put simply, social media works on a scale that's too big to study, but when we reduce the scale to something manageable, it's not social media anymore! In an effort to find a compromise, we've designed some activities that guide students in applying the rules of notice to excerpts from social media texts. While our examples are disconnected from the broader texts and conversations they're part of (for example, a whole sequence of posts and pages on different platforms and publications on a trending topic) they'll offer students opportunities for practice. The second part of the lesson asks students to apply what they've learned to authentic, live social media texts.

A note on classroom access is necessary. While our students live in a world where social media is deeply embedded, we are not often able to engage with social media platforms in schools. While there are very good reasons not to involve social media in classes, we believe it is still imperative to teach safe and responsible use. The Pew Research Center reports that nearly a fifth of Americans currently report getting the majority of their news via social media (Mitchell et al., 2020), and Common Sense Media reports that numbers are even higher for teens: "More than half (54%) of teenagers say they find news at least a few times a week from social media platforms such as Instagram, Facebook, and Twitter . . . 50% get news from YouTube" (Robb & Wronski, 2019).

The importance of critical consumption can hardly be overstated! As a possible extention of this lesson, you could give students the opportunity to design a (playful!) social media conspiracy in which they demonstrate their knowledge of the rules of notice through the design choices that they make.

Purpose

- To practice applying the rules of notice to social media texts

- To continue to notice and catalog calls to attention, reader response, ruptures, and direct statements

Length

- 90–135 minutes

Materials

- A way of projecting images from the internet to a larger screen, or smaller screens for students to work on individually or in groups

- Digital devices, if available

- Writing materials, either on a computer or paper (a shared document with preloaded writing frames would be an advantage; otherwise you can share frames on the board or print them out)

- Whiteboard, chart paper, or other means of continuing to record students' responses

- Handout 4.3A: Social Media Handout

- Handout 4.3B: Writing Frame for Social Media

Resources

The following resources may prove useful in providing material for group work. We recommend using social media apps in class, but we realize this may not be possible in some schools. If you can't have students access material in class, screenshots printed out or made available digitally will allow students to access the material. Please remember that content filters fail, and you should check the content of sites before assigning them. We also recognize that social media is a volatile industry. Indeed, as this book was going into production, Twitter was in turmoil after its change in ownership. Moreover, students' social media preferences change. Here and throughout the book when we provide a link or make a suggestion for using digital materials you may need or want to search for other comparable materials.

YouTube

https://bit.ly/3MZce9l

https://bit.ly/3SuwnoL

https://bit.ly/3D3izfp

Make sure to read the comments and follow any links that seem interesting.

Facebook

The following pages may be helpful:

https://www.facebook.com/AXJ.NIBIRU

https://www.facebook.com/yowusa

https://www.facebook.com/NibiruPlanetXAnunnakiGlobalWarming

Instagram

The following hashtags may prove useful:

#niburu

#planetx

#zechariasitchin

#annunaki

The following posts, live at the time of publication, referenced Nibiru and associated conspiracy theories:

https://bit.ly/3N0eyN4

https://bit.ly/3DmOTdp

https://bit.ly/3FbDtve

https://bit.ly/3DtIyy2

Twitter

The following hashtags may prove useful:

#niburu

#planetx

#zechariasitchin

#annunaki

The following tweets, live at the time of publication, referenced Nibiru and associated conspiracy theories:

https://bit.ly/3U8wEz9

https://bit.ly/3Dp1b67

https://bit.ly/3D0fqwN

https://bit.ly/3W011Ju

LESSON STEPS

Step 1

Introduce the lesson and its purpose, by saying something like this:

"We've considered fairly traditional text forms so far, although some of those, like newspapers, have changed dramatically because they've moved online. Now we're going to think about social media, a whole environment that was born digital, and one where it's really difficult to judge what's true and what's not because perhaps it's not really about truth at all."

Step 2

- Introduce students to consider social media–borne conspiracy stories by asking, "What makes apocalyptic theories so compelling?"

- List student answers where they can be seen, and draw students to consider how conspiracies develop from enduring questions—fear of, or curiosity about, the past or future is important to us. As we argued in Chapter 2, *misinformation is calculated to attack deeply human needs and desires.*

Note. You may wish to break between Steps 2 and 3 if your lesson is split between class periods.

Step 3

- Explain the Planet X, AKA Doomsday Planet Nibiru conspiracy theory.

- Watch the video at https://bit.ly/3D35T87 and have students respond to the following scale:

NASA sees theories about Planet X as

Evidence of enthusiasm for its work ———— Dangerous conspiracies

- When students have noted their claim, ask them to provide data. Challenge them to nominate rules of notice, for example:
  - calls to attention like the NASA logo
  - the call to attention/rupture of "It is not, however . . ." at 1.20
  - the "You know" direct statement that opens the video
  - the reader response techniques included crediting viewers as intelligent participants, and so on

- Ask students to divide a page of notes into a quadrant corresponding to your class rules of notice. Watch the video again to see if students can add more examples.

- Record student observations and examples on your class anchor chart, and ask students if any of them would like to change their marking on the scale after a second viewing. This question emphasizes the importance of collecting evidence and adopting positions accordingly.

Step 4

- Explain that the class will now consider how Nibiru theories develop on different platforms. Explain that they are going to look at a select number of posts on YouTube, Twitter, Instagram, Facebook, and news sites.

- Assign students groups and a platform to each group. It may be worth breaking the YouTube assignment into more groups because it will require the most time. Each group will review a set of media items that they will mentally organize into a text, completing Handout 4.3A.

Step 5

- On the board, a document projected on a screen, or a large piece of paper, add the text "Nibiru Conspiracy." Invite students to feed back, or collaboratively write up, what their text contributes to the conspiracy and how they saw, via the rules of notice, an argument being made using the affordances of their technology.

- Draw students' attention to the ways the rules of notice help us see the affordance and limitations of the technology in enabling original posts and responses. Often responses, for example in YouTube videos, strongly counter the original post to the effect that the argument is most strongly made by the comments rather than the post.

- If you have access to a shared document, for example through One Drive or Google Drive, open the document and allocate students the frame in Handout 4.3B to complete. Otherwise, have students copy the frame from the board or give out printed copies.

Step 6

Invite students to consider and discuss how conspiracy theories emerge by asking what are the most popular theories among their peers today and on what social media platforms are they most often found.

Reflection Questions

- Do you use social media yourself? Do you notice differences between your social media use habits and those of your students?

- Did any of your students continue to hold to misinformation or conspiracy theories they've encountered online? Do you have a sense of why they remain unconvinced by counterarguments?

Access lesson handouts and more resources at
resources.corwin.com/fightingfakenews.

Overarching Claim Made in Our Reading						
RULE OF NOTICE	EXAMPLE	HOW AND WHY USED	EXAMPLE	HOW AND WHY USED	EXAMPLE	HOW AND WHY USED
Calls to attention						
Ruptures						
Direct statements						
Reader response						

In our group, we analyzed the way the Nibiru conspiracy was presented on [INSERT SOCIAL MEDIA PLATFORM] _____ _____. Among the claims we found were [DESCRIBE SOME OF THE CLAIMS YOU SAW] _____

_____

_____

_____.

The dominant claim was [DESCRIBE THE DOMINANT CLAIM] _____

_____

_____.

This claim was made both through original posts and through responses. One of the ways this argument was made and supported [IN AN ORIGINAL POST/A RESPONSE] was through the use of [EXPLAIN HOW A RULE OF NOTICE WAS USED AND TO WHAT EFFECT]

_____

_____

_____.

Another way we saw this argument develop [IN AN ORIGINAL POST/A RESPONSE] was through the use of [EXPLAIN HOW ANOTHER RULE OF NOTICE WAS USED AND TO WHAT EFFECT] _____

_____

_____

_____.

In addition [EXPLAIN HOW OTHER RULES OF NOTICE WERE USED AND TO WHAT EFFECTS] _____

_____

_____

_____.

CHAPTER 5

Lessons for Teaching Point of View in Digital Media

A story to start: For the last 9 years Michael has been working as part of the Pathways Project, a project designed to prepare students from a neighborhood comprehensive school for the rigors of college reading, writing, and quantitative reasoning. (Before he finished his doctoral studies, Hugh was a research assistant on the project.) According to *U.S. News & World Report,* the total minority enrollment of the school is 92% and 100% of students are economically disadvantaged. On Michael's last visit, students were working on an assignment in which they were evaluating websites for their usefulness in helping students figure out how they might be able to fund their college attendance.

One student started by looking at the website of his first-choice college. His eyes were immediately drawn to the array of pictures of diverse groups of students flashing on the top of the landing page.

"You see," he said, "my college is really diverse."

One of the team members responded, "You know, those pictures are carefully chosen to create the impression the college wants you to believe. You have to take them with a grain of salt."

A lightbulb went off. "I guess I'd better check for myself," he said while looking up the college's demographics.

His checking paid off because he found that while the college had some diversity, that diversity was overrepresented in the curated photos. As part of his work on the project, he wrote about the importance of not simply accepting a website without considering the point of view of its creator. It is this kind of healthy skepticism that we aim to foster.

THE IMPORTANCE OF POINT OF VIEW

Understanding point of view is critically important. Indeed, Scholes and Kellogg (1966) go so far as to say that point of view controls "the reader's impression of everything else" (as cited in Lanser, 1981, p. 12). Little wonder that teaching point of view is part of most ELA teachers' instruction in literature. And living in an age in which politics has been "reduced to 'us' versus 'them,' that most basic (and dangerous) of human dynamics" (Kolbert, 2021, par. 18) makes understanding point of view maybe even more crucial in life than it is in literature. But in our experience many fewer teachers work to help their students apply what they've learned about literature to the myriad other kinds of texts they encounter every day. In this chapter we

- Think about the essential aspects of understanding point of view

- Examine five key differences between digital reading and literary reading

- Share two detailed lessons that work to create a bridge between developing students' literary understandings and their capacity to be critical consumers of digital media

Here's the challenge: Even in what would seem to be the most obvious of cases, for example, on websites that are explicitly labeled as satiric, readers don't always accept the invitation to reconstruct the surface meaning of a text based on the point of view and the reliability of the point of view that is the source of readers' information. *The Daily Beast* (Fallon, 2017) compiled a list of news organizations' epic fails stemming from taking *The Onion* seriously, ranging from *The People's Daily* (China's official newspaper) to the *New York Times*.

Other pop culture stories make the stakes of the game clear. National Public Radio (2019) recently ran a story about the persistent misinterpretation of Bruce Springsteen's "Born in the USA" as an unproblematic celebration of America. The *Huffington Post* (Chassin, 2014) reports that Kendrick Lamar's "Swimming Pools," a song with a strong (albeit ironically delivered) antidrinking message, has somehow become a drinking anthem.

So what to do? We assert that the skills one needs to understand point of view in literary texts are directly applicable to being a more critical consumer of digital and popular media texts. However, because digital texts differ from literary texts in important ways, we have to build bridges between our teaching of literary and digital reading.

UNDERSTANDING POINT OF VIEW IN LITERARY TEXTS

In our experience, teaching point of view often focuses on developing a vocabulary for labeling different points of view. For example, when we looked up teaching point of view, the source at the top of the queue was from Ereading Worksheets.

The site takes what seems to us to be a traditional approach to teaching point of view. The site explains that "[s]tudents are often required to identify the narrator's point of view on reading standardized tests. This page will show you an effective way of teaching students how to identify the narrator's view point." It then goes on to define and explain five different points of view: first person, second person, third-person objective, third-person limited, and third-person omniscient.

Our first problem with this approach is revealed in the infinitive in the sentence that states the site's goal. The page is designed to teach students "to identify" the point of view. Our concern: Identifying is just not enough. Identifying may be where interpretation starts, but it's sure not where it ends. The key is to use one's knowledge of point of view to engage with the author and the text to interpret its meanings, and then to decide whether to accept, adapt, or resist those meanings.

> Identifying point of view may be where interpretation starts, but it's sure not where it ends.

The second problem is that the traditional labels the site uses just aren't that useful. Booth's (1961/1983) *The Rhetoric of Fiction* is perhaps the classic critical examination of how stories are told. He explains why labels aren't useful this way: "To say that a story is told in the first or third person will tell us nothing of importance unless we become more precise and describe how the particular qualities of the narrators relate to specific effects" (p. 150). What matters is deciding how much we can trust the source from whom we're getting information in a text and what we should do when that source of information isn't trustworthy. What matters is being mindful of the effects that an author's choice of point of view has on our experience as we read.

Lanser (1981) explains that there are three crucial factors to consider in evaluating point of view: *status, stance,* and *contact*. The terms aren't important in themselves but we think the ideas they represent certainly are. The most important factor, in our opinion, is what Lanser calls *status*.

- *Status: "the authority, competence, and credibility which the communicator is conventionally and personally allowed"* (p. 86).

  We cited *The Daily Beast* above, but we know it doesn't have the same status as the *New York Times*. To use traditional terms, third-person omniscient narrators have a higher status than limited omniscient narrators. Less knowledgeable first-person narrators have less status, at least initially, than do more knowledgeable first-person narrators. Status is a matter of trust, and as experienced readers, we know that some sources and some narrators are more worthy of our trust than others.

- *Stance: the relationship a speaker has with the content.*

  When NPR discusses "Born in the USA" as part of its NPR's American Anthem series in which they examine "songs that Americans embrace in ways that reveal who we are," we know that they value the song. But the speaker of the song seems to have at best an ambivalent attitude to his country, the content about which he sings. He can't get a job and he laments that he has "nowhere to run ain't got nowhere to go." But he was "born in the USA" and fought and sacrificed for his country, which means that he expects more.

- *Contact: the relationship a speaker or writer establishes with the audience.*

  Another way to understand contact is to think about a person nudging someone with an elbow and then telling a racist or sexist joke. The joke teller typically is presuming that the audience is complicit in the joke's racism or sexism. In like manner, Chris Cillizza of CNN seems to expect readers of "The 32 Most Bizarre Lines from Donald Trump's Latest Interview with Sean Hannity" to share his politics.

As we have explained elsewhere (Smith & Wilhelm, 2010), Lanser's (1981) work convinces us that we should ask three primary questions when we examine a source of information:

1. What is the status of the source of information? That is, to what extent is the source reliable?

2. How does the source of information feel about the content of its message?

3. What relationship does the source of information have with its readers? That is, to what extent does the source trust and respect its audience?

And as we have argued elsewhere (Smith, 1992; Smith & Wilhelm, 2006, 2010), answering the first question requires us to ask a couple more. The most important of those seem to us to be as follows:

4. Is the source of information too self-interested to be reliable?

5. Does the source of information have enough knowledge, awareness, and experience to be reliable?

The lessons that we share in this chapter are designed to help students see the value of asking these questions for both literary and digital texts to determine if a source is indeed reliable or unreliable. But before we share them, let's think about five key differences between digital texts and literary texts so we can see why it's not enough to simply ask students to apply what they've learned about literature to their reading of digital texts (see Figure 5.1).

FIGURE 5.1 The Five Key Differences Between Literary Texts and Digital Texts

LITERATURE	DIGITAL MEDIA
Meant to be understood	Sometimes meant to deceive
Typically we know whose reliability we are to assess	The source of information may be obscured
Commercial dimension is not too important	Commercial dimension is critical
Both windows and mirrors	More likely mirrors
Within-text information helps us determine reliability	Determining reliability requires reading across texts

Difference 1: Irony in literature is meant to be understood whereas some digital media are meant to deceive.

When we read *The Adventures of Huckleberry Finn* we recognize that Huck's understandings are not to be trusted. When Huck complains in paragraph 3 that "[w]hen you got to the table you couldn't go right to eating, but you had to wait for the widow to tuck down her head and grumble a little over the victuals, though there warn't really anything the matter with them," we know that he's misunderstanding the widow's prayers, just the first of his many misunderstandings we have to recognize.

We're not saying that unreliable narrators are always easy to interpret. Indeed, some of our most powerful reading experiences have come when we initially trusted a narrator and then had to radically change our thinking when we realized that our trust was misplaced. But we are saying that authors expect their readers to engage in that effort. And if they don't, well, according to Mueke (1969), they become as much the victims of the irony as those who are directly targeted. Indeed, throughout history, writers have been so concerned about readers' understanding irony that some have suggested special punctuation to designate ironic utterances, such as a mark that looks like a Christmas tree or a backward question mark or a squiggly exclamation point.

In contrast, much of what students encounter on the internet is deliberately designed to deceive. The most obvious example is the growing incidence of deepfakes. As the Government Accounting Office (GAO; 2020) explains, a deepfake is a video, photo, or audio recording that is designed to seem real but that has, in fact, been created or manipulated by artificial intelligence. Perhaps the most famous example is actor, comedian, director, and writer Jordan Peele's warning about the potential problem of deepfakes cast in the form of a deepfake of President Obama saying decidedly unpresidential things. The increasing sophistication of deepfakes causes the GAO (and many others) to be concerned about the potential that deepfakes might influence elections and cause civil unrest. Indeed, California has passed legislation designed to curb the spread of deepfakes during the election cycle.

As this book was going into production, the increasing sophistication of deepfakes was made manifest when the company Metaphysic competed in the semi-finals of *America's Got Talent* with a deepfake of Simon Cowell, Howie Mandel, and Terry Crews singing opera. The *Washington Post* reports that the three "singers" were effusive in their praise. But, the *Post* reports, critics worry that such sophisticated fakery "blur[s] a line between fiction and reality that's barely clear now" (Zeitchik, 2022). The *Post* continues by quoting Hany Farid, a professor at the University of California with a joint appointment in electrical engineering and computer sciences and the School of Information, who says, "We're quickly entering a world where everything, even videos, can be manipulated by pretty much anyone who wants to" and then asks ironically, "What can go wrong?"

What could go wrong indeed? The point here is not to offer a history of deepfakes but rather to point out that whereas the intended effect of satire and irony depends on the reader's recognizing it, the intended effect of deepfakes depends on just the opposite.

Difference 2: As hard as it is to identify the source of information in a literary text, it's even harder to identify the source of information in digital media.

As experienced readers, we're always on the alert when we are reading a text with a dramatized first-person narrator. Although as we argued above, determining the reliability of a dramatized first-person narrator isn't always easy, we know that it's our job to make that determination. And, at least in the case of dramatized narrators, we know typically know just who we are to assess. Here's the first sentence of *Huck Finn*: "You don't know about me without you have read a book by the name of *The Adventures of Tom Sawyer*; but that ain't no matter." The first sentence of *Gatsby* is only slightly less direct: "In my younger and more vulnerable years my father gave me some advice that I've been turning over in my mind ever since." In both of these canonical texts, we know right from the start that a character and not the author is the one who is telling us the story.

Sometimes it's not so easy to figure out the source of our information. Here are the first few sentences of Reynolds's (2019) *Look Both Ways: A Story Told in Ten Blocks*: "All I can tell you is if you ever see John Watson, Francy Baskin, Trista Smith, or especially Britton 'Bit' Burns—the Low Cuts—better watch your pockets." Who's the unnamed I? Can we trust "I"'s perspective, that is, should we watch our pockets if we encounter the Low Cuts?

And here is the first paragraph of the chapter in *Frindle*, a best-selling and award-winning novel for young people that is sufficiently popular that a play was made about it over two decades after its publication, which introduces Mrs. George, the teacher who is fifth-grader Nick Allen's antagonist in the novel:

> Fifth grade was different. That was the year to get ready for middle school. Fifth grade meant passing classes. It meant no morning recess. It meant real letter grades on your report cards. But most of all, it meant Mrs. Granger. (Clements, 1996)

Just who is the source of information? The first two sentences could conceivably be coming from an adult perspective. The next three seem decidedly more kid-like. Should Nick be worried about Mrs. Granger? As experienced readers, we know that we shouldn't rush to judgment. We know that regardless of the complexity of assessing the source of information in a literary text, in the end what matters is the extent to which the judgments of the source of information are congruent with those of the author, who is ultimately responsible for the text.

But in digital media, determining who is ultimately responsible for the text is more complex. Imagine a digital text written by an author that appears on a website sponsored by an organization. Now imagine that there are embedded links in that digital text from texts written by other authors that appeared on other websites sponsored by other organizations. Yikes! Sorting who's ultimately responsible for the content of a website is a trickier business, and certainly as important, if not more so.

Difference 3: The salience of the commercial dimension of digital texts is far greater than it is for most literary texts.

When we ask whether a literary narrator is too self-interested to be reliable, we're usually asking a reputational question. For example, in *The Hate U Give* the narrator Starr witnesses the police murder her oldest friend. Starr lives a complex life. She lives in an all-Black impoverished neighborhood and goes to a virtually all-White suburban private school with mostly wealthy kids. She struggles to find a way to live comfortably in both worlds. Her school friends don't know she was a witness to the murder, and they ask her if she knows the young man who was killed. Despite the fact that she knows it's a betrayal she says, "No," and says to herself: "But I had to do it. I had to," justifying her response a few seconds later by saying, "I don't want all the pity" (Thomas, 2017, p. 114). We suspect Starr's judgment because she's defending herself, and we know from our own experience that accurately assessing one's own behavior is a difficult proposition. It's just too easy to make excuses.

There's another dimension to self-interest on the internet: the commercial aspect. Of course, Angie Thomas, the author of *The Hate U Give,* wants to sell books as does her publisher Balzer & Bray, a HarperCollins Publisher imprint. But the commercial dimension in the conventional publishing world is not front and center.

The internet, on the other hand, is far more conspicuously commercially oriented. Just take a look at how the streaming service Hulu uses the availability of the movie *The Hate U Give* to entice visitors to the website to sign up for a free trial of the service. The commercial dimension of the internet is why webpages need to be updated for currency and have to be linked to encourage traffic. It's why sites need to continue to grow and grow to continue. It's why domains have to be maintained and optimized for search engine recognition, and so on. As a consequence, each page, and even every component within a page, must be understood within a complex matrix of commercial and institutional interests. That is, in looking at a website we have to ask: What allows this site to make money? What does the site do to create the traffic on which it depends? And perhaps most important: What impact does the drive for traffic have on what the site presents?

Difference 4: Digital texts are much more apt to be mirrors than windows.

Style (1988) poses a powerful metaphor for thinking about curriculum, arguing that curricula need "to function both as window and as a mirror, in order to reflect and reveal most accurately both a multicultural world and the student herself or himself." (This construct was elaborated on and popularized by Sims Bishop [1990].) Style introduces the contrast with reference to two *Peanuts* strips. In the first Snoopy types, "Always remember that beauty is only skin deep" and then thinks for a minute and revises his advice to say "fur deep." He's seeing things from his own perspective, so that's a mirror. The next day at the behest of his bird friend Woodstock, he revises yet again: "Always remember that beauty is only feather deep." He's seeing things through another's perspective, so that's a window. *The Hate U Give* is a window for the four of us because we're White, middle-class, and gracefully aging (remember what we said about the problem of evaluating your own behavior and perspective?).

The mirrors and windows metaphor is one useful way to think about what Lanser (1981) calls contact, that is, the relationship an author has with their readers. Let's take *The Hate U Give* as an example again. It seems to us that Angie Thomas, the author, presumes that her book is a window for at least some of her readers, which means that she can't trust their understanding of the environment about which she writes. As a consequence, she has to work harder than she might otherwise have to, for example, create empathy for Starr's father, a former gang member and ex-convict. One way she does so is by making him a very caring gardener through passages like this one:

> While I feed Brickz [the family dog] and refill his water bowl, Daddy picks bunches of collard greens from his garden. He cuts roses that have blooms as big as my palms. Daddy spends hours out here every night, planting, tilling, and talking. He claims a good garden needs good conversation. (p. 37)

Literary authors can't presume shared values with their readers, so they have work to do to establish a common ground. In this case it seems to us that Thomas deliberately challenges possible stereotypes that White readers might have to establish that common ground.

But digital authors often can presume shared values. Algorithmic technologies that personalize information create the impression of a vast information landscape when, in truth, every internet reader may be gathering information on a very small information island that is used by, built by, and maintained by people who are just like them (Rainie & Anderson, 2017). Not to put too fine a point on it, but here's a headline from Alex Jones's InfoWars site: "Mask-wearers detest people who don't blindly follow advice from 'medical experts.'" Much like the *CNN* headline writer we cited earlier, the headline writer in this site pretty clearly expects readers to share a disdain for those mask-wearers and "medical experts." On the other hand and from a different place of the political spectrum, the headline writer at *The Daily Beast* who penned the headline "The Hot New Far-Right Trend: Claiming a Disability to Avoid Wearing a Mask" pretty clearly expects readers to share a disdain for those on the "far-right" who try to avoid wearing a mask during a pandemic.

Difference 5: In literature we can use within-text information to help us determine reliability; in digital texts we often have to read across texts.

Regardless of who's telling the story in a literary narrative, there are both unquestioned facts on which we can base our interpretations and a variety of perspectives beside the storyteller's that we can weigh. In *The Hate U Give*, for example, Starr tells us that she isn't brave for testifying against the police officer who killed her friend. But her mom thinks otherwise as do a number of other characters. And we never question her reporting of the events of the killing or how she is treated at the police station. Those facts help readers assess whether she is brave or not.

But as we just explained, many websites don't provide a variety of perspectives against which readers can check their own. To get anything approaching the full picture, one has to read laterally, or intertextually, putting texts about related content in conversation with each other. Indeed McGrew and colleagues (2017) explain that that's just the strategy that professional fact checkers take: "They left a site in order to learn more about it. This may seem paradoxical, but it allowed fact checkers to leverage the strength of the entire internet to get a fix on one node in its expansive web" (p. 8). That is, to learn about a site, they had to read other sites that address the same content.

We've seen that assessing point of view in literary texts has some crucially important similarities with assessing point of view in digital texts as well as some significant differences. Take a moment now to reflect on some of your own experiences with digital reading.

Reflection Questions

- Think about some digital reading you've done lately. To what extent were the five key differences reflected?

- Which ones seemed especially important to you? Why?

Now let's take a look at two lessons that will help students apply and extend what they learn about literature to their digital reading.

LESSON SUMMARIES

Lesson 5.1: Who's Telling the Story and Why Does That Matter? This lesson is designed to help students understand how point of view influences readers' understanding of and response to literary texts. In it, students will work with a variety of texts, including a fable by Aesop and two poems from Edgar Lee Masters's *Spoon River Anthology*.

Social Media Extension: The social media extension asks students to apply what they've learned to their analysis of Twitter feuds.

Lesson 5.2: Applying Literary Understandings to Digital Texts. This lesson asks students to apply what they have learned to their critical reading of websites that focus on celebrities and health.

Social Media Extension: The social media extension asks students develop criteria for the reliability of posts on issues that matter to them.

LESSON 5.1, PART I

Who's Telling the Story and Why Does That Matter?

LESSON BACKGROUND

This lesson is designed to engage students in recognizing how authors use different points of view to create specific meanings and effects. The lesson starts with a short real-world activity to engage students. It then moves to a text with which many students will be familiar, a fable by Aesop. Manipulating that fable in various ways will help students see why point of view matters. Following that activity, students will watch and then write about a video from multiple perspectives to solidify those conceptual understandings. Finally, they will apply what they've learned to the reading of literature. We selected two poems from Edgar Lee Masters's *Spoon River Anthology* for three reasons:

- The poems are in the public domain so we can include them here

- They are very short, so they are manageable to teach

- They provide a clear illustration of the importance of point of view

Taken together, the activities in this lesson are a good illustration of our instructional approach.

- Students get plenty of practice in both reading and writing.

- We move from materials that are familiar to those that are less familiar.

- We integrate reading and writing.

- We introduce terms in a context that makes it clear why the terminology matters.

Please note: As has been the case thoughout the book, we've tried to write this lesson sufficiently specifically so that you can teach it as it has been written. But we realize that you might want to modify them by changing texts (by replacing the student emails we refer to below with different texts, for example, comments on a blog that raises an issue of local interest and importance; by changing the grouping suggestions that we make; by changing the format for whole-class discussion, etc.).

Purpose

- To understand how authors use different points of view to create specific meanings and effects

- To evaluate the reliability of different points of view and understand how this evaluation affects and informs our interpretations

Length

- Approximately 90–135 minutes

Materials

- Writing materials

- A class set of Handout 5.1A: Two Student Emails

- A class set of Handout 5.1B: The Ants and the Grasshopper

- A class set of Handout 5.1C: The Ants and the Grasshopper (From the Grasshopper's Perspective)

- A class set of Handout 5.1D: The Pantiers

- Whiteboard, chart paper, or other means of recording students' responses

- LCD projector and screen

LESSON STEPS

Step 1

- Introduce the lesson and its purpose by telling students that they've been doing so well that they're getting a promotion today and that for the first activity they should pretend they're principals. Explain that one thing principals have to do is try to discover what really happened on the basis of what they are told by others. Explain that figuring out the truth of the situation based on an analysis of the information we receive and the source from whom we receive it is the focus of today's lesson. Tell students to imagine that they received two emails from the same class after the distance learning instruction they received during the pandemic and that their task is to figure out what, if anything, they should do in response to the emails. (Provide handout or display emails. See Handout 5.1A.)

- Read Dana's email aloud. Ask students to fill out the scale that follows it. Get a sense of the whole by asking students to indicate where they placed it on each scale (i.e., How many gave this a 1?). Probe for their reasoning with something like this: "Okay, you said that you gave it a 1, that you'd definitely do something in response to Dana's email. What makes you say so? Why is that important?" Student responses might include that Dana wanted more work, not less, which makes Dana more believable; that Dana seems to be a good and serious student; and that the email has an appropriately formal tone. Solicit other responses, especially any that provide different ratings.

- Repeat the process for Chris's email. Students might notice the misspellings, which undercut Chris's authority, the overly familiar tone, and the self-interest indicated in the idea that two assignments a week is too many, but they might also notice the legitimacy of Chris's concerns about doing the work in light of family obligations.

- Ask students how reading the two emails together affects their understanding of what's not under dispute in the situation. For example, a student might note that Ms. Edwards really doesn't communicate much with either student and that both students agreed that the class received two assignments each week. Lead a whole-class discussion on the impact of their reading across emails on the ratings they provided.

- Explain how this little activity establishes that both in life and in literature we must identify the claims that people are making, think about the relationship between the person making the claims and those to whom the claims were made, and decide how much we trust whoever is making the claim.

- If you want to, you can explain that stories told through letters or emails, for example, *Letters From the Inside*, are one kind of first-person narration.

Step 2

- Explain that you're going to cast them in a different role this time: the author. Read the fable (Handout 5.1B) aloud.

- Explain that there are other ways to tell the story and that those different ways might affect how we understand it. Ask students who Aesop wants readers to sympathize with, the Ants or the Grasshopper. Probe for how they know. Explain that the point of view from which the fable is told is omniscient (or objective omniscient).

- Explain that adding, changing, or moving details can suggest a change in the author's stance. Explain that if those details come from a narrator who looks into the mind of just one of the characters that's called *limited omniscient*. Explain that you want them to indicate a different stance on the Grasshopper. Provide or display Handout 5.1C.

- Model what you want them to do by writing the first insertion called for in Handout 5.1C. Think aloud as you do so. You might say something like this: "Okay, what if the Ants were among those insects who really wanted the music? What if the reason that the Grasshopper didn't collect the food was to please the other insects? How's this? 'The Grasshopper knew the Ants loved his music and indeed had long told him that his music helped them keep at work. He played for others and not himself, sacrificing the future to keep smiles on faces in the present.'" Have students work in triads to complete the other insertions and a new moral. If students are having difficulty developing a moral, ask them to look up sayings relevant to the additions that they made. For example, note that your think-aloud sentences were about the power of music, so in noodling around on the internet you found this possibility: "The joy of music is food for the soul."

- Explain to students that another way to tell the story is by pretending that you are one of the characters and that this is called *first-person narration*. Have students stay in the same triads and rewrite the fable from the Ants' point of view but make them appear unsympathetic. If students have difficulty getting started you can prompt them with this possible beginning: "Here comes that lazy old Grasshopper. Always quick with a smile for anyone but never quick to get to work."

- Circulate as triads are working. If students are having difficulty writing a moral, you might once again suggest using the internet to help find one. (If their revision is about work, the proverb "All work and no play makes Jack a dull boy" could work. If it's about sharing, this quote from Booker T. Washington might work: "We all should rise, above the clouds of ignorance, narrowness, and selfishness.")

- Have triads read their revisions. Note that the revisions show how the impact of the point of view is a function of how the authors used their narrators to manipulate details to achieve different effects.

- Explain to students that one way readers can make their own judgments about the situation independent of the narrators is to check the facts. Have them identify what's not under dispute (e.g., that the Ants are drying grain, that the Grasshopper is a musician, that the Grasshopper is without food) and what is under dispute (e.g., the reason the Grasshopper didn't prepare for the winter).

Step 3

- Explain to students that they're now going to apply what they learned to a more contemporary text. Show a video that went viral of a student critiquing his teacher's practice (https://bit.ly/3W0WZk7). (It would be fine to substitute any similar video if you find one more relevant to your classroom context.)

- Explain to students that you want them to demonstrate how narrators can manipulate details to achieve different effects. Assign each person in each triad a number from 1 to 3. Make new triads by having the 1s move counterclockwise and the 2s move clockwise. Assign each new group to write from one of these perspectives: omniscient, first person from the student's perspective, limited omniscient from the perspective of the student, first person from the teacher's perspective, or limited omniscient from the teacher's perspective.

- Circulate as students write. Probe for what stance they are taking on the event and/or the characters. Make sure that each person in the triad has a copy of the writing or have groups use a voice recording program like Otter so they have a version they can share.

- Divide students into groups of five to share their revisions with one person who wrote each of the different points of view in each group. After sharing, have groups discuss the similarities and differences among the stories, focusing especially on how the source of information affects their understanding of the situation.

- Show a news report on the confrontation (https://bit.ly/3TNUGiD).

- Ask students to indicate what feeling about the student (Jeff Bliss) the news editor and reporters wanted the audience to have.

Completely unsympathetic   Very sympathetic

- As you did previously, get a sense of the whole by asking students to indicate where they placed it on each scale (i.e., How many gave this a 1?). Probe for their reasoning by asking something like this: "Okay, you said that you gave it a 1, that the story was designed to create a completely unsympathetic portrait; what makes you say so?"

Step 4

- Tell students that in the next activities you want them to apply what they've been learning to the reading of literature. Explain that you're going to be looking at two poems from Edgar Lee Masters's *Spoon River Anthology* and that the idea of the book is that the residents of a small town in Illinois speak from the grave about their lives. Explain that you're going to be working with two poems, one spoken by a husband and the other by his wife. Read the poems aloud (Handout 5.1D).

- Divide students into triads and have them discuss these questions:
  ○ What facts can readers be sure of?
  ○ What do they think happened to the marriage? What do they have to go on in making these inferences?
  ○ With whom does Masters want readers to sympathize? How do they know?

- Assign triads to write about the Pantiers (in prose or in a poem) from the perspective of another townsperson, which would mean they could include only the details that would be observable to someone outside the marriage, or from the omniscient point of view. Tell them they could use this first line regardless of the point of view: "Every marriage has its story—and that story has at least two sides . . ."

- As students write, circulate. Solicit volunteers to read aloud as you do so.

- Have volunteers read. Lead brief discussions on how and why the versions were similar and/or different and what different meanings and effects stemmed from the differences.

Step 5

- Note that the class's work establishes that it's crucial to understand the impact of point of view on how stories are told and the kind of interpretive work readers have to do to interpret those stories.

- Ask students to write an exit ticket in which they explain how recognizing the perspective from which a story is told will affect them as a reader in the future.

Extension

Have students rewrite a song from a different perspective. You could note, as an example, that Post Malone's "Better Now" explicitly calls on hearers to recognize that his imagined audience has a different perspective on the breakup than he does. If you have time, students could play their song, read their rewrite, and explain what effects they were trying to achieve through the change in point of view.

Reflection Questions

- One of the major strategies this lesson employs is casting students as writers to help them become better readers. What do you think of this strategy?

- How might you use it in other lessons?

Dear Principal Jones:

I am writing to express my concern about the online instruction my class and I have received from Ms. Edwards, my English teacher, during the COVID pandemic. My class received assignments twice a week that took me on average 1 hour to complete. Most of the materials were review, but she did not provide instruction for any of the new material. My other teachers all provided various ways for me to ask questions or seek clarification. Ms. Edwards did not. All she did was post the work. I understand that some teachers are less comfortable than others with digital platforms, but I also understand that the District provided training for how to engage classes using Zoom and other technologies. I feel as though I lost a semester. I realize nothing can be done for me, but I hope that your intervention might result in other students having a richer experience moving forward.

Sincerely,

Dana Williams

Now that you've read Dana's email, mark the following scale:

Dana's email convinces
me I need to do something

I can ignore
Dana's email

Principle Jones,

You need to talk to Ms. Edwards right away. I got a D in her class just cause I didn't do all of the work. But who could? She gave us assignments twice a week. I have other classes you know. And I have to watch my little sister when my mom's at work. And most of it was busy work anyways. So why do it? I feel as though nobody should get a bad grade under the circamastances. Plus, she should of told me I was going to get a bad grade, but all she ever do was post work. It's just not fair. You need to do something right away!

Chris Miller

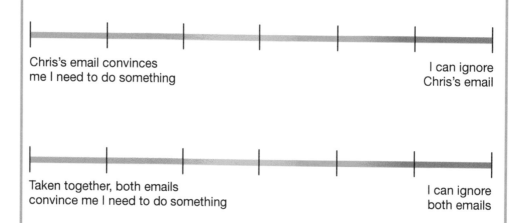

Chris's email convinces
me I need to do something

I can ignore
Chris's email

Taken together, both emails
convince me I need to do something

I can ignore
both emails

One bright day in late autumn a family of Ants were bustling about in the warm sunshine, drying out the grain they had stored up during the summer, when a starving Grasshopper, his fiddle under his arm, came up and humbly begged for a bite to eat.

"What!" cried the Ants in surprise. "Haven't you stored anything away for the winter? What in the world were you doing all last summer?"

"I didn't have time to store up any food," whined the Grasshopper. "I was so busy making music that before I knew it the summer was gone."

The Ants shrugged their shoulders in disgust.

"Making music, were you?" they cried. "Very well; now dance!" And they turned their backs on the Grasshopper and went on with their work.

There's a time for work and a time for play.

One bright day in late autumn a family of Ants were bustling about in the warm sunshine, drying grain they had gathered during the summer. Upon seeing them, a starving Grasshopper, his fiddle under his arm, came up and humbly begged for a bite to eat. [Insert a sentence or two here about what the Grasshopper is thinking that would make the Grasshopper more sympathetic.]

"What!" cried the Ants in surprise. "haven't you stored anything away for the winter? What in the world were you doing all last summer?"

"I didn't have time to store up any food," whined [change this verb to make the Grasshopper more sympathetic] the Grasshopper. "I was so busy making music that before I knew it the summer was gone." [Insert a sentence or two here about what the Grasshopper is thinking that would make the Grasshopper more sympathetic.]

The Ants shrugged their shoulders in disgust.

"Making music, were you?" they cried. "Very well; now dance!" And they turned their backs on the Grasshopper and went on with their work. [Insert a sentence or two here about what the Grasshopper is thinking that would make the Grasshopper more sympathetic.]

Write a new moral based on your revised story.

Benjamin Pantier

TOGETHER in this grave lie Benjamin Pantier, attorney at law,

And Nig, his dog, constant companion, solace and friend.

Down the gray road, friends, children, men and women,

Passing one by one out of life, left me till I was alone

With Nig for partner, bed-fellow; comrade in drink.

In the morning of life I knew aspiration and saw glory,

The she, who survives me, snared my soul

With a snare which bled me to death,

Till I, once strong of will, lay broken, indifferent,

Living with Nig in a room back of a dingy office.

Under my Jaw-bone is snuggled the bony nose of Nig

Our story is lost in silence. Go by, Mad world!

Mrs. Benjamin Pantier

I know that he told that I snared his soul

With a snare which bled him to death.

And all the men loved him,

And most of the women pitied him.

But suppose you are really a lady, and have delicate tastes,

And loathe the smell of whiskey and onions,

And the rhythm of Wordsworth's "Ode" runs in your ears,

While he goes about from morning till night

Repeating bits of that common thing;

"Oh, why should the spirit of mortal be proud?"

And then, suppose;

You are a woman well endowed,

And the only man with whom the law and morality

Permit you to have the marital relation

Is the very man that fills you with disgust

Every time you think of it while you think of it

Every time you see him?

That's why I drove him away from home

To live with his dog in a dingy room

Back of his office.

LESSON 5.1, PART II
Social Media Extension

LESSON BACKGROUND

In this lesson we discuss points of view and reliability. In online culture, questions of reliability and authenticity are endemic. Followers and fans are often hugely loyal, even to the extent of participating in the personal feuds of their favorites. To have students reflect on the ways they engage in arguments online, have them rank the social media techniques they find most persuasive. This extension activity offers students the opportunity to think about reliability and points of view in social media. The first step is to complete a ranking activity, which is then the prompt for discussion in Step 2.

Step 1

Have students complete the following chart by saying something like the following: "Imagine you've stumbled into an internet feud between two media personalities. From the following options, rank the things that would get you to take one side or the other. For example, if you really feel a connection when your favorite TikTok-er shares personal information, give that a 1. If you find positive posts (#blessed) a bit too unconvincing or fake, give that a 14."

CRITERIA	RANK	REASON
Having a lot of followers		
Creating high-quality content		
Creating high-volume content		
Sharing lots of personal details		

CRITERIA	RANK	REASON
Personal appeals (please support me/take my side) made directly to the audience through video		
Personal appeals made directly to the audience in writing		
Supportive comments, tweets, or posts made in response by other users		
Supportive comments, tweets, or posts made by other prominent or famous users		
Video used as evidence		
Screen-caps used as evidence		
Use of trending hashtags		
Raw emotion: anger, expletives, tears		
Positive vibes, especially in response to negativity		
Apologies, especially those that reference growth or personal development		

Step 2

Have students share their top three and bottom three with their neighbors and discuss how their choices compare.

LESSON 5.2, PART I
Applying Literary Understandings to Digital Texts

LESSON BACKGROUND

This lesson is designed to engage students in applying what they learned about point of view to digital texts. The lesson is also designed to recognize both what students can transfer rather unproblematically and the five key differences between literacy and digital texts that we discussed earlier. For ease of reference, we list them again here:

- Difference 1: Irony in literature is meant to be understood whereas some digital media are meant to deceive.

- Difference 2: As hard as it is to identify the source of information in a literary text, it's even harder to identify the source of information in digital media.

- Difference 3: The salience of the commercial dimension of digital texts is far greater than it is for most literary texts.

- Difference 4: Digital texts are much more apt to be mirrors than windows.

- Difference 5: In literature we can use within-text information to help us determine reliability; in digital texts we often have to read across texts.

As you'll see, we start with materials that we think will be of high interest to students, focusing on popular cultural figures. Then we move into an examination of three controversial health- and wellness-related sites. We chose to have students examine health/wellness websites instead of, say, political ones because we thought they would not have performed evaluations whereas their minds might already be made up about political issues. But choosing any three sites would work as long as they have a similar content focus.

Purpose

- To apply what students learned about point of view to their evaluation to digital media

Length

- Approximately 90 minutes

Materials

- Writing materials

- A class set of Handout 5.2A: Analyzing Websites I

- A class set of Handout 5.2B: Analyzing Websites II

- At least six devices that have internet access

- Some way to display websites

- Whiteboard, chart paper, or other means of recording students' responses

LESSON STEPS

Step 1

- Introduce the lesson by reminding students that in the previous lesson they worked on understanding the fact that different points of view resulted in different interpretations of the same event and so in literature, as in life, we have to be very aware of who we trust and why. Explain that the internet makes our critical engagement and judgment even more crucial.

- Play Jordan Peele's Obama deepfake (https://bit.ly/3N3fRLj; Warning: The clip includes the word *dipshit*). Note that deepfakes are only one example of problematic information. Explain that there are plenty of other examples of either deliberate or accidental misinformation. Note that even when information is shared, writers and website creators might have a different interpretation of the information that they'll have to sort through. Explain that in this lesson they're going to engage in developing criteria for the assessment of websites as a way to adapt what they learned from literary reading to this new kind of reading.

Step 2

- Explain that the class is going to start by reading and thinking about popular cultural figures.

- Say something like the following: "Okay, in our last lesson we had to think about how much we could trust the perspective of the students who wrote the emails, the perspective of the Grasshopper and the Ants, the people from the video, and the speakers from *Spoon River*." Explain that today the class will be doing the same thing but will be focusing on websites. Note that one thing people do on the internet is check up on celebrities. Tell students that you wanted to find out more about Lady Gaga because you heard a song of hers you liked and this site came up in your queue (https://bit.ly/3D0Xpyw). (*Note*. If Lady Gaga isn't relevant to your students, choose a celebrity who is. Please note also that we deliberately chose a site that is problematic. If you choose a different site, choose one that will allow you to raise students' attention to reading both within and across sites to evaluate the reliability of the author and the sponsor of the site. One more note: What follows is a model think-aloud. We mean it to be a model and not a script.) Say something like "I know I need to understand the source of my information and that means I need to check out the site and the author." Click the menu icon, then About Us, which featured this text at the time this chapter was composed:

  > Hey! Hi. Hello! We're Team *Cosmopolitan*. We work to deliver you content on your screens, in our mag, and across your feeds that's just like you: fearlessly authentic, unapologetically honest, and really damn interesting.

As the biggest young women's media brand in the world, we're in an intimate relationship—and ongoing conversation—with our audience, and our 75 editorial staffers (more on us below) hustle hard to pack every Cosmopolitan platform with fresh, funny, and fundamental intel about what millennials truly care about (from how to survive a <u>tough Tinder date</u> to <u>how to run for political office</u>).

Say something like "Yikes, I'm sure not the intended audience. It's appealing specifically to young women. Look at the language, right from the start 'Hey! Hi. Hello!' Hmm. I think that what they're going to tell me is what they think young women might like. We'll see."

- Recall that when the class looked at the texts in the last lesson we used internal clues to come up with our interpretation. Explain that it's important on the internet to read across sites, that is to read intertextually as well as intratextually. Look at Google reviews of the *Cosmopolitan* magazine website. Note that there seems to be a wide variety of opinions from a 1.5 rating on Yelp to a 4.4 on influenster.com, and explain that you don't know quite what to make of that. If students are interested, read some of the reviews to see what accounts for the differences in ratings.

- Recall that the self-interest of the Ants or the Grasshopper or each of the Pantiers affected what they said; so too does the self-interest of an author or a site. Explain that one key aspect of self-interest in digital media is how a site makes money. Explain that it looks as though there are two ways here: subscriptions to the print magazine and ads. Explain that ad revenue depends on clicks, so they want to attract attention and provide clickbait. Note that one way they seem to do that is that all but one of the links are linked to other *Cosmopolitan* stories. Note that another is to use photos and some moving images to attract attention. Note also that they seem to invite clicks with what seems to be a false familiarity with Michelle Obama by referring to her only by her first name.

- Click back to the story and say, "Okay, I see this was written by Starr Bowenbank. If I click her name I can see that she's an editorial assistant. I wonder why not a writer. But man, she writes so many stories. That means she can't take too much time with any of them. That worries me."

- Continue to talk about the focus of the article. Explain that it's striking to you that the bulk of the story is made up of quotes or paraphrases but that it seems that they all stem from the interview Lady Gaga did on *The Kyle and Jackie O Show*. Explain that this undercuts the author's authority in your eyes as does the false familiarity suggested by referring to Lady Gaga simply as Gaga in the last sentence.

- Solicit any questions the class has about your think-aloud or any comments they have about what they noticed that you didn't discuss.

Step 3

- Explain that you want students to put into practice the kind of analysis you just did, this time with a different popular cultural figure: Jay-Z.
  (*Note*: Once again, if Jay-Z isn't relevant to your students, choose a celebrity who is. Choose three sites that take different perspectives on that celebrity.)

- Divide students into six groups and assign two groups to investigate each of the following three sites:
  - https://bit.ly/3zblZvo
  - https://genius.com/artists/Jay-z
  - https://bit.ly/3VY3J27

- Have students use Handout 5.2A: Analyzing Websites I to aid in the analysis. Tell them that they can't do the final rating until they get together with their triad group.

- Circulate as groups work. The key in listening is to make sure they are engaging in each level of analysis. The process of their analysis is what's important, not the product.

- Once the groups have completed their work, combine the groups who worked on the same site to share their analyses.

- Once that sharing is complete, create jigsaw triads comprised of one person who did each website. Each member of the jigsaw should share their work and then complete the final rating.

- Have a whole-class discussion of their ratings. As you have done before, get a sense of the whole by asking students to indicate where they placed it on each scale (i.e., How many gave this a 1?). Then probe for their reasoning with something like this: "Okay, you said that you gave it a 1, that you find Jay-Z extremely admirable. What makes you say so? Why do you find that evidence credible?" Then move to someone who had a different view. Highlight the evidence they used and how they assessed its credibility.

Step 4

- Explain that you want students to get some more practice, this time looking at an entire website instead of just a single article. Explain that you're going to focus on three health-related sites that have had their share of controversy.

- Divide students into six groups. (If the previous small groups worked well, you might want to use them again.) Assign two groups to investigate each of the following three sites (they will have to use their phones if other devices aren't available):
  - www.mercola.com
  - www.goop.com
  - www.doctoroz.com

- Have students use Handout 5.2B: Analyzing Websites II to aid in the analysis.

- Circulate as groups work. Once again, the key in listening is to make sure they are engaging in each level of analysis. The process of their analysis is what's important, not the product.

- Once the groups have completed their work, combine the groups who worked on the same site to share their analyses.

- Once that sharing is complete, create a jigsaw triad comprised of one person who did each website. Each member of the jigsaw should share their work.

- Have a whole-class discussion of what they've learned. Ask students to share what aspects of their analysis they found most useful and which ones they found least useful in assessing reliability.

Step 5

- Thank students for their hard work deliberately practicing and using expert strategies.

- Ask students to write an exit ticket in which they explain how assessing the reliability is similar to and different than assessing the reliability of the source of information in linear texts and how they can see using what they have learned in the immediate future.

Extension

Have students choose an issue they care about and investigate how it is discussed on social media. Have them identify one tweet or Instagram, TikTok, or Facebook post that they find credible and one that they find unreliable and explain why they made the determination that they did.

Analyze the message of the site. The topic of each site is Jay-Z. What comment is the site making about Jay-Z?

Analyze the sponsor of the site:

- Look for internal evidence (how it's written, how it makes money, who its imagined audience is)

- Look for external evidence (What, if anything, do other sites say about the sponsor?)

Analyze the author of the information:

- Look for internal evidence (How much does the author know about the subject? What else has the author written?)

- Look for external evidence (What, if anything, do other sites say about the author?)

On the basis of what you've discovered, rate the reliability of the source of information:

Extremely reliable   Totally unreliable

What makes you say so?

Based on your analysis of your site and the reports that you've heard from your classmates, rate your feeling about Jay-Z:

Extremely admirable   Not admirable at all

What makes you say so?

Identify a claim that the author/site is making:

Topic: _____

_____

Comment: _____

_____

Analyze the sponsor of the site:

• Look for internal evidence (how it's written, how it makes money, who its imagined audience is)

• Look for external evidence (What, if anything, do other sites say about the sponsor?)

Analyze the author of the information (if there is no author cited, do the same analysis of the site in general):

• Look for internal evidence (How much does the author know about the subject? What else has the author written? How does the author use links or references to social media? Do the links/use of social media go to credible sources? Do they clearly support the point the author was trying to make?)

• Look for external evidence (What, if anything, do other sites say about the author?)

What do other sources have to say about the claim made by the site you investigated?

On the basis of what you've discovered, rate the reliability of the source of information:

Extremely reliable   Totally unreliable

What makes you say so?

LESSON 5.2, PART II
Social Media Extension

LESSON BACKGROUND

We've already done a lot of work on born-digital texts in this lesson, but we'd like to see if students can apply the work we've been doing to a social media text. This activity involves Instagram but can be adapted for other platforms. We are going to look for the ways that internal and external evidence are used on Instagram, and how they contribute to argument. Our steps are written for using the app, but if that is not possible or is something you are not comfortable with, you might screenshot and print out material.

LESSON STEPS

Step 1

Put the class into groups of two or three.

Step 2

Have them look up a prominent Instagrammer or influencer's account. At the time of this writing the top five Instagram users were Cristiano Ronaldo, Ariana Grande, The Rock, Selena Gomez, and Kylie Jenner, but there are many more possibilities. Check content before assigning users.

Step 3

Have students read over their landing page (look at their profile picture, bio, links) then carefully look at their last five or so posts. After a few minutes ask them to complete this scale.

This Instagrammer's posts suggest:

They're developing
a brand

They're sharing
their values

To back up their claim, students will need to think more specifically about the evidence they based their observations on. Have them note the evidence they are drawing on.

Internal Evidence (photos, including content, location, frequency, captions):

-

-

-

External Evidence (links, partnerships, comments, likes):

-

-

-

 Access lesson handouts and more resources at
resources.corwin.com/fightingfakenews.

CHAPTER 6

Lessons for Examining News, Nonfiction, and Digital Texts Through Literary Lenses

Rachel teaches English Language Arts at a high school that was named after the first governor of Minnesota. A career Union officer, he led several cavalry brigades responsible for the slaughter of many Native people. In recognition of both this heinous history and that the school stood on Native land, the name of the school was changed to Two Rivers, reflecting the confluence of the Mississippi and Minnesota rivers. As with nearly all recent name changes of schools, streets, and professional teams, a backlash ensued, one that spilled into the classroom. Rachel was teaching her students to read fake news critically, using contemporary literary theory. She saw the uproar about renaming the school as an opportunity to employ her pedagogical strategies of critical lenses with her new curricular emphasis on fake news.

First, as part of a continuing effort to demonstrate to students that fake news is not new and that Native Americans have long been victimized and marginalized by inaccurate and racist portrayals, Rachel offered a fake news story written by none other than Benjamin Franklin in 1782 and posted in a facsimile of the *Boston Chronicle* (https://bit.ly/3DojYyl). In that story, he "reported" a completely fabricated account of Native Americans ruthlessly scalping colonists and sending their scalps to the king. Rachel then showed her class a series of fake Facebook pages (https://bit.ly/3eV7WTX; see Indianz, 2018), circulating in both the United States and Europe that were purported to be "Native American pages." These pages were not created by or posted by Native people and represented stereotyping and an appropriation of Native identity.

Rachel then introduced the postcolonial lenses (see the postcolonial theory card in the Appendix) and asked students to consider both the historical and the current fake news from a postcolonial perspective.

She then turned to the question of the renaming of the school and asked the students in small groups to consider the relationship between how Natives were treated in the fake news and the controversy surrounding renaming the school. Viewing the naming from both a historical context and through the postcolonial lens gave students a different perspective on the naming controversy.

Rachel's experience using fake news and critical lenses in her classroom is at the heart of this chapter. In this chapter, we focus on the power of using critical lenses as a tool for understanding nonfiction texts including news items, nonfiction, and digital texts. More specifically, the chapter focuses on the following:

- How adolescents are affected by the information explosion and the info wars

- The importance of civil discourse

- The developmental characteristics of adolescent thought

- The ways in which examining ideology is at the heart of helping adolescents become critical consumers of media

- How using a variety of critical lenses can enliven the teaching of both print and digital texts, providing the grounds for rich and varied interpretations and compelling classroom discussions about positioning and credibility

- Five lessons that demonstrate how critical lenses help students detect, critique, and if necessary, resist the biases and ideological positions of authors of nonfiction, news, and digital texts. These lessons include
  - Lesson 6.1: Fake News and Fairy Tales
  - Lesson 6.2: A Not-So-Modest Proposal
  - Lesson 6.3: Barack Obama: In the Running?
  - Lesson 6.4: A Theory Relay
  - Lesson 6.5: How to Tell a True War Story: Tim O'Brien and Ukraine

THE INFORMATION EXPLOSION

In previous chapters we have discussed what happens when young people read and receive information that may not be factual, information that might indeed be false. Upon reflection, we are bucking a tradition where students generally assumed that what was presented to them in classrooms was unquestionably true. The assertions, facts, and even opinions that were found in textbooks or from the teacher were, for the most part, supposed to be unproblematically accepted. The authority of the text or other classroom material was connected to the authority of the teacher. Students were not encouraged to question the veracity of the material that was presented to them. In fact, educators once thought that the primary goal of education was to transmit information, to teach students to absorb, retain and remember and, if we were lucky, apply that information to different contexts. Of course, given the structure or format of typical standardized tests, they were never assessed on their ability to do so.

In the 21st century, much has changed as we consider how adolescents receive and internalize information. First, despite the enduring emphasis on fact consumption, memorization, and regurgitation, which is perpetuated by the persistence of those standardized tests and the Common Core movement, there has been an increased emphasis on critical thinking and on a more constructivist approach to teaching. As Applebee (1993) defines constructivism, "instruction becomes less a matter of transmittal of an objective and culturally sanctioned body of knowledge, and more a matter of helping individual learners learn to construct and interpret for themselves" (pp. 200–201). Applebee goes on to say that "[t]he challenge for educators is how in turn to embed this new emphasis into the curricula they develop and implement."

Next, as we have described in previous chapters, there is what some observers have understatedly called the *information explosion*. Multitudes of information outlets from television networks to social media platforms have made it more important than ever for adolescents to be able to process information judiciously and to carefully select and vet their sources of information. According to a recent Pew report on the role of adolescence and social media, "95% of teens now report they have a smartphone or access to one" (Anderson & Jiang, 2018). These mobile connections are in turn fueling more persistent online activities: 45% of teens now say they are online on a near-constant basis (Anderson & Jiang, 2018).

> 45% of teens now say they are online on a near-constant basis (Anderson & Jiang, 2018).

ADOLESCENTS AND THE INFO WARS

Today's adolescents, those secondary school students sitting in our classrooms, are assaulted from all sides with both legitimate and illegitimate sources. Increasingly, those who promulgate untruths are more easily able to deceive, from the sonorous tones of obfuscating Fox anchors to visuals on Instagram or TikTok that have been literally doctored. As young people become barraged from so many sources, it is natural to wonder how they are ever supposed to tell fact from fiction.

Well, as we have argued throughout the book, it turns out, they can't. Young people are easily duped. Despite their relative sophistication on many different levels as well as their digital native status, adolescents have proven to be casual about the information they receive at best and gullible at worst. Recent compelling research demonstrates this. Over the past few years, a team of researchers from Stanford led by Sam Wineburg (2016) found that despite their apparent technological skills, adolescents are easily duped by misleading or false information. Wineburg and his colleagues studied the responses of over 7,000 secondary and college students. They systematically presented the adolescents with screenshots of ads, Facebook posts, news magazines, and other sources. They then used a series of carefully constructed assessments. As Wineburg's team (2016) concluded:

> Overall, young people's ability to reason about the information on the Internet can be summed up in one word: bleak. Our "digital natives" may be able to flit between Facebook and Twitter while simultaneously uploading a selfie to Instagram and texting a friend. But when it comes to evaluating information that flows through social media channels, they are easily duped. (p. 4)

Wineburg's study is critically important to teachers for several reasons. The dire results are perhaps more telling and more urgent than any collection of NAEP scores. We are clearly not teaching the critical thinking and reasoning skills that would help young people be able to distinguish fact from fiction. This leaves students vulnerable to deception by everything from dishonest ads to bogus claims from peers to doctored or even catfished social media accounts. Perhaps even more important, these thinking and reasoning skills are necessary to become productive members of society and to engage in what Wineburg and his colleagues (2016) call *civic reasoning*. In our post-Trumpian (what some have called post-truth) nation, it is easy to see why this kind of skill is imperative. To be productive citizens to preserve our democracy, the next generations of citizens need to be able to detect and resist unreliable sources and understand that even a president can be a purveyor of falsehoods, and dangerous ones at that.

CIVIC DISCOURSE

The significance of this important skill is reframed in important ways by Mirra and others (2021), who identify the ability to discern fact from fiction, truth from untruths, as a requisite for effective civic discourse. They argue that it is not merely the discerning consumption of news that needs to be considered as we think about the intellectual predispositions of adolescents; it is also an acknowledgment of the "multiple, expansive, and varied textual influences on young people's developing civic identities beyond narrow conceptions of 'news.'" Therefore, in our quest to help students become better consumers of information, we are not simply concerned with helping students avoid factual mistakes or misunderstandings, which may lead them into problematic situations or cause them to cobble together a set of beliefs that are based on falsehoods. We also want them to be able to inhabit an intellectual disposition that will help them learn to move meaningfully through the world as people and as citizens. This includes encouraging young people to develop empathy, which rests on students' ability to consider ideas, events, information, and opinions from the perspectives of others.

THE DEVELOPMENTAL ASPECTS
OF ADOLESCENT THOUGHT

Although it is understandable to lament the flawed thinking of adolescents when it comes to understanding information, it's important to keep in mind their cognitive development and what we can rightfully expect for secondary students. William Perry (1970) has posited that early adolescents are dualistic in their thinking processes. Things are right or wrong, real or not real, true or false, me or not me. As dualistic thinkers they are unable to sustain multiple possibilities, to see things from different perspectives, especially if they are contradictory. Students may eventually develop a more relativistic manner of thinking simply by virtue of the process of cognitive development as they move through the developmental stages as articulated by Perry. To facilitate that development, students benefit from cognitive dissonance to help them think more relativistically, and ultimately, from the perspective of multiplicity.

Offering at least two differing perspectives on a single issue and inviting students to inhabit perspectives other than their own can help prompt cognitive growth. As F. Scott Fitzgerald (1945) remarked, "The test of a first-rate intelligence is the ability to hold two opposed ideas in the mind at the same time, and still retain the ability to function" (p. 69).

We want to reiterate our goals about the importance of helping students be able to discern fact from fiction. One thread that seems to be apparent throughout is the idea of metacognitive instruction. That is rather than presenting students with what to read, we also want to teach them how to read and, ultimately, how to curate their own reading. So we want to be explicit about how they should approach reading.

IDEOLOGY

As with the recent controversies surrounding the 2020 election, the subsequent January 6 insurrection, mandated vaccination and masking, and the Russian invasion of Ukraine and the West's response, these controversies are about more than just themselves. They are ideological. By ideological we mean the body of doctrine, myth, belief, and so on that guides an individual, social movement, institution, class, or large group. In *In Search of Authority*, Stephen Bonnycastle (2007) perhaps says it best:

> In essence an ideology is a system of thought, or "world view," which
> an individual acquires (usually unconsciously) while growing up. An
> ideology determines what you think matters in life, how you
> distinguish between good people and evil people, what you think
> "polite" behavior is, how you see male and female roles in life, and a
> host of other things. You can visualize your ideology as a grid, or a set
> of glasses, through which you can see the world. (p. 40)

THE IMPORTANCE OF MULTIPLE PERSPECTIVES

The concept of multiple theoretical lenses, which Deborah has described in detail elsewhere (Appleman, 2014), can be directly applied to the variety of dispositions adolescents need to read critically. We think encouraging multiple perspectives through various literary lenses is a useful tool to help foster this kind of intellectual predisposition. There is much to be said for the power of multiple perspectives to trouble a single, often erroneous, reading by triangulating information through different points of view.

Teaching literature, nonfiction literature, and other kinds of current events and social media texts through contemporary literary theory promotes what many in the field of literacy education have come to regard as a constructivist approach. When teachers introduce literary theory into their literature classes, they invite students to construct both interpretive method and literary meaning into their study of literature. No longer will students respond within a preselected theoretical paradigm. They construct the theoretical context as well as the content of their meaning-making. This kind of intellectual activity is directly tied to students' ability to discern fact from fiction, real from fake, since, as Bonnycastle (2002) writes:

> [t]he main reason for studying theory at the same time as literature is that it forces you to deal consciously with the problem of ideologies . . . There are many truths and the one you will find depend[s] partly on the ideology you start with. [Studying theory] means you can take your own part in the struggles for power between different ideologies. It helps you to discover elements of your own ideology, and understand why you hold certain values unconsciously. It means that no authority can impose a "truth" on you in a dogmatic way—and if some authority does try, you can challenge that "truth" in a powerful way, by asking what ideology it is based on . . . Theory is subversive because it puts authority in question. (p. 34)

Multiplicity, or the ability to see many different sides of stories, is central to the idea of helping adolescents to view a story, an article, a news item, or a website critically and skeptically. Students' ability to read texts, the world, and their own lives is enhanced not only by the study of individual theories themselves but also by the notion of multiple perspectives. Henry Louis Gates, Jr.'s (1987) metaphor for theory as a prism, one that changes the entire nature of what is viewed when we view it through a different angle of the prism, is useful here:

Theory is subversive because it puts authority in question.

> Literary theory functioned in my education as a prism, which I could *turn* to refract different spectral patterns of language use in a text, as one does with daylight. Turn the prism this way, and one pattern emerges; turn it that way, and another pattern configures. (p. xvii)

We can help our students understand what it means to read thoughtfully and with discrimination if we value multiple readings (or interpretations) over a single authoritative reading. Literary theory helps us understand that there are many ways to know texts, to read and interpret them.

READING WORLDS

Critical encounters with literary theory also help students read the world around them. As teachers, we hope that students will be able to integrate successful strategies for learning in school and adapt those strategies to life as well. Students need to learn to read the world around them to function as literate participants in an increasingly complex society. Thomson (1993) has written, "All our regular institutional and social practices, including our social rituals and ceremonies, are texts to be read and interpreted" (p. 130). In *The Crafty Reader,* Scholes (2001) reminds us that "[t]he human condition . . . is a textual one and has always been so" (p. 78). Learning to read the world as text is an important result of high school literature instruction that includes theory.

Because reading from multiple perspectives helps students be able to see things from more than one point of view, it plants the idea that there is more than one way of looking at things, more than one way to read the story in front of us. In a much-lauded TED talk, which we discuss again in Chapter 7, Chimamanda Adichie reminds us of the danger of a single story. She cautions that it not only narrows our gaze, but it can also lead us to misinterpretations, into a mistaken notion of the reality, the facts, the people, and the stories that are presented to us.

When we teach theory, we are, more than anything else perhaps, helping young people move through the texts of our lives as the kind of enlightened witnesses that bell hooks (1997) envisions:

> It's really about being enlightened witnesses when we watch representations, which means we are able to be critically vigilant about both what is being told to us and how we respond to what is being told. (p. 8)

The lessons that conclude this chapter are designed to provide that enlightenment.

Reflection Questions

- Consider your students' lived experiences, both in and out of school. What are some examples of contemporary events that need to be read from multiple points of view?

- How might the use of critical lenses help your students understand aspects of their own experiences? Why are critical lenses particularly well suited to learning to critically read fake news?

LESSON SUMMARIES

Lesson 6.1: Fake News and Fairy Tales. This lesson uses *The True Story of the Three Little Pigs* to illustrate how the teller of the tale determines what the "true" story is.

Lesson 6.2: A Not-So-Modest Proposal. This lesson uses the classic text by Jonathan Swift, "A Modest Proposal," to demonstrate how to look at a text from a variety of critical perspectives, each yielding a different reading.

Lesson 6.3: Barack Obama: In the Running? This lesson centers on a real fake news article that claimed Barack Obama was running for president of Kenya. Students will use a variety of lenses to excavate the ideology behind the fake claims.

Lesson 6.4: A Theory Relay. In small groups, students will encounter five different fake news websites. Armed with theory cards, they will use different theoretical perspectives to consider the motivations behind each of the websites.

Lesson 6.5: How to Tell a True War Story: Tim O'Brien and Ukraine. This lesson begins with a discussion of the difference between fact and fiction as animated in Tim O'Brien's classic story, "How to Tell a True War Story" from *The Things They Carried*. We then look at news dispatches from different sources covering the war in Ukraine and discuss the degree to which fact and fiction are intermingled.

LESSON 6.1
Fake News and Fairy Tales

LESSON BACKGROUND

Before teaching this lesson, the students will have considered point of view (see Chapter 5) and perspective through a variety of lenses focusing on both fiction and nonfiction. They will also have been introduced to critical lenses.

Purpose

- To be able to detect bias in the text
- To learn that there are multiple truths to any story
- To learn that the truth of any story resides and is affected by the teller of the tale

Length

- Two 50-minute class periods

Materials

- Book: *The True Story of the Three Little Pigs, as Told by A. Wolf* by Jon Scieszka

You can use the text or one of these read-alouds:

  - https://www.youtube.com/watch?v=hXUwONM-gVA
  - https://www.youtube.com/watch?v=pF0h7NqpJQc
  - https://www.youtube.com/watch?v=4ZtUdk2UlT8

LESSON STEPS

Step 1

Students will, in small groups, retell the traditional story of the three little pigs.

Step 2

Student versions of the story of the three little pigs will be shared with the entire class and compared for points of emphasis.

Step 3

- Students will then read the children's book *The True Story of the Three Little Pigs, as Told by A. Wolf.*

- Tell students that they are going to compare this version to the original and their own to detect bias and self- and group interest and to identify how perspective can pollute basic information.

Step 4

Students will consider the story from the following critical perspectives:

- Reader response lens

- Formalist/New Critical lens

- Social Class/Marxist lens

Step 5

- **Discuss in small groups:** Who is the more reliable narrator here: the wolves or the pigs? Remember when thinking about narrator reliability to do the following:

  1. Ask, Would all reasonable readers completely accept the surface meaning? If some of the surface meaning is questionable or needs to be rejected, then . . .

  2. Decide what is not under dispute in the work (i.e., what critical readers can believe and accept).

  3. Apply knowledge of the world to generate a reconstructed meaning of what is under dispute, and if possible, check what you think against knowledge of the author.

In this case, consider:

- How might the truth lie somewhere in between the stories of the pigs and the wolf?

Step 6

Write an informal essay that describes the ways in which the book *The True Story of the Three Little Pigs, as Told by A. Wolf* might be an example of information pollution and how it might express biases and try to play on the reader's cognitive biases.

Step 7

- Follow up/potential extensions: Students will watch the documentary *Outfoxed*, which exposes the bias inherent in Rupert Murdoch's Fox network, despite its claims of being "fair and balanced."

- Students could also consider other two-sided stories where a traditional tale is retold from another perspective.

- Consider how bias is at work and how readers' or viewers' cognitive biases are being worked.

Step 8

Final reflection: Students will consider and note:

- Why they need to consider bias

- What they need to notice to consider if a text might be telling only one "truth" or taking on the "truth"

LESSON 6.2
A Not-So-Modest Proposal

LESSON BACKGROUND

Although "A Modest Proposal" by Jonathan Swift is frequently used to teach irony, this lesson takes a different approach. We use several lenses to help students read this canonical text from a variety of perspectives. Prior to reading the text, students will need to learn about the historical context in which Swift was writing, specifically, the Irish Famine.

Purpose

- To help students notice when they might not want to read a text at face value
- To apply the techniques of literary interpretation to an expository text
- To contrast literal reading with interpretive reading
- To view a text using critical lenses

Length

- Two 55-minute class periods or one 80-minute block period

Materials

- Background material: Satire in "A Modest Proposal" (https://www.youtube .com/watch?v=gByfoDgdN2c)

- An annotated version of the text "A Modest Proposal" (https://bit.ly/ 3D3nCMT)

LESSON STEPS

Step 1

Students will read a few historical documents and study the background:

- https://bit.ly/3gx8ks1
- https://bit.ly/3z6t5RK

Step 2

Tell students that they are going to read a classic text that was misunderstood at the time because many readers did not understand when to reject the face value of a text or to use a lens to reconstitute what the text might mean to different groups and explain that this lesson will help them do better!

Step 3

Students read "A Modest Proposal" in buddy groups of two to four.

Step 4

Divide students into groups using the following lenses

- The Class lens

- The Gender lens

- Historical lens

- Reader response lens

Step 5

Students convene into jigsaw groups and discuss their reading through their assigned lens.

Step 6

- Reconvene as a whole class. Discuss what stood out and what was brought into sharper relief by using the lenses.

- Discuss what is missed. How can we be misled if the lenses are not in our reading repertoire?

Step 7

- Have each student individually identify a real-world event (in their personal lives, at your school, or in your community) where reports might not be acceptable at face value. Then share in triads.

- Find (or have students find) contemporary examples of misleading documents that can be more richly understood by using the lenses.

Step 8

As an exit ticket, jot down some ideas about how using a lens can help you reject some of or all the text's face value.

LESSON 6.3
Barack Obama: In the Running?

LESSON BACKGROUND

This lesson centers on a fake news article that claimed Barack Obama was running for president of Kenya. Students will use a variety of lenses to excavate the ideology behind the fake claims. This lesson follows the format of "two truths and a lie." In other words, there will be two true stories and one fake story.

Purpose

- To encourage students to read headlines with appropriate skepticism and learn that news is frequently neither factual nor objective

- To apply critical lenses to help discern the underlying point of view and ideology that lies underneath a particular story or claim

Length

- One class period, approximately 55 minutes

Materials

- Article about Barack Obama running for president of Kenya (https://bit.ly/3ss5Mhq)

- Two other legitimate articles about Barack Obama

- Handout 6.3A: Group Activity Sheet

LESSON STEPS

Step 1

Show three news articles about Barack Obama to the class. Two of the stories will be regular run-of-the-mill short articles, and the other will be fake.

Step 2

Use a clicker (https://www.iclicker.com) to poll the class on the veracity of each of the articles using the following question: "Do you believe this article is true? Yes or no?" (The class should be able to see instantaneous results for each of the articles.)

Step 3

Divide students into groups with each group assigned to one of the following lenses:

- Reader response
- Postcolonial
- Class
- Critical race[*]

[*]Given the current controversies about critical race theory, teachers may elect not to use this lens and so substitute another.

Step 4

Each group fills out the Group Activity Sheet (Handout 6.3A).

Step 5

Students are assigned to new jigsaw groups so that each theory is represented by one or more members of each group. They then respond to the following questions:

- What did your literary lens help you see?
- What did you discover about the point of view of the article?
- What red flags did this activity raise for you?

Step 6

Conclude the lesson by having a whole-class discussion, creating five tips for reading articles skeptically so that you won't be fooled.

Names:

Literary Lens:

Briefly define the lens you are using. What does it bring into sharper relief? What questions does it raise?

Now, using that lens, consider these questions on the three articles:

QUESTIONS FOR CONSIDERATION	ARTICLE 1	ARTICLE 2	ARTICLE 3
What is the source of the article?			
What, if anything, do you know about the political or ideological point of view of the source?			
What are some neutral words that the article uses?			
What are some laden or loaded words?			
Using this lens, what questions arise for you about this article?			
What did this lens help you see about this article that you couldn't see before?			
Is this article factual?			

LESSON 6.4
A Theory Relay

LESSON BACKGROUND

This lesson uses multiple literary theories to help students learn to discern the ideological perspective of news articles and to detect "fakes."

Purpose

- To increase students' familiarity with a variety of literary lenses and to apply them to real-world texts
- To encourage agile thinking and processing

Length

- One 80-minute class period or two 50-minute class periods

Materials

- Twenty-five sets of theory cards (see Appendix)
- Theory relay sheets (Handout 6.4A)
- Four theory stations
- Printouts of five fake news articles from the following source: https://library-nd.libguides.com/fakenews/examples

LESSON STEPS

Step 1

Before class begins, set up five theory stations, each with two to three articles and some instructional material about the lenses. This material will supplement the material outlined on the theory cards.

Step 2

Introduce the activity to the class.

Step 3

Divide the class into four groups with five to six students in each group.

Step 4

Distribute a complete set of theory cards (Appendix) and the theory relay sheet (Handout 6.4A) to each student.

Step 5

Direct the class to activity stations, switching every 5 minutes.

Step 6

Conduct a whole-class discussion focusing on these questions:

- What theories seemed to be the most useful?

- Have you used any of the theories outside of class to read or interpret something?

- In what ways can the theories help you detect fake news?

Step 7

- Collect students' relay sheets and journal entries.

For the next 40 minutes or so, in groups of three or four, please consider *some fake news articles* from a variety of theoretical perspectives:

☐   Historical/biographical

☐   Reader response

☐   Social class

☐   Gender

We'll be doing this as a kind of relay. There are four theory stations around the room. Each station includes a set of fake news articles as well as a glossary of the theories under consideration. Spend approximately 10 minutes at each station. Each group should turn in one of these sheets to your teacher. Make certain you've completed the journal entry at the end of the sheet.

Name:

Group Members:

Station 1: Reader Response

Reread the explanation of reader response. In the space below, write three personal characteristics that are relevant to one of the articles, three important aspects of that article, and three meaning statements that are the result of your personal interaction with that article.

1.

2.

3.

Station 2: Historical/Biographical

Skim the introduction from *Lies My Teacher Told Me* (https://bit.ly/3gEm6ZZ).

What do you need to know about history to be able to evaluate the veracity of the articles?

To what degree are historical events open to interpretation?

(Continued)

(Continued)

Station 3: Feminist/Gender

When you consider *these articles* from a feminist perspective, what considerations are brought into greater relief? Write your response below.

Station 4: Social Class

When you consider *these articles* from a social class lens perspective, what characters, incidents, or themes are brought into greater relief? Write your response below.

Journal entry for all students

Reflect on your group's efforts this hour to read *fake news* through a variety of critical lenses. Respond to the following questions in an entry of at least two paragraphs:

- Which lens seemed to be most helpful?
- Which lens was the most difficult to apply?
- Which was the most informative?

LESSON 6.5
How to Tell a True War Story: Tim O'Brien and Ukraine

LESSON BACKGROUND

This lesson begins with a discussion of the difference between fact and fiction as animated in Tim O'Brien's classic story "How to Tell a True War Story" from *The Things They Carried*. We will then look at news dispatches from different sources covering the war in Ukraine and will discuss the degree to which fact and fiction are intermingled.

Purpose

- To help students adopt a stance of thoughtfulness and healthy skepticism as they consume news, especially about war
- To invite students to think about the subjectivity of truth, especially when it comes to war

Length

- Two class periods

Materials

- Twenty-five copies of "How to Tell a True War Story" by Tim O'Brien
- Handout 6.5A: Literary Theory: Among the Things We Carry
- The following news stories:
    - https://www.bbc.com/news/60589965
    - https://bit.ly/3zakKfI

LESSON STEPS

Step 1

Have students read "How to Tell a True War Story" by Tim O'Brien.

Step 2

Ask students to consider the story from several literary theories using the activity sheet, "Literary Theory: Among the Things We Carry" (Handout 6.5A).

Step 3

- Divide students into groups of three and distribute the two fake news stories about Ukraine.
- Ask students to consider what is true and what is false about each story.

Step 4

Reconvene as a class and read the following story: https://bit.ly/3MYhZnL

Step 6

Lead a whole-class discussion, focusing on the following questions:

- Which lenses would be useful to help us see the truth of a story?

- Is the truth about war stories important?

- How did the reading of Tim O'Brien's story influence your reception of the other stories?

Step 7

Write an exit ticket, describing which literary lens you might use next time you read a story about war and why you think that lens would be especially helpful.

Reflection Questions

- Which of these lessons seems most appealing to you? Which lenses do you think your students might most readily use? Which might they resist?

- How might you build the use of critical lenses into your curriculum for reading other texts you are currently teaching?

Access lesson handouts and more resources at
resources.corwin.com/fightingfakenews.

Please consider "How to Tell a True War Story," the story from Tim O'Brien's *The Things They Carried*, from the perspective of the four theories listed below. Each group will consider a particular lens and then we will discuss this together as a whole class.

	READER RESPONSE	POSTCOLONIAL	FEMINIST/ GENDER	MARXIST/ SOCIAL CLASS
Cite specific textual passage(s) that support this kind of reading.				
Interpret at least one character through this lens.				
If you look through this lens, what questions emerge?				
Do you believe in this reading? Why or why not?				

(Continued)

(Continued)

Literary Theories

A Sampling of Critical Lenses

Literary theories were developed as a means to understand the various ways people read texts. The proponents of each theory believe their theory is *the* theory, but most of us interpret texts according to the "rules" of several different theories at a time. All literary theories are lenses through which we can see texts. There is nothing to say that one is better than another or that you should read according to any of them, but it is sometimes fun to decide to read a text with one in mind because you often end up with a whole new perspective on your reading.

What follows is a summary of some of the most common schools of literary theory. These descriptions are extremely cursory, and none of them fully explains what the theory is all about. But it is enough to get the general idea.

Archetypal Criticism. In criticism *archetype* signifies narrative designs, character types, or images that are said to be identifiable in a wide variety of works of literature, as well as in myths, dreams, and even ritualized modes of social behavior. The archetypal similarities within these diverse phenomena are held to reflect a set of universal, primitive, and elemental patterns, whose effective embodiment in a literary work evokes a profound response from the reader. The death-rebirth theme is often said to be the archetype of archetypes. Other archetypal themes are the journey underground, the heavenly ascent, the search for the father, the Paradise-Hades image, the Promethean rebel-hero, the scapegoat, the earth goddess, and the fatal woman.

Gender/Feminist Criticism. A feminist critic sees cultural and economic disabilities in a "patriarchal" society that have hindered or prevented women from realizing their creative possibilities and women's cultural identification as a merely negative object, or "other" to man as the defining and dominating "subject." There are several assumptions and concepts held in common by most feminist critics.

- Our civilization is pervasively patriarchal.

- The concepts of "gender" are largely, if not entirely, cultural constructs, affected by the omnipresent patriarchal biases of our civilization.

- This patriarchal ideology also pervades those writings that have been considered great literature. Such works lack autonomous female role models, are implicitly addressed to male readers, and leave the woman reader an alien outsider or else solicit her to identify against herself by assuming male values and ways of perceiving, feeling, and acting.

This lens is somewhat like the Social Class/Marxist lens, but instead of focusing on the relationships between the classes, it focuses on the relationships between the genders. Under this theory you would examine the patterns of thought, behavior, values, enfranchisement, and power in relations between the sexes. For example, "Where Are You Going, Where Have You Been" can be seen as the story of the malicious dominance men have over women both physically and psychologically. Connie is the female victim of the role in society that she perceives herself playing— the coy young lass whose life depends on her looks.

Social Class/Marxist Criticism. A Marxist critic grounds their theory and practice on the economic and cultural theory of Karl Marx and Friedrich Engels, especially on the following claims:

- The evolving history of humanity, its institutions and its ways of thinking, are determined by the changing mode of its *material production*—that is, of its basic economic organization.

- Historical changes in the fundamental mode of production effect essential changes both in the constitution and power relations of social classes, which carry on a conflict for economic, political, and social advantage.

- Human consciousness in any era is constituted by an ideology—that is, a set of concepts, beliefs, values, and ways of thinking and feeling through which human beings perceive and by which they explain what they take to be reality. A Marxist critic typically undertakes to explain the literature in any era by revealing the economic, class, and ideological determinants of the way an author writes and to examine the relation of the text to the social reality of that time and place.

This school of critical theory focuses on power and money in works of literature. Who has the power/money? Who does not? What happens as a result? For example, it could be said that "The Legend of Sleepy Hollow" is about the upper class attempting to maintain their power and influence over the lower class by chasing Ichabod, a lower-class citizen with aspirations toward the upper class, out of town. This would explain some of the numerous descriptions you get of land, wealth, and hearty living through Ichabod's eyes.

Formalism/New Criticism is directed against the critics whose focus is concerned with the lives and psychology of authors, with social background, and with literary history. There are several points of view and procedures that are held in common by most New Critics:

1. A poem should be treated as primarily poetry and should be regarded as an independent and self-sufficient object.

2. The distinctive procedure of the New Critic is explication, or close reading; that is, detailed and subtle analysis of the complex interrelations and ambiguities of the components within a work.

3. The principles of New Criticism are basically verbal. That is, literature is conceived to be a special kind of language whose attributes are defined by systematic opposition to the language of science and of practical and logical discourse. The key concepts of this criticism deal with the meanings and interactions of words, figures of speech, and symbols.

4. The distinction between literary genres is not essential.

Psychological and Psychoanalytic Criticism. Psychological criticism deals with a work of literature primarily as an expression, in fictional form, of the personality, state of mind, feelings, and desires of its author. The assumption of

(Continued)

(Continued)

psychoanalytic critics is that a work of literature is correlated with its author's mental traits:

1. Reference to the author's personality is used to explain and interpret a literary work.

2. Reference to literary works is made to establish, biographically, the personality of the author.

3. The mode of reading a literary work itself is a way of experiencing the distinctive subjectivity or consciousness of its author.

This theory requires that we investigate the psychology of a character or an author to figure out the meaning of a text (although to apply an author's psychology to a text can also be considered biographical criticism, depending on your point of view). For example, alcohol allows the latent thoughts and desires of the narrator of "The Black Cat" to surface in such a way that he ends up shirking the self-control imposed by social mores and standards and becomes the man his psyche has repressed his whole life.

Reader Response Criticism. This type of criticism focuses on the activity of reading a work of literature. Reader response critics turn from the traditional conception of a work as an achieved structure of meanings to the responses of readers as their eyes follow a text. By this shift of perspective, a literary work is converted into an activity that goes on in a reader's mind, and what had been features of the work itself—including narrator, plot, characters, style, and structure—are less important than the connection between a reader's experience and the text. It is through this interaction that meaning is made.

Students seem most comfortable with this school of criticism. Proponents believe that literature has no objective meaning or existence. People bring their own thoughts, moods, and experiences to whatever text they are reading and get out of it whatever they happen to, based on their own expectations and ideas. For example, when Deborah reads "Sonny's Blues" she is reminded of her younger sister who loves music. The story really gets to Deborah because sometimes she worries about her sister and their relationship. Deborah wants to support her sister in a way that Sonny's brother does not support Sonny.

New Historicism. New Historicism asks us to consider literature in a wider historical context than does traditional historicism. Unlike traditional historicism, new Historicism asserts that our understanding of history itself is a result of subjective interpretation rather than a linear objective set of events. New Historicists also believe that it is not simply enough to understand the sociocultural and historical contexts in which a piece of literature was written; we must also consider how our own place and time in history affects our interpretations since we bring to a text some perceptions, assumptions, and beliefs that were not at play when the text was written. For example, the questions that we ask about how women are portrayed in Shakespeare's plays are shaped by contemporary feminist thought and the changes that women's roles in society have undergone in the intervening centuries since Shakespeare's era. New Historicism then tells us that literature is influenced by history and that our historical understanding is also influenced by literature. The author, the reader, and the critic are all influenced by our own cultural and historical location. Moreover, our understanding of and appreciation for particular texts will change over time.

Other theories we'll be discussing in class include

Deconstructionist Criticism. Deconstruction is, by far, the most difficult critical theory for people to understand. It was developed by some very unconventional thinkers who declare that literature means nothing because language means nothing. In other words, we cannot say that we know what the "meaning" of a story is because there is no way of knowing. For example, in some stories (like "Where Are You Going, Where Have You Been") that do not have tidy endings, you cannot assume you know what happened.

Historical Criticism. Using this theory requires that you apply to a text specific historical information about the time during which an author wrote. History, in this case, refers to the social, political, economic, cultural, and/or intellectual climate of the time. For example, William Faulkner wrote many of his novels and stories during and after World War II, which helps explain the feelings of darkness, defeat, and struggle that pervade much of his work.

CHAPTER 7

Lessons for Teaching Students to Evaluate Evidence and Research

The day after Kobe Bryant died, Michael was working with students on the Pathways Project, the college access program that we mentioned in the introduction to Chapter 5. Michael thought there would be some talk about Kobe's death. After all, Bryant's dad played for the Philadelphia 76ers and Kobe spent his teenage years in a Philadelphia suburb. But he was unprepared to find that so many Pathways students believed that he was murdered.

"What makes you say that?" Michael asked.

The reply from some: "I've done my research."

We've all heard that line before and most often it comes in defense of the most outlandish claims. Of course, none of the students did any investigation of Kobe's death. What "I've done my research" means is that "I read something on the internet." Look up "It must be true, I read it on the internet" and see all the memes. But we wonder whether characteristic ways of teaching text-based arguments might contribute to that misapprehension. In this chapter, we take up that question. More specifically we

- Examine the importance of evidence as foundation for argument

- Consider the extent to which evidence in text-based argument is different from the evidence used in other kinds of arguments

- Delineate five key questions to ask when evaluating research used as evidence

- Share lessons that will help students become more critical consumers of the evidence they cite

Evaluating the evidence upon which arguments are based is essential to our students. They have to do it as they consider the choices they confront every day: iPhone or Android? McDonald's or Wendy's? TikTok or Instagram? They have to do it in their classrooms. Andrews (2009) contends that argument is "the most highly prized type of academic discourse" (p. 1). But for the purposes of this book, what is even more important is that they have to do it to be an informed citizen.

EVIDENCE PROVIDES THE FOUNDATION FOR ARGUMENTATION

The most intractable public policy argument of our lives is the debate about abortion. We think its intractability is instructive for us as teachers because it points out a fundamental truth about arguments: Effective arguments, and hence reasoned public discourse, depend on opposing sides' willingness to at least provisionally accept the evidence on which they are based. Put another way, for an argument to have a chance of succeeding or even fostering dialogue it has to be founded on evidence that is safe.

Let's explain. We believe the reason the abortion debate is so complicated is that the opposing sides don't (and will never) agree on the starting point. There are distinctly different views of when personhood begins, from the moment of fertilization at one end of the spectrum, to birth, at the other, with a number of positions in between. We are not going to engage in this debate. We simply want to point out that each starting point brings with it a different argument about whether and when abortion should be legal. But because the data for each of these arguments will not be accepted by the opposing side, no one will ever be persuaded and indeed no real conversation across positions is likely to ensue.

> Effective arguments depend on opposing sides' willingness to at least provisionally accept the evidence on which they are based.

Our operationalizing (Smith & Imbrenda, 2018; Smith et al., 2012) Toulmin's (1958) model of everyday argumentation helps us understand the stakes of the game. Arguments are always based on someone's asserting a position, sometimes unprovoked, sometimes in response to the question "Where do you stand?" sometimes at the beginning of a conversation, sometimes after a story in which the person establishes their credibility or establishes their interest in an issue. For an argument to proceed, a *claim* has to be both controversial and defensible. It has to be interesting or significant in some way, maybe by furthering understanding or informing action. If a claim doesn't have these features, it's greeted with a statement akin to "Duh" or "Tell me something I don't know." Think about someone's saying the following:

"LeBron James is a great basketball player."

"McDonald's is a popular fast-food restaurant."

"Young people today pay attention to social media."

Such claims don't lead to exploration, extension of understanding, or new insights and learning. Rather they lead simply to assent or an eye roll because of their obviousness. On the other hand, think of claims like these:

"Michael Jordan couldn't even make a team today."

"Eating even one McDonald's hamburger will kill you."

"The social media scene hasn't really changed much over the last 20 years."

We think that these claims are also likely to resist serious exploration because on their face they seem so silly. Now think of these claims:

"LeBron is the greatest player of all time."

"The state government should put a significant tax on fast food to reduce its consumption."

"TikTok is a positive force in today's society because it provides a way for young people to meaningfully affect their worlds."

If you make a claim that is both controversial and defensible, as we think the three claims above are, then your interlocutor will likely ask something like this:

"What makes you say so?" or "What do we have to go on?"

The answer to those questions is *data*. As we argued in our discussion of the abortion debate, the *sine qua non* of data is that it has to be safe. That is, your audience has to be willing to accept it, at least provisionally. If not, then the statement isn't really data but is rather a claim. Let's look at a conversation that might help make the point.

Imagine that two people are discussing an issue that's quite controversial at the time of this writing, whether colleges should require their students to get vaccinated before returning to campus:

1. A: So where do you stand?

2. B: Easy answer for me: "Yes."

3. A: What makes you say so?

4. B: Pfizer's and Moderna's vaccines are over 90% effective.

5. A: So what?

6. B: A big part of college is the social interaction. An effective vaccine will allow students to have campus social interactions again. How about you?

7. A: I don't think colleges should require the vaccine.

8. B: Really? What makes you say so?

9. A: You can't tell people what to do.

10. B: What makes you say so?

11. A: Our bodies, our choice.

12. B: But what about the other vaccines you have to get? What about seatbelts?

Speaker B presents a claim in line 2. After being asked for evidence, Speaker B provides it in line 4. Speaker A does not challenge the evidence, and because Speaker A accepts the evidence, the argument can proceed. In contrast, something different happens with Speaker A's argument. Speaker A makes a claim in line 7 and provides evidence in line 9. But Speaker B challenges that evidence rather than accepting it. So rather than proceeding with the argument, Speaker A will first have to rehabilitate that evidence or provide different evidence for the argument to proceed.

Of course, things could have gone differently. Speaker A could have challenged the evidence in line 4: "They are not. That's just government propaganda." And if Speaker A did so, the argument might have devolved into a shouting match or an agreement to change the subject. What is certain is that discussion can only ensue if people share some common understandings. Those understandings are evidence, which, because they are at least provisionally accepted by both sides, provide a foundation on which to build.

Easier said than done. In today's polarized political world, people are hesitant to provisionally accept even the most innocuous evidence. Perhaps the most famous example of this hesitancy came in an exchange between Chuck Todd, the host of *Meet the Press*, and Kellyanne Conway, former counselor to former President Trump, in which she explained the administration's insistence on claiming that President Trump's inauguration was more heavily attended than President Obama's despite absolutely definitive visual evidence to the contrary. Conway explained that when press secretary Sean Spicer claimed that "[t]his was the largest audience to ever witness an inauguration—period—both in person and around the globe," Spicer was simply presenting "alternative facts" (Meet the Press, 2017).

> Our job as teachers is to help our students develop the tools that they need to ascertain when evidence is worth trusting and when it is not.

It's easy to feel smugly superior to such a ridiculous pronouncement. However, The Conversation (2017), an organization that describes itself as "dedicated to unlocking the knowledge of experts for the public good" because of "deep-seated concerns for the fading quality of our public discourse" and the recognition that "uninformed views are amplified by social media networks that reward those who spark outrage instead of insight or thoughtful discussion" makes what we think is a compelling point: "In politics, facts are contestable. This has always been the case: the status of facts and their use in politics hasn't changed as a result of Trump's election" (para. 7).

Our job as teachers, then, is to help our students develop the tools that they need to ascertain when evidence is worth trusting and when it is not. We began exploring this idea in Chapter 3, but it's so important that we're revisiting it here in the context of teaching argumentative writing. In fact, we think this issue is so important that we should be teaching and reteaching it all the time, across grade levels and subject areas.

Imbrenda (2018) makes the argument that in doing so when we teach argumentative writing, we need to confront students' misconceptions about facts and opinions and how they work in academic and civic discourse. He explains that students in his study manifested a conceptual orientation to argument that includes these elements:

1. Written texts come in two varieties: enumerated facts and elaborated opinions.

2. Facts are facts. They belong to no one in particular and they are more or less irrefutable.

3. Opinions are completely subjective and belong only to their authors.

4. Everyone is entitled to an opinion. Regardless of the underlying reasoning behind an opinion, no opinion is more important or valid than any other.

5. To be convincing, a written text must enumerate relevant facts. Written texts that elaborate opinions, on the other hand, can be dismissed if the reader disagrees with them.

Unfortunately, this conceptual orientation did not serve students well, instead providing "a recurring barrier to their evaluation and generation of effective academic arguments" (Imbrenda, 2018, p. 336). If facts are irrefutable, students won't question them and will not feel the need to explain them. If everyone is entitled to an opinion, there is no need to explain your own and no way to critique the opinion of others.

Writing conventional text-based arguments does not challenge the conceptional orientation Imbrenda documents. Let's take a look at a question eNotes proposes on Frost's "The Road Not Taken," a poem we selected because of its familiarity and because it's in the public domain, which means we can print it here. We chose eNotes because, according to Wikipedia, it specializes in literature and is one of the most popular education websites in the United States, receiving more than 11 million unique visitors each year, and 1 million unique visitors each month, making it among the most-visited education properties in the United States.

Just to refresh your memory, here's the poem:

The Road Not Taken

By Robert Frost

Two roads diverged in a yellow wood,

And sorry I could not travel both

And be one traveler, long I stood

And looked down one as far as I could

To where it bent in the undergrowth;

Then took the other, as just as fair,

And having perhaps the better claim,

Because it was grassy and wanted wear;

Though as for that the passing there

Had worn them really about the same,

And both that morning equally lay

In leaves no step had trodden black.

Oh, I kept the first for another day!

Yet knowing how way leads on to way,

I doubted if I should ever come back.

I shall be telling this with a sigh

Somewhere ages and ages hence:

Two roads diverged in a wood, and I—

I took the one less traveled by,

And that has made all the difference.

Here's the question eNotes poses: What is the message of the poem "The Road Not Taken" by Robert Frost? Here's the beginning of the answer the site provides by "certified educator" Reynolds (n.d.). The sample was provided before having to sign up for a free trial or pay for access:

> "The Road Not Taken" is traditionally taken to mean that it can be better to take the less conventional path in life. In the poem, a man is walking through the woods, when he comes to a fork in the path. He has to make a decision about which way to turn. He takes a long time trying to decide, and notices that one path is slightly less traveled, saying, "it was grassy and wanted wear." However, he also notes that the differences between the two paths are subtle—they are "really about the same"—and both were untraveled that day: "And both that morning equally lay / In leaves no step had trodden black."

Whatever you think of the interpretation or the writing, what is clear is that the primary evidence for the argument is a summary statement about the plot of the poem or direct quotes from the poem. Indeed, in our experience the most common exhortation to students about text-based interpretive arguments is that they must be based on textual evidence. And that makes sense because textual evidence is unproblematic. It provides something solid on which to build. As we noted previously, Toulmin (1958) points out that if the audience of a claim objects to the evidence, those objections have to be cleared away before the argument can proceed. Evidence has to be beyond dispute. We call that *providing a safe starting point*, a solid foundation on which to build. To be sure, although textual evidence is beyond dispute, the way that evidence signifies is not. In contrast to what is the case in policy arguments, because textual evidence is beyond dispute, writers do not have to establish it as a safe starting point. Rather, after selecting appropriate evidence they have to explain why that evidence matters. In a public policy argument, in contrast, the essential first step is establishing the safety of the evidence so that one can reason forward from it.

What is true in English classes might be even more true in social studies classes. Indeed, according to Nokes and De La Paz (2018) students perceive textbook accounts, still at the center of many social studies classes, as entirely unproblematic. Writing from textbooks, therefore, "distorts students' understanding of the nature of historical writing" (p. 560). That is, students see historical writing as unproblematic knowledge telling instead of argumentation in which establishing the credibility of evidence is crucially important.

As Sinatra and Lombardi (2020) point out, learning how to evaluate evidence is also crucially important in science classes. While they applaud efforts teachers make to evaluate the source of evidence, they note that the most common efforts to do so, for example, teaching students to make evaluative judgments on the basis of domain names, are "woefully insufficient" (para. 12). What follows is our discussion of a set of questions that are designed to do much more.

> Teaching students to make evaluative judgments on the basis of domain names is "woefully insufficient."

FACTS AREN'T FACTS

As we noted above, one aspect of the conceptual orientation to argument that the students in Imbrenda's (2018) study manifested is the belief that "facts are facts" and so are beyond dispute. But that is seldom the case with the research that informs public policy debates. Evaluating competing research claims is difficult work, but we've identified what we think are five key questions that will help students evaluate studies.

FIVE KEY QUESTIONS TO HELP STUDENTS EVALUATE STUDIES

Question 1: Who's doing the study?

There are two aspects to this question.

1. Do writers or speakers identify the study or studies on which they are drawing? We want our students to be suspicious of arguments that begin with "Research shows." Sometimes such pronouncements are hot-linked. And sometimes those links go to the source study itself while others go to other popular press reports or even to previous articles the author has written. We want to cultivate the understanding that clarity about the source of evidence allows readers to make assessments about whether or

not to accept it, while a lack of transparency should make them at least somewhat skeptical.

2. What do we know about possible conflicts of interest? We want students to assess whether the authors or sponsors of a study had some sort of financial or ideological stake in it. The importance of looking at funding sources and financial interest was perhaps most notoriously established by the tobacco industry's manipulation of research. (See, for example, Bero, 2005.) The importance of understanding the impact of *a priori* ideological commitments is made clear simply by flipping between news channels that appeal to different ends of the political spectrum as our discussion of cognitive bias in Chapter 2 makes clear.

Question 2: Who are the participants?

We want our students to take a critical look at who the participants are in any study they read. Here are some examples that demonstrate the importance of this consideration:

- People of color are underrepresented in biomedical research (Konkel, 2015), which makes us skeptical of many generalizations drawn from that research.

- Women in general are underrepresented in research on virtual reality (Peck et al., 2020), so we approach that research skeptically as well.

- In contrast, the Pew Study of technology use takes great pains to report that its sample is consistent with the gender, age, education, and race from the U.S. Census Bureau's 2019 American Community, which makes us more open to believing its findings are widely applicable.

Question 3: What causes what?

If students are to be critical consumers of online texts, they have to be aware of one of the foundational concepts of statistics: *correlation does not equal causation.* If Event A and Event B co-occur, A may cause B, B may cause A, C may cause either or both A and B, or the co-occurrence may be coincidental. There are funny examples you can use to illustrate the point. Both crime and ice cream consumption rise during the summer, so obviously eating ice cream causes crime, right?

But confusing correlation with causality can distort public policy debates, too. *USA Today* (Rouan, 2020) recently reported on an Ohio doctor who jokingly posted on Facebook that "My mind is slowly being taken over by the hive mind" after he was vaccinated. He died months later and his Facebook post was published along with his memorial notice by Earthley, a wellness site (https://bit.ly/3TAKsCC), leading readers (read the comments) to conclude that his death was caused by the vaccine, when, as *USA Today* reports, it was caused by an undiagnosed aortic dissection. It may seem rudimentary, but it seems important to us to help our students from leaping too quickly to accept causal claims.

Question 4: What instruments are used?

Many public policy debates are fueled by the results of survey research or polling, and the wording of those questions has a big impact on the results a survey or poll obtains. Bernstein (2020) provides a compelling example, noting that the Trump campaign asked this question during the 2020 campaign: "'Who do you trust more to protect America from foreign and domestic threats?' and offers choices of (a) President Trump or (b) a corrupt Democrat."

Not to be outdone, the Democratic National Committee, Bernstein points out, asked voters to enumerate the aspects of the Trump presidency that were most disturbing, in so doing assuming the stance a respondent might take.

Question 5: Can I reason from a single story?

Chimamanda Adichie's (2009) TED Talk "The Danger of a Single Story" makes the compelling point that any single story is inherently incomplete and so robs people of their dignity and humanity. But single stories are regularly used to inform people's understanding of public policy. Ronald Reagan made political hay through his attack on welfare programs made through stories of a "welfare queen." (In 2019, Josh Levin wrote a book exploring the exceedingly complex life of Linda Taylor, the woman on whom Reagan based his characterization.)

When we first drafted this chapter (May 2021) InfoWars' argument against vaccination was being carried in no small measure by the side effects experienced by rock guitarist Eric Clapton while David Brooks argues in the *New York Times* that President Biden's orientation toward the role of government was largely informed by the experience of his father. Both of these seem related to the *availability bias*, which we discuss in Chapter 2 and which the American Psychological Association (n.d.) dictionary defines as a "common strategy for making judgments about the likelihood of occurrence in which the individual bases such judgments on the salience of the information held in his or her memory about the particular type of event." If our students are making judgments on the basis of a single story, we want them to do so deliberately, and after considering if there might be different stories and perspectives.

OPINIONS AREN'T OPINIONS

As we noted earlier, another aspect of the conceptual orientation to argument that the students in Imbrenda's (2018) study manifested is the belief that because everyone is entitled to their opinion, all opinions are equal. This would imply that one ought not to make what could be called an *argument from authority*. But people do so all the time. And as Walton and Koszowy (2014) note, arguments from authority were "traditionally categorized as an informal fallacy by the logic textbooks, but in recent years a revolution has taken place, and it is now regarded as a legitimate argument" (p. 1). But, they warn, such argument must be made very cautiously and can only hold if the credibility of the authority can be established.

We're not going to belabor the point here since we talk about it at length in Chapter 5, but we want our students to understand that some opinions are more credible than others, and so provide a safer starting point. The heart of the matter, it seems to us, is evaluating the status (Lanser, 1981), that is, the reliability of the person on whose judgment one is drawing in making a point. As we explain in that chapter, two key questions can guide our assessment of a speaker's status:

1. Is the source of information too self-interested to be reliable?
2. Does the source of information have enough knowledge, awareness, and experience to be reliable?

Walton and Koszowy (2014) would add two questions to this list:

3. On what evidence did the source of information draw in asserting a position?
4. To what extent is the assertion consistent with those of other experts?

Our work on evidence should make the connection between understanding literature and understanding policy implications of data, and the place to start is creating lessons supporting writing about literature that complicates the question of evidence.

Reflection Questions

- Think about an intractable argument you've been part of, either in your personal life or in the public sphere.

- Think about the evidence that the opposing sides drew on. To what extent did the evidence contribute to the argument's intractability?

LESSON SUMMARIES

Lesson 7.1: Thinking About Evidence in Text-Based Arguments. This lesson focuses on having students write about the extent to which Atticus Finch is a role model and in doing so evaluating evidence from both within and outside the text.

Social Media Extension: This asks students to examine and evaluate responses to *To Kill a Mockingbird* on Twitter and Facebook.

Lesson 7.2: Thinking About Evidence in Topical Issues. This lesson focuses on preparing students to write an argument about the impact of social media on youth by evaluating the way that research is presented in digital sources.

Social Media Extension: This asks students to evaluate the research presented on a tweet endorsing a personal care product.

LESSON 7.1, PART I
Thinking About Evidence in Text-Based Arguments

LESSON BACKGROUND

As we noted, the request for textual evidence makes a huge amount of sense, but that request does not help students cultivate the ability to discriminate among different pieces of evidence. In this lesson, we suggest using a writing topic that allows for the use of both textual evidence as well as other kinds of evidence. This allows students to develop and apply criteria for the safety and effectiveness of data and gives them practice transferring a skill they use when reading and writing literature to knowing, thinking, doing, and arguing in real life and in policy and positioning spheres.

We illustrate our approach by using *To Kill a Mockingbird*, a very commonly taught book. As is true throughout the book, we've tried to write this lesson sufficiently specifically so that you can teach it as it has been written. But we also hope that you will be able to modify the lesson as needed, for example, by changing the text on which the lesson is based so that it can be used across the curriculum and across grade levels.

Purpose

- To evaluate the effectiveness and safety of different kinds of evidence

Length

- Approximately 90–135 minutes

Materials

- Writing materials
- A class set of Handout 7.1A: Who's the Best Role Model?
- A class set of Handout 7.1B: Assessing Textual Evidence
- A class set of Handout 7.1C: Assessing Evidence From Outside the Text
- A class set of Handout 7.1D: *Mockingbird* on Social Media
- Whiteboard, chart paper, or other means of recording students' responses

LESSON STEPS

Step 1

- Introduce the lesson by telling students that now that they've finished reading *To Kill a Mockingbird*, they are going to be writing about it. Note that there's some controversy about teaching the book that focuses on concerns about the use of the N-word, but also about whether it's appropriate that *To Kill a Mockingbird* is one of the, if not *the*, most commonly taught books about race in American schools even though it is told by a White author from a White character's point of view. Explain that that controversy is also informed by the extent to which people feel Atticus is a role model. Explain that this is the issue that they're going to take up in their writing.

- Note that before they think about Atticus that you want them to consider what it means to be a role model more generally and that their discussion should help them think not only about Atticus but also about the historical figures they are reading about in their history classes.

- Distribute Handout 7.1A: Who's the Best Role Model? Have students do the ranking independently. (*Note.* This activity could be used across subjects, for example, in a history class that is considering whether a historical figure is a positive role model or a different set of scenes could be developed that would have students develop criteria for a different construct, for example, what makes a good leader.)

- Divide students into heterogeneous small groups to discuss their rankings. As groups discuss, circulate around the room. Encourage participation by noting areas of disagreement, something like "I see your rating was different. What makes you say so?"

Step 2

- Have a whole-class discussion about students' ranking.

- While there is still energy in the small group discussions, reconvene the class. Get a sense of the whole by asking, "Who gave Marissa a 1? 2? 3? 4?" Repeat the process with the other characters. Tally responses using a matrix like this:

	1	2	3	4
Marissa				
James				
Zoey				
Miles				

- Choose the character about whom there is the greatest disagreement among the students. Ask a student who gave it a 1 to explain why. Ask, "What makes you say so?" If students provide evidence that you judge not to be safe (for example, saying about James something like "He never did anything"), ask again, "What makes you say so?"

- Once you judge the evidence to be safe, ask students to explain how the evidence signifies by asking, "So what?" As students talk, write the criteria for role models that they articulate (e.g., She influenced others) on an anchor chart.

- Turn to a student who gave the claim a low ranking and repeat the process. Continue to call on students as long as there is energy in the discussion.

- Repeat the process with the other three characters.

Step 3

- Engage students in applying the criteria to *To Kill a Mockingbird* by reminding them that their assignment is to write an argument about whether Atticus is a role model and that the class discussion of the scenes gave rise to criteria that they can use to make their judgment.

- Remind students that in the class discussion you asked, "What makes you say so?" to elicit evidence for their ranking. Recall that sometimes they gave evidence, but you still asked them "What makes you say so?" because the evidence wasn't sufficiently established. Give examples from the classroom discussion. Here are some possibilities that students might have offered: saying that Marissa's problems outweighed her achievements; saying that James didn't do anything; saying that Zoey had sold out; and saying that Miles just wanted to focus attention on himself.

Step 4

- Explain that they're going to look at some evidence they might choose to use in arguing either for or against the proposition that Atticus is a role model and determine whether it provides a safe starting point.

- Provide students with Handout 7.1B: Assessing Textual Evidence. Make sure students understand how to use the scales.

- Have students work in pairs to mark the scales. Once they are all marked, tally the responses using a scale that is written on the board. Ask students to justify their rating by asking, "What makes you say so?"

- As conversation is going on, track the criteria students are articulating. Remind students that safe evidence is only the starting point and that they still have to answer "So what?" by explaining why the evidence matters.

Step 5

- After the discussion, have students work in pairs to rewrite one of the pieces of evidence that isn't safe to make it safer.

- Have students share their revisions and the moves they made to create safe evidence. Add those moves to the anchor chart.

Step 6

Provide Handout 7.1C: Assessing Evidence From Outside the Text. Repeat the same discussion process with that handout.

Step 7

Ask students to write an exit ticket explaining why safe evidence matters and what makes evidence safe.

LESSON 7.1, PART II
Social Media Extension

LESSON BACKGROUND

Social media offers the opportunity to create and disseminate texts rapidly. A search on any social media platform for polar perspectives on any current issue will yield many results quickly. While we tend not to encounter these perspectives in classrooms, we often look to social media for others' perspectives on controversial topics; you'll always find someone online who shares your love/hate for that ice cream flavor, sports team, city, talent show competitor, and so on. How you respond to that point of view involves some complex, yet often taken-for-granted reading skills. In this activity, we return to *To Kill a Mockingbird* but view the book through the lens of social media commentators. We think this task works best on Twitter or Facebook.

LESSON STEPS

Step 1

Introduce the task by providing Handout 7.1D and explaining that you're going to split the class into groups of two or three and that half the groups will search "To Kill a Mockingbird racist"; the others will search "To Kill a Mockingbird best book."

- Students' assignments are below. They should weigh the evidence used in the posts, evidence that can be from, for example:
  - The text
  - Plot summaries
  - Descriptions of characters
  - Quotations from outside the text
  - Whether the poster is a certified user
  - How long the post is
  - Whether the post includes a persuasive or amusing image as a way to sway readers
- Circulate as groups work.

Step 2

Have groups report to the class on what they found.

Reflection Question

- Think about another literature-related writing project that would require students to draw on evidence beyond the literary text. What other sources of evidence would students have to evaluate?

Each of the following scenes features someone who could be considered a role model. Read each scene carefully and then rank them from the one who you think is the best role model (1) to the person who is the worst role model (4). Make sure you can support your decisions. You'll be talking about your rankings in small groups, and then we'll be sharing them as a class. Make sure that you're ready to explain the evidence on which you are basing your judgments and why that evidence affected your ranking.

1. Marissa was one of the first women to make it big in reggaeton. She was a real inspiration to both women and men trying to break into the business. She started with nothing, and now she has a worldwide following. But with fame and money came problems. Lots of them. Her marriage failed because she was so devoted to her music that she had time for nothing else. She's in the midst of a drug rehab that seems to be working but it's early yet. She's alienated from her family because they think she should be doing more good, not to them (she's always been very generous to her family with her money) but to the community. But the music keeps getting better and more and more young women are trying to follow her lead.

   Ranking for Marissa _____

2. After 50 years with the same company, James is finally retiring. He didn't advance very far in his career, but he found a niche that suited him and kept at it. Never late for work, never sick. James was the kind of guy people tended not to notice. He didn't do anything flashy or spectacular. But he worked hard and everyone who worked with him knew that they could count on him to do his part. At his retirement party, the president of the company said that she wished there were more like him, but that kind of loyalty was very rare these days. His kids appreciated all the kind words but wondered why there had been so few recognitions and raises during such a long career. "Don't worry," said James. "What matters is showing up and doing your job, not what others think."

   Ranking for James _____

3. Zoey always had a knack for talking with high school kids. That's why she was such a great high school English teacher. She was the kind of teacher who inspired others. The kids in her class learned to love to read novels and write about them. Every year she would receive a handful of letters from former students saying that she changed their lives, and every year she was voted outstanding teacher. Zoey loved to teach but doing it right took so much time. And while she made a good living, she didn't make the kind of salary that the doctor and lawyer friends she went to high school with made. It gnawed at her, especially since her 10-year reunion was coming up. At that reunion she ran into a former classmate who was starting up a new line of vaping products. He needed someone who could talk to kids and develop a social media presence to make them try his brand. He was so impressed with Zoey that he offered her a job right there and at 50% more than she was making, with promises of an ownership stake if the products took off. Zoey decided to take the risk. After all, she was young. It was time to put her skills to use and make some real money.

   Ranking for Zoey_____

4. If there was an injustice in the city, you could be sure Miles knew about it. And he didn't just learn about it, he always tried to do something. He started a campaign to try to get the city to provide more housing for the homeless by staging a one-person sit-in outside the mayor's office. He got some press coverage and a promise to study the issue, but no tangible results yet. His latest cause was trying to get the school district to adopt an explicitly anti-racist curriculum that focused on how America itself and the city were built on White supremacy. He was booed when he spoke at a school board meeting and even threatened by some who called him anti-patriotic. He knew he had little chance of prevailing in his politically conservative city. But while winning from time to time would have been nice, what mattered, thought Miles, was fighting the good fight.

   Ranking for Miles _____

Assess the safety of each of the six pieces of textual evidence below. That is, decide how likely it is that your audience would accept the piece of evidence. Remember, even after you establish safety, you still have to answer the "So what?" question and explain why the evidence matters.

In favor of Atticus as a role model:

Throughout the novel, it always seemed as though Atticus knew what to do.

Completely safe   Not safe at all

Miss Maudie says, "Atticus Finch won't win, he can't win, but he's the only man in these parts who can keep a jury out so long in a case like that" (p. 246).

Completely safe   Not safe at all

Atticus lives up to the definition of courage that he applies to Mrs. Dubose. Atticus says to Jem, "I wanted you to see what real courage is, instead of getting the idea that courage is a man with a gun in his hand. It's when you know you're licked before you begin but you begin anyway and see it through no matter what" (p. 128).

Completely safe   Not safe at all

Against Atticus as a role model:

At the end of the book, Atticus and Heck Tate conspire to lie about what really happened to Bob Ewell.

Completely safe   Not safe at all

Atticus never calls adults out for their bad and racist behavior.

Completely safe   Not safe at all

Atticus never wanted to take Tom Robinson's case. He tells his brother, "You know, I'd hope to get through life without a case of this kind, but John Taylor pointed at me and said, 'You're it'" (p. 100).

Completely safe   Not safe at all

Assess the safety of each of the six pieces of textual evidence below. That is, decide how likely it is that your audience would accept the piece of evidence. Remember, even after you establish safety, you still have to answer the "So what?" question and explain why the evidence matters.

In favor of Atticus as a role model:

According to Casey Cess in an article in the *New Yorker*, "Atticus has inspired legions of lawyers, been memorialized with a public sculpture, had professional-achievement awards and a nonprofit organization named after him, and been invoked admiringly by Barack Obama, who quoted one of the character's folksy father-isms in his farewell address as president: 'You never really understand a person until you consider things from his point of view, until you climb into his skin and walk around in it.'"

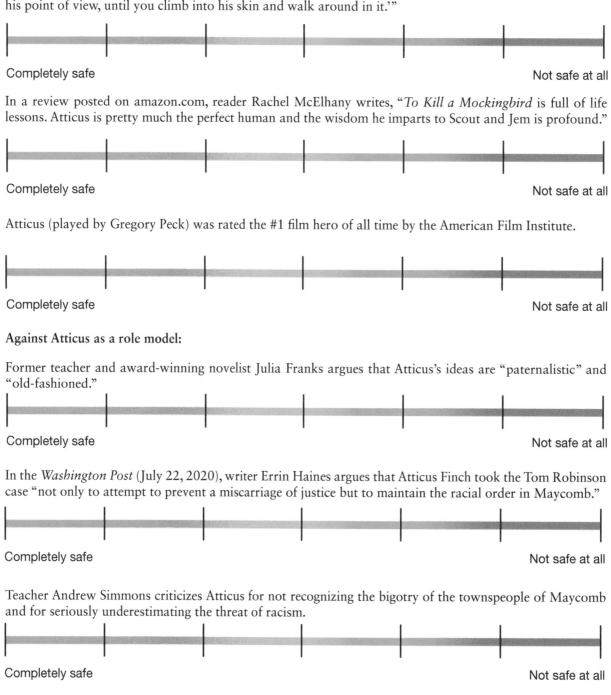

Completely safe   Not safe at all

In a review posted on amazon.com, reader Rachel McElhany writes, "*To Kill a Mockingbird* is full of life lessons. Atticus is pretty much the perfect human and the wisdom he imparts to Scout and Jem is profound."

Completely safe   Not safe at all

Atticus (played by Gregory Peck) was rated the #1 film hero of all time by the American Film Institute.

Completely safe   Not safe at all

Against Atticus as a role model:

Former teacher and award-winning novelist Julia Franks argues that Atticus's ideas are "paternalistic" and "old-fashioned."

Completely safe   Not safe at all

In the *Washington Post* (July 22, 2020), writer Errin Haines argues that Atticus Finch took the Tom Robinson case "not only to attempt to prevent a miscarriage of justice but to maintain the racial order in Maycomb."

Completely safe   Not safe at all

Teacher Andrew Simmons criticizes Atticus for not recognizing the bigotry of the townspeople of Maycomb and for seriously underestimating the threat of racism.

Completely safe   Not safe at all

Task Group A

1. On your device, open Twitter or Facebook and type in "To Kill a Mockingbird racist."

2. Skim the first five to ten results.

3. Choose one post that you think makes a strong argument. Note its content briefly in the table that follows. Then note what evidence makes this a strong argument.

4. Choose another post that you think makes a weak argument. Note its content briefly in the table that follows. Then note what evidence makes this a weak argument.

SEARCH:	
Strong argument:	
What makes me/ us say so?	
Weak argument:	
What makes me/ us say so?	

Task Group B

1. On your device, open Twitter or Facebook and type in "To Kill a Mockingbird best book."

2. Skim the first five to ten results.

3. Choose one post that you think makes a strong argument. Note its content briefly in the table that follows. Then note what evidence makes this a strong argument.

4. Choose another post that you think makes a weak argument. Note its content briefly in the table that follows. Then note what evidence makes this a weak argument.

SEARCH:	
Strong argument:	
What makes me/ us say so?	
Weak argument:	
What makes me/ us say so?	

LESSON 7.2, PART I
Thinking About Evidence in Topical Issues

LESSON BACKGROUND

As we noted, if students are to be informed citizens, they have to be able to evaluate the research on which public policy debates are often based. The purpose of this lesson is to help students develop that ability by focusing on an issue that we think will matter to most of them: the impact of social media on youth. We want students to

- learn the five questions we explained earlier in the chapter

- apply them to the research they encounter in seeking to develop a position on social media and youth

- and then apply them in their investigations of other issues

Our focus in this lesson is social science research. But we think that the healthy skepticism and curiosity that we seek to cultivate will serve them well when they encounter scientific research as well. Once again, we've tried to write this lesson sufficiently specifically so that you can teach it as is, but as always, our hope is that you can use the lesson format and change the details to better match your teaching context and use it as a model to create your own lessons around issues that fit your content area and grade level.

Purpose

- To develop a mental model for how to evaluate social science research

Length

- Approximately 90–135 minutes

Materials

- Computer or some other device to connect to the internet for each student (phones would work)

- Some kind of projection device

- Class set of Handout 7.2A: Social Media Survey

LESSON STEPS

Step 1

- Introduce the lesson and its purpose by telling students that now that they've finished writing about a contested literary issue they are going to write about a contested current issue: The impact of social media on youth.

- Note that debates about current events are often based on at least some reference to research. To demonstrate, ask students to look up "Research shows."

- Ask students to select two examples of the use of the phrase and to fill out the following scale on each. Note that if the site provides hyperlinks, they should follow the links before making their assessment. Here are two examples of what we found on the day that this lesson was composed:

  o https://nyti.ms/3slQxa1

  o https://bit.ly/3z9DVX8

Clearly explains details
of the research

Does not explain details
of research at all

- Divide students into heterogeneous small groups to discuss their rankings. Circulate as they do so. Encourage participation by noting ratings and prompting them with something like "I see you gave that site a 5. What makes you say so?"

Step 2

- While there is still energy in the small group discussions, reconvene the class. Ask the groups to report. If possible, have groups share one of the sites so that everyone can see it.

- Summarize the class discussion. It should be clear that there are considerable differences in how transparent authors and sites are about the research that they cite and the extent to which they establish clear connections between their evidence and their claims.

Step 3

- Discuss why transparency might matter, beginning with the question of who's doing/reporting on the study by recalling the two status questions that students asked in the point of view chapter:

  o Is the source of information too self-interested to be reliable?

  o Does the source of information have enough knowledge, awareness, and experience to be reliable?

- Display this site: https://bit.ly/3gyIAvo

- Ask students to rate the transparency and reliability of the site using these scales:

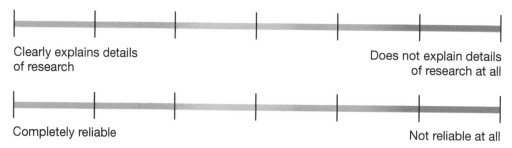

Clearly explains details
of research

Does not explain details
of research at all

Completely reliable

Not reliable at all

- Please note: Discussion should focus on the fact that the publisher is an adolescent rehabilitation center but that it hyperlinks to the actual study. Students' ratings aren't important in and of themselves. What is important is that their consciousness is raised about the implications of asking, "Who's doing the study?"

Step 4

- Engage students in thinking about the importance of the participants by asking students to pretend they wanted to find out what the climate of the school is. Brainstorm for possible constituencies. If students identify a general category, ask them to specify. For example, if someone calls out "Students," probe for what kind of students (e.g., grade levels, demographic differences, interest groups).

- Explain that the idea of random selection is supposed to eliminate the need for representative samples, but that they always need to check for the ultimate makeup of the participant pool.

- Ask students what they think about using a study that surveyed these participants to make an argument on the impact of social media on young people:

    Eighty-two people (average age 19.52, 53 females; 60.5% European American, 28.4% Asian, 6.2% African American, and 4.9% other) were recruited for a study on Facebook through flyers posted around Ann Arbor, Michigan. Participants needed a Facebook account and a touch-screen smartphone to qualify for the study. They received $20 and were entered into a raffle to receive an iPad2 for participating.

- Divide students into pairs to list the advantages and disadvantages of the sample. Encourage them to look up Ann Arbor if they are not familiar with it.

- Have a whole-class discussion on the advantages and disadvantages of the study population. Students might note that volunteers might have stronger feelings about the issue, for example, or that African Americans are underrepresented, or that Ann Arbor is a university town. Make sure that students explain why what they note might matter to interpreting and applying the data. Once again, it doesn't really matter what students say, but it does matter that they are thinking about the participants and who they represent or don't represent.

Step 5

- Engage students in thinking about causal claims by reminding them that their assignment is to write a paper on the extent to which social media has a positive or negative impact on the youth of America. Explain that to do so they will need to evaluate the causal claims that people make about social media, for example, on the positive side, that it reduces loneliness, or, on the negative side, that it causes negative body image.

- Note that many of the studies that they'll see will make an argument about causes by documenting how often when one thing occurs (e.g., social media use) another thing occurs (e.g., negative body image). Explain that the co-occurrence of A and B could happen under four circumstances: If A causes B, if B causes A, if C causes both A and B, or coincidence.

- Display three examples of co-occurrence and ask students to discuss which of the four alternatives they think explains them. Have students work in pairs with a different partner for each example.
  - "When Ice Cream Sales Rise, So Do Homicides" (https://bit.ly/3DsmZ0F)
  - Per capita consumption of cheese and the number of people who died by becoming tangled in their bedsheets (https://bit.ly/3gqLTof)
  - The more coffee you drink, the longer you stay awake (https://bit.ly/3TyLDlN)

- Discuss each alternative. The first example pretty clearly exemplifies the C causes A and B explanation in that hot weather contributes to both murders and ice cream eating. The second example pretty clearly could only be coincidental. The third example is more complex. Coffee could cause a lack of sleep, or the need to stay awake could cause coffee consumption. But as before, what matters is not that students agree but rather that they come away from the discussion with an understanding that correlation does not equal causation.

- Apply their understanding to a new case. Project the following:

  However, social media use can also negatively affect teens, distracting them, disrupting their sleep, and exposing them to bullying, rumor spreading, unrealistic views of other people's lives, and peer pressure.

  The risks might be related to how much social media teens use. A 2019 study of more than 6,500 12- to 15-year-olds in the U.S. found that those who spent more than three hours a day using social media might be at heightened risk for mental health problems. Another 2019 study of more than 12,000 13- to 16-year-olds in England found that using social media more than three times a day predicted poor mental health and well-being in teens.

Other studies also have observed links between high levels of social media use and depression or anxiety symptoms. A 2016 study of more than 450 teens found that greater social media use, nighttime social media use, and emotional investment in social media—such as feeling upset when prevented from logging on—were each linked with worse sleep quality and higher levels of anxiety and depression. (Mayo Clinic Staff, 2022, paras. 5–7)

- Have students imagine that this site was being used to argue that social media has a negative effect on teens. Have them fill out the following scale:

Completely persuasive   Not persuasive at all

- Have a whole-class discussion of their ratings. Make sure to probe asking students, "What makes you say so?" and "So what?"

Step 6

- Engage students in considering the extent to which the formulation of survey and poll questions might affect the results.

- Note how some surveys are seemingly designed to give people the answers that they are looking for. Give examples that we discussed in the introduction to this chapter:

  ○ The Trump campaign asked, "'Who do you trust more to protect America from foreign and domestic threats?' and offered the choices of (a) President Trump or (b) a corrupt Democrat."

  ○ Note that on the other side of the aisle, the Democratic National Committee asked voters to enumerate the aspects of the Trump presidency most disturbing, a similarly biased question designed to elicit only particular kinds of responses.

- Distribute Handout 7.2A: Social Media Survey.

- Have students work in triads to identify two questions on the social media survey that they might find leading and problematic and to rewrite those items to make them less leading and problematic.

- Have a whole-class discussion, making sure that students' revised questions and answers are displayed in some fashion. Once again, the key is not exactly what students say but rather that they come away with an understanding of how to question formulation or other forms of prompting can skew responses, making the data less reliable.

Step 7

- Engage students in thinking about reasoning from a single story by noting that politicians often make or at least introduce their policy arguments with a specific story. Note that immigration is a very complex issue but that it's sometimes framed in terms of a single story, a noncitizen who makes a big success, on the one hand, or commits a terrible crime, on the other. Note that the president typically invites guests to the State of the Union speech whose individual stories speak to some policy or another.

- Explain that they are going to look at two *New York Times* articles (https://nyti.ms/3DmZNjl and https://nyti.ms/3zd4tH3) that take different positions about whether students experienced catastrophic learning loss during the pandemic. Note that each uses a particular story to help establish their position. Tell students that you want them to think about how effective the stories of the Coleman family and the Bonillas are in helping the author make her point using this scale:

Exceptionally effective   Not effective at all

- Read the stories aloud. Give students a few minutes to mark the scales, making sure that they mark a separate scale for each news story.

- Divide students into groups to discuss their ratings. As groups discuss, circulate around the room. Encourage participation by noting areas of disagreement, something like "I see your rating was different from theirs. Why is that? What makes you say so?"

- When the energy in the groups begins to dissipate, have a whole-class discussion on the ratings. In the discussion, the key move is to highlight the "So what?"s the students provide, that is, the criteria for judgment they rely on. So, for example, if a student argued that the Coleman story was very effective because it was consistent with the studies alluded to in the news story, then write, "Consistent with more generalized findings" on an anchor chart.

- Explain to students that you want to have them apply the criteria to a new case, one related to the issue of the impact of social media on youth, the topic on which they will be writing.

- Display this story: https://bit.ly/3DsnV5b. Ask students to rate how effective they think Sonia's story would be in making an argument on the impact of social media on youth. Have students individually fill out the scale, tally the responses, and lead a whole-class discussion of their ratings, once again using the "What makes you say so?" probe and once again highlighting the criteria they applied.

Step 8

- Introduce the writing assignment by explaining to students that their assignment is to write a position paper on whether, on balance, social media has a more positive or negative effect on youth. Explain that they need to cite at least two studies in their writing and justify their selection of the studies they included in terms of the work they've been doing by considering
  - who did the study
  - who the participants were
  - what instruments/kinds of question formulations were used
  - whether any causal claims were reasonably justified

- Set due dates and procedures that are consistent with classroom practice.

1. How often do you spend on social media a day?
   - ☐ 1 hour or less
   - ☐ 2–3 hours
   - ☐ 4–5 hours
   - ☐ 6 hours or more
   - ☐ Never

2. How dependent are you on technology?
   - ☐ I can't live without it.
   - ☐ I use it regularly but not all day.
   - ☐ I rarely use technology.

3. Do you feel like you spend too much time on social media?
   - ☐ Yes, I'm constantly checking messages, status updates, posts, pictures, etc.
   - ☐ I use it moderately and check it every once in a while.
   - ☐ I rarely check social media.
   - ☐ I don't have any social media.

4. How do you feel when you are without social media for a long period of time?
   - ☐ Anxious, depressed, lonely, like I'm missing out on things.
   - ☐ I feel like I might be missing out but it's not a big deal.
   - ☐ It doesn't affect me in any way.

5. Have you ever been subjected to cyberbullying while on social media?
   - ☐ All the time
   - ☐ Rarely
   - ☐ Sometimes
   - ☐ Never

6. How much personal information do you share on social media?
   - ☐ Everything.
   - ☐ I share a lot.
   - ☐ Some things, but most information is hidden from the public.
   - ☐ I share very little information.
   - ☐ I don't share any information.

7. Do you feel like the number of "likes" you get on photos or posts makes you feel better about yourself?
   - ☐ Yes
   - ☐ A little bit
   - ☐ Not at all

(Continued)

(Continued)

8. Do you ever get jealous of other people's seemingly extravagant lives on social media?

☐ All the time, I'm constantly comparing lives.

☐ Sometimes, but it doesn't bother me too much.

☐ Not really, I don't pay attention.

9. Do you feel that social media has more positive or negative effects?

☐ Negative

☐ Positive

10. Do you think that social media has affected your life positively or negatively?

☐ More positively, I can stay connected with friends and family and be updated about world events.

☐ More negatively, I spend too much time comparing my life to others and feel lonely without social media or technology.

☐ I think that social media has affected me both negatively and positively.

LESSON 7.2, PART II
Social Media Extension

LESSON BACKGROUND

In this lesson, we've discussed the impact of social media on young people and studies that cite various forms of evidence to present arguments on the topic. We think that when engaging with social media, issues of transparency (where the information comes from, how it was developed or established, who's sharing it, who's involved in the data gathering, and whether causal claims are being made and can be justified) are especially important.

LESSON STEPS

Step 1

- Provide data by displaying or distributing the screenshot provided (of a post we created for this task), or have students search for a claim made on social media. We suggest using health and personal care products as they provide easy access for this activity.

- Divide students into heterogeneous groups of four.

Step 2

- Have students complete the scales for the post they're viewing.
- Tally ratings.
- Lead a discussion on rating, focusing especially on points of controversy.

ANALYZING EVIDENCE IN SOCIAL MEDIA

Transparency

Who's sharing this information and why:

Is clear   Is unclear

What makes you say so?

Participants

The participants in this study:

Represent a diverse
population   Don't represent a diverse
population

What makes you say so?

Causal claims

This post suggests

A clear link between
cause and effect   No clear link between
cause and effect

What makes you say so?

Any causal links

Are clearly justified with
explanation and reasoning   Not justified

What makes you say so?

Conclusion
Some Final Words

We all came to this project with an awareness of the importance of helping our students become more critical consumers of digital media. But each of us came with a different straw that broke the camel's back—a different occurrence that made it clear to us that we had to do more than we had done to help our students become more critical digital readers.

For Hugh, it was when one of the eleventh graders with whom he worked in the Pathways Project announced his belief that the mainstream media is lying to us all the time, so whatever the opposing narrative is, it's true. The student believed, for example, that Earth is flat, that 9/11 was an inside job, that the moon landing was faked, and that the Sandy Hook and Parkland shootings never happened, a veritable greatest hits of conspiracy theories.

Michael was spurred to think about what more he could do to address digital reading when he was conferring with one of the twelfth graders in that same project and the student proudly announced that he planned to go to a local for-profit college, a decision he made in part because of what he found out on the college's website, but one that was not informed by any knowledge that the for-profit college he had chosen had been sued on multiple occasions for its predatory lending practices.

For Deborah and Jeff, it was less an error of commission than one of omission that brought them to this project. Deborah recounts the time one of her students refused to believe that Notre Dame was burning because everything on the internet is fake. Jeff's motivation resides in part in his experience of two ninth-grade boys telling him that they had decided not to read or watch the news because they had no idea how to tell what was real and what was fake. They figured they were better off just not being exposed to news. Throughout this book we've shared more causes for alarm, and many of them have much bigger consequences than the ones that brought us to this project.

Indeed, the proliferation of fake news was one of the greatest challenges in writing this book. Throughout the book, we've selected examples to illustrate the issues we've discussed. And soon after providing each example we'd see another example of fake news that might be even more egregious. An embarrassment of riches that made writing hard but that makes teaching even harder. And more important. How important? According to a Pew Research Center survey of 6,127 U.S. adults conducted between February 19 and March 4, 2019, respondents called "made-up news" a greater problem than violent crime, climate change, and racism (Mitchell et al., 2019)!

Respondents called "made-up news" a greater problem than violent crime, climate change, and racism (Mitchell et al., 2019)!

So here we are: Our students are bombarded with different texts from different sources every day, all positioned in some way or another, and many developed with the intent to deceive. If we want to help our students navigate their world, if we want them to be well informed, and if we want them to be responsible citizens, then we have to help them become more critical consumers of digital media. The stakes could not be higher. We hope we have persuaded you that this goal is one we as teachers must resolve to embrace.

Our focus in this book has been on ELA teachers, though in each of our chapters we have worked to demonstrate that the kind of teaching we're advocating could and should be done across disciplines. Why should ELA teachers take up this resolution? Because we're morally obliged to prepare our students for the future. To be sure, we believe deeply that effective teaching of reading and composing in all forms has the capacity to change people's lives both in the here-and-now and in the future. That's why we have dedicated our professional lives to trying to foster high-quality instruction. But we also believe deeply that whatever instruction we provide has to recognize that only a very small proportion of our kids will become English majors. Indeed, according to the reports of the ADE Ad Hoc Committee on the English Major (2018), only 2.3% of the undergraduate majors at Carnegie doctoral-granting institutions are English majors. That statistic means that a secondary school English teacher who teaches five classes of thirty will likely teach between three and four future English majors over the course of a day. Fewer than one a class.

Of course, we hope that we are making our students lifelong readers, but according to the Pew Research Center (Anderson & Jiang, 2018), the average American reads four books a year. Not too bad. But consider this: According to the 2018 Digital Future Report by the Center for the Digital Future at the University of Southern California Annenberg, the average American spends 22.5 hours per week online, 17.8 of them at home. Fifty percent of people report clicking a link from a public organization at least once a day, 34% report clicking a link from a private company at least once a day, and 34% report going online to check a fact at least once a day. If we want to prepare our students for the future they are sure to have, instead of for the future that a select few of them may have, we have to attend to digital reading.

We also hope that we have persuaded you that attending to digital reading requires a recognition that we have to do more than we are currently doing. This resolution is grounded in two key understandings.

- First, as we explored in Chapter 1, although teachers work to cultivate critical reading and thinking skills, students are unlikely to be able to fully transfer those critical reading and thinking skills to the fake news and information pollution they encounter—because while digital reading resembles other reading, it poses unique challenges.

- Second, as we explored in Chapters 2 and 3, fake news is effective because it taps into cognitive biases and shortcomings that we all share.

For both of these reasons, if we are going to address the problem of information pollution, we have work to do.

But here's the good news: Although helping students become more critical users of digital media requires explicit attention, doing so is absolutely compatible with what we are already doing. Close reading is a practice that is important to all disciplines in which texts are central. As we explored in Chapter 4, we can build bridges between our efforts to teach close reading of print-based linear texts to our efforts to help students become more critical users of multi-modal digital texts. Understanding point of view is central to reading literary and historical texts. In Chapter 5 we explored how we can build bridges between our work on point of view and our efforts to help students become more discerning readers of digital texts. Theories are central to the work experts do across disciplines. In Chapter 6 we explored the power of engaging students in applying different critical lenses and in doing so helping them see how they can apply their new theoretical understandings to their digital reading.

Students write from sources across disciplines, and one mantra of writing teachers everywhere is about the importance of providing evidence. In Chapter 7 we explored how instruction in identifying high-quality evidence will enhance the academic writing students do and can provide the foundation for helping them become more conscious of criteria they can apply when they are assessing the digital texts that inform their opinions.

In short, in Chapters 3 through 7 we provided lessons that you can use or adapt to enhance the instruction you are currently offering while also providing the opportunity to build bridges to the crucially important work you need to be doing in the digital domain.

Let's face it, in the current climate, we need to be careful and protect ourselves. We need to integrate democracy-building instruction into what is clearly understood as something we already have to do. No one is going to be upset by an English teacher's teaching close reading or point of view, or by a social studies teacher's helping students look at the origins of primary source materials, or by a science teacher's encouraging students to critically evaluate the evidence used to support scientific models. Recognizing the connection between expert knowledge in our subject areas and the new knowledge that students need to understand the new kinds of texts they encounter daily means that we have the time we need to pursue this instruction since these new strategies become part of what we already do. And this recognition means also that we are offered a safe space to do this work.

We know that the demands on teachers have never been higher. But we also know that it has never been more important for us to take on one more demand: teaching the critical reading of digital texts. We hope that this book has provided both a compelling rationale for as well as theoretically rich and practical ways of doing just that.

Appendix: Theory Cards

GENDER/FEMINIST CRITICISM	SOCIAL CLASS/MARXIST CRITICISM
Assumptions	**Assumptions**
1. The work doesn't have an objective status, an autonomy; instead, any reading of it is influenced by the reader's own status, which includes gender or attitudes toward gender.	1. The German philosopher Karl Marx argued that the way people think and behave in any society is determined by basic economic factors.
2. In the production of literature and within stories themselves, men and women have not had equal access.	2. In his view, those groups of people who owned and controlled major industries could exploit the rest of the population, through conditions of employment and by forcing their own values and beliefs onto other social groups.
3. Men and women are different: They write differently, read differently, and write about their reading differently. These differences should be valued.	3. Marxist criticism applies these arguments to the study of literary texts.

GENDER/FEMINIST CRITICISM	SOCIAL CLASS/MARXIST CRITICISM
Strategies	**Strategies**
1. Consider the gender of the author and/or the characters: What role does gender or sexuality play in this work?	1. Explore the way different groups of people are represented in texts. Evaluate the level of social realism in the text and how society is portrayed.
2. Specifically, observe how sexual stereotypes might be reinforced or undermined. Try to see how the work reflects, or distorts, or recuperates the place of women (and men) in society.	2. Consider how the text itself is a commodity that reproduces certain social beliefs and practices. Analyze the social effect of the literary work.
3. Look at the effects of power drawn from gender within the plot and/or form.	3. Look at the effects of power drawn from economic or social class.

BIOGRAPHICAL CRITICISM	ARCHETYPAL CRITICISM
Assumptions	**Assumptions**
1. Because authors typically write about things they care deeply about and know well, the events and circumstances of their lives are often reflected in the literary works they create.	1. Meaning cannot exist solely on the page of a work, nor can that work be treated as an independent entity.
2. The context for a literary work includes information about the author; their historical moment; the systems of meaning available at the time of this writing.	2. Humankind has a "collective unconscious," a kind of universal psyche, that is manifested in dreams and myths and harbors themes and images that we all inherit.
3. Interpretation of the work should be based on an understanding of its context. That context can provide insight into themes, historical references, social oppositions or movements, and the creation of fictional characters.	3. These recurring myths, symbols, and character types appear and reappear in literary works.

BIOGRAPHICAL CRITICISM	ARCHETYPAL CRITICISM
Strategies	**Strategies**
1. Research the author's life and relate that information to the work.	1. Consider the *genre* of the work and how the genre affects the meaning; for example, comedy, romance, tragedy, irony.
2. Research the author's time (the political history, intellectual history, economic history, etc.), and relate that information to the work.	2. Look for story patterns and symbolic associations from other texts you've read such as black hats, springtime settings, evil stepmothers, and so forth.
3. Research the systems of meaning available to the author and relate those systems to the work.	3. Consider your associations with these symbols as you construct meaning from the text.

READER RESPONSE CRITICISM

Assumptions

1. An author's intentions are not reliably available to readers; all they have is the text.

2. Out of the text, readers actively and personally make meaning.

3. Responding to a text is a process, and descriptions of that process are valuable.

FORMALIST/NEW CRITICISM

Assumptions

1. The critic's interest ultimately should be focused on the work itself (not the author's intention, or the reader's response).

2. The formalist perspective pays particular attention to these issues of form and convention.

3. The formalist perspective says that a literary work should be treated as an independent and self-sufficient object.

READER RESPONSE CRITICISM

Strategies

1. Move through the text in super slow motion, describing the response of an informed reader at various points.

2. Or describe your own response moving through the text.

3. React to the text as a whole, embracing and expressing the subjective and personal response it engenders.

FORMALIST/NEW CRITICISM

Strategies

1. Read closely. You can assume that every aspect is carefully calculated to contribute to the work's unity—figures of speech, point of view, diction, recurrent ideas or events, everything.

2. The methods used in this perspective are those of close reading: a detailed and subtle analysis of the formal components that make up the literary work, such as the meanings and interactions of words, figures of speech, and symbols.

3. Say how the work is unified, how the various elements work to unify it.

HISTORICAL CRITICISM	POSTCOLONIAL CRITICISM
Assumptions	**Assumptions**
1. When reading a text, you have to place it within its historical context.	1. Colonialism is a powerful, often destructive historical force that shapes not only the political futures of the countries involved but also the identities of colonized and colonizing people.
2. History refers to the social, political, economic, cultural, and/or intellectual climate of the time.	2. Successful colonialism depends on a process of "othering" the people colonized. That is, the colonized people are seen as dramatically different from and lesser than the colonizers.
3. Specific historical information will be of key interest: about the time during which an author wrote, about the time in which the text is set, about the ways in which people of the period saw and thought about the world in which they lived.	3. Because of this, literature written in colonizing cultures often distorts the experiences and realities of colonized people. Literature written by colonized people often includes attempts to articulate more empowered identities and reclaim cultures in the face of colonization.

HISTORICAL CRITICISM	POSTCOLONIAL CRITICISM
Strategies	**Strategies**
1. Research the fundamental historical events of the period in which the author wrote.	1. Search the text for references to colonization or current and formerly colonized people. In these references, how are the colonized people portrayed? How is the process of colonization portrayed?
2. Consider the fundamental historical events of the period in which the literary work is set, if it is different from the period in which the author wrote.	2. Consider what images of "others" or processes of "othering" are present in the text. How are these others portrayed?
3. View the text as part of a larger context of historical movements and consider how it both contributes to and reflects certain fundamental aspects of human history.	3. Analyze how the text deals with cultural conflicts between the colonizing culture and the colonized or traditional culture.

STRUCTURALIST CRITICISM

Assumptions

1. Draws on linguistic theory.

2. There are structural relationships between concepts that are revealed in language.

3. Linguistic *signs* are composed of two parts—the *signifier* (sound patterns) and the *signified* (the concept or meaning of the word).

4. Through these relationships, meaning is produced, which frames and motivates the actions of individuals and groups.

DECONSTRUCTIONIST CRITICISM

Assumptions

1. Meaning is made by binary oppositions, *but* one item is unavoidably favored (or "privileged") over the other.

2. This hierarchy is probably arbitrary and can be exposed and reversed.

3. Further, the text's oppositions and hierarchy can be called into question because texts contain within themselves unavoidable contradictions, gaps, spaces, and absences that defeat closure and determinate meaning. All reading is misreading.

STRUCTURALIST CRITICISM

Strategies

1. Focus on the text alone, not external information.

2. Examine the underlying *system* or patterns of language. By examining the pattern of linguistic signs, we can establish the paradigm that will reveal meaning.

3. Identify and analyze contrasting elements (binary oppositions) to determine the important elements in the text.

4. Look at structural elements such as words, stanzas, chapters or parts, or characters, narrators, or speakers to see how they can reveal important contrasts and differences.

5. What system of relationships governs the work as a whole or links this work to others?

DECONSTRUCTIONIST CRITICISM

Strategies

1. Identify the oppositions in the text. Determine which member appears to be favored and look for evidence that contradicts that favoring.

2. Identify what appears central to the text and what appears to be marginal and excluded.

3. Expose the text's indeterminacy. Whereas formalism assumes that you should read a literary work closely as if it made sense, deconstruction assumes the opposite: that if you read closely enough, the text will fail to make sense—or at least will contradict itself.

POLITICAL CRITICISM

Assumptions

1. Literary texts do not have an objective meaning; instead, any reading of it is influenced by the reader's own status, which includes gender, or attitudes toward gender, and social class or attitudes toward social class.

2. Literary texts are commodities that reproduce certain social beliefs and practices. For example, historically the production and reception of literature have been controlled largely by men; it is important to insert a feminist viewpoint to bring to our attention neglected works as well as new approaches to old works.

3. Literary texts represent and are influenced by the particular ideological viewpoint of the author, whether it is their political perspective, gender, or social class.

POLITICAL CRITICISM

Strategies

1. Consider the gender and the social class of the author, the characters: What role does gender, sexuality, or social class play in this work?

2. Observe how social stereotypes might be reinforced or undermined. Try to see how the work reflects, or distorts, or interrupts our commonly held assumptions about others based on their gender or class.

3. Explore the way different groups of people are represented in texts. Evaluate the level of social realism in the text: How is society portrayed?

4. Determine the ideological stance of the text: What worldview does the text represent?

Access this appendix and more resources at
resources.corwin.com/fightingfakenews.

References

Abrams, J. (2009). *Having hard conversations*. Corwin.

ADE Ad Hoc Committee on the English Major. (2018, July). *A changing major: The Report of the 2016–17 ADE Ad Hoc Committee on the English Major*. The Association of Departments of English. https://www.maps.mla.org/content/download/98513/file/A-Changing-Major.pdf

Adichie, C. N. (2009). *The danger of a single story* [Video]. TED Conferences. https://www.ted.com/talks/chimamanda_ngozi_adichie_the_danger_of_a_single_story

Albert and Shirley Small Special Collections Library. (n.d.). *Educators: Cabells and education*. https://small.library.virginia.edu/collections/featured/the-cabell-family-papers-2/contributions/educators/

Allport, G. W., & Postman, L. (1947). *The psychology of rumor*. Henry Holt.

American Psychological Association. (n.d.). *Availability heuristic*. https://dictionary.apa.org/availability-heuristic

Anderson, K. (2017). *Fantasyland: How America went haywire—a 500-year history*. Random House.

Anderson, K. (2022). *Fantasyland: How America went haywire*. https://www.kurtandersen.com/fantasyland

Anderson, M., & Jiang, J. (2018). *Teens, social media and technology 2018*. Pew Research Center. https://www.pewresearch.org/internet/2018/05/31/teens-social-media-technology-2018/

Andrews, R. (2009). *The importance of argument in education*. Institute of Education, University of London.

Applebaum, A., & Pomerantsev, P. (2021, April). How to put out democracy's dumpster fire. *The Atlantic*, 43–52.

Applebee, A. N. (1993). *Literature in the secondary school, studies of curriculum and instruction in the United States*. National Council of Teachers of English.

Appleman, D. (2014). *Critical encounters in high school English: Teaching literary theory to adolescents* (3rd ed.). Teachers College Press and National Council of Teachers of English.

Bakhtin, M. M. (1981). *The dialogic imagination: Four essays by M. M. Bakhtin*. (C. Emerson & M. Holquist, Trans.; M. Holquist, Ed.), University of Texas Press.

BBC News. (2021, February 14). *Trump impeachment trial: Biden warns democracy is fragile*. https://www.bbc.com/news/world-us-canada-56061100

Bernstein, J. L. (2020). An exercise on question wording and political polling. *Cengage*. https://blog.cengage.com/an-exercise-on-question-wording-and-political-polling/

Bero, L. A. (2005). Tobacco industry manipulation of research. *Public Health Reports, 120*(2), 200–208. https://doi.org/10.1177/003335490512000215

Bishop, B. (2009). *The big sort: Why the clustering of like-minded America is tearing us apart*. Houghton Mifflin Harcourt.

Boghossian, P., & Lindsay, J. (2019). *How to have impossible conversations: A very practical guide*. Hachette Books.

Bonnycastle, S. (2002). *In search of authority: An introductory guide to literary theory* (2nd ed.). Broadview Press.

Bonnycastle, S. (2007). *In search of authority: An introductory guide to literary theory* (3rd ed.). Broadview Press.

Booth, W. C. (1961/1983). *The rhetoric of fiction* (2nd ed.). University of Chicago Press.

Center for the Digital Future. (2018). *The 2018 Digital Future Report: Surveying the digital future*. https://www.digitalcenter.org/wp-content/uploads/2018/12/2018-Digital-Future-Report.pdf

Chassin, J. (2014, September 10). How did a song with a strong anti-drinking message turn into a drinking anthem? *Huffington Post*. https://www.huffpost.com/entry/kendrick-lamar-lyrics_b_5548671

Cho, B.-Y. (2014). Competent adolescent readers' use of internet reading strategies: A think-aloud study. *Cognition and Instruction, 32*, 253–289.

Chrissy, G. (n.d.). Ice cubes. *Food.com*. https://www.food.com/recipe/ice-cubes420398

Clements, A. (1996). *Frindle*. Simon & Schuster.

Coiro, J. (2015). Purposeful, critical and flexible: Vital dimensions of online reading and learning. In R. J. Spiro, M. DeSchryver, M. S. Hagerman, P. M. Morsink, & P. Thompson (Eds.), *Reading at a crossroads? Disjunctures and continuities in current conceptions and practices* (pp. 53–64). Routledge.

Coiro, J., & Dobler, E. (2007). Exploring the online reading comprehension strategies used by sixth-grade skilled readers to search for and locate information on the internet. *Reading Research Quarterly, 42*, 214–257.

The Conversation. (2017). *Alternative facts do exist: Beliefs, lies and politics.* https://theconversation.com/alternative-facts-do-exist-beliefs-lies-and-politics-84692

De Bono, E. (2004). *How to have a beautiful mind.* Random House.

Dewey, J. (1916). *Democracy and education.* The Free Press.

Eco, U. (1978). *The role of the reader.* Indiana University Press.

Ericsson, A., & Pool, R. (2016). *Peak: Secrets from the new science or expertise.* Houghton Mifflin Harcourt.

Fallon, K. (2017, July 14). Fooled by 'The Onion': 9 most embarrassing fails. *The Daily Beast.* https://www.thedailybeast.com/fooled-by-the-onion-9-most-embarrassing-fails

Fisher, M. (2021). "Belonging is stronger than facts": The age of misinformation. *The New York Times.* https://www.nytimes.com/2021/05/07/world/asia/misinformation-disinformation-fake-news.html

Fitzgerald, F. S. (1945). *The crack-up: With other uncollected pieces, note-books and unpublished letters* (Together with Letters to Fitzgerald from Gertrude Stein; Edith Wharton; T. S. Eliot; Thomas Wolfe, and John Dos Passos), edited by Edmund Wilson.

Franklin, B. (1782). *"Supplement to the Boston Independent Chronicle", [before 22 April 1782].* https://founders.archives.gov/documents/Franklin/01-37-02-0132

Friedman, R. A. (2020, July 24). *Why humans are vulnerable to conspiracy theories.* https://doi.org/10.1176/appi.ps.202000348

Gardner, H. E., Csikszentmihalyi, M., & Damon, W. (2001). *Good work: When excellence and ethics meet.* Basic Books.

Gates, H. L., Jr. (1987). *Figures in black: Words, signs, and the "racial" self.* Oxford University Press.

Gates, H. L., Jr. (1992). *Loose cannons: Notes on the culture wars.* Oxford University Press.

Government Accounting Office. (2020, February 20). *Science & teach spotlight: Deepfakes.* https://www.gao.gov/products/gao-20-379sp

Greene, S. (1992). Mining texts in reading to write. *Journal of Advanced Composition, 12*(1), 151–170.

Harris, J. (2006). *Rewriting: How to do things with texts.* Utah State University Press.

Hartman, D. K., Hagerman, M. S., & Leu, D. J. (2018). Toward a new literacies perspective of synthesis: Multiple source meaning construction. In J. L. G. Braasch, I. Bråten, & M. T. McCrudden (Eds.), *Handbook of multiple source use* (pp. 55–78). Routledge.

Haskell, R. E. (2000). *Transfer of learning: Cognition, instruction, and reasoning.* Academic Press.

Hofstadter, R. (1962). *Anti-intellectualism in American life.* Vintage Books.

hooks, b. (1994). *Teaching to transgress: Education as the practice of freedom.* Routledge.

hooks, b. (1997). *Cultural criticism and transformation.* Media Education Foundation. http://www.mediaed.org/transcripts/Bell-Hooks-Transcript.pdf

Imbrenda, J. P. (2018). "No facts equals unconvincing": Fact and opinion as conceptual tools in high school students' written arguments. *Written Communication, 35*(3), 315–343.

Indianz. (2018). *Facebook takes down fake 'Native' pages that posted fake news.* https://www.indianz.com/News/2018/02/02/facebook-takes-down-fake-native-pages-th.asp

Jamieson, K. H., & Campbell, K. K. (1997). *The interplay of influence: News, advertising, politics and the mass media.* Wadsworth.

Johnston, P. H. (2012). *Opening minds: Using language to change lives.* Stenhouse.

Kahan, D. M. (2013). Ideology, motivated reasoning, and cognitive reflection. *Judgment and Decision Making, 8*(4), 407–424.

Kahan, D. (2021). Motivated numeracy and enlightened self-government. *Behavioural Public Policy, 1,* 54–86.

Kahan, D., Peters, E., Wittlin, M., & Slovic, P. (2012). The polarizing impact of science literacy and numeracy on perceived climate change risks. *Perceived Climate Change Risks.* George Washington University Law School, GWU Scholarly Commons. https://scholarship.law.gwu.edu/cgi/viewcontent.cgi?article=1298&context=faculty_publications

Kahneman, D. (2013). *Thinking fast and slow.* Farrar, Straus & Giroux.

Kershner, J. (2005). *The elements of news writing.* Pearson Allyn and Bacon.

Klaas, B. (2022, July). America's self-obsession is killing its democracy. *The Atlantic.* https://www.theatlantic.com/ideas/archive/2022/07/american-democracy-breakdown-authoritarianism-rise/670580/

Kolbert, E. (2021, December 27). How politics got so polarized. *New Yorker.* https://www.newyorker.com/magazine/2022/01/03/how-politics-got-so-polarized

Konkel, L. (2015). Racial and ethnic disparities in research studies: The challenge of creating more diverse cohorts. *Environmental Health Perspectives, 123*(12), A297–A302. https://doi.org/10.1289/ehp.123-A297

Kovach, B., & Rosenstiel, T. (2007). *The elements of journalism: What newspeople should know and the public should expect* (1st ed.). Three Rivers Press.

Kress, G. R. (2003). *Literacy in the new media age.* Routledge.

Lakoff, G. (2008). *The political mind: A cognitive scientist's guide to your brain and its politics.* Viking Penguin.

Lanser, S. S. (1981). *The narrative act: Point of view in prose fiction.* Princeton University Press.

Lehman, D. (2019). 1/11/18 fake news. In D. Lehman (Ed.), *Playlist: Poems.* University of Pittsburgh Press.

Leonhardt, D. (2021, February 19). *Vaccine alarmism: And what else you need to know today.* https://www.nytimes.com/2021/02/19/briefing/ted-cruz-texas-water-iran-nuclear.html

Levitsky, S., & Ziblatt, D. (2018). *How democracies die.* Broadway Books.

Masters, E. L. (1915). *Spoon River anthology.* Macmillan.

Mayo Clinic Staff. (2022, February 26). *Teens and social media use: What's the impact?* https://www.mayoclinic.org/healthy-lifestyle/tween-and-teen-health/in-depth/teens-and-social-media-use/art-20474437

McGrew, S., Ortega, T., Breakstone, J., & Wineberg, S. (2017). The challenge that's bigger than fake news: Civic reasoning in a social media environment. *American Educator, 41*(3), 4–9, 39.

McManus, J. H. (1992). What kind of commodity is news? *Communication Research, 19*(6), 787–805. https://doi.org/10.1177/009365092019006007

Meet the Press. (2017, January 22). *Conway: Press Secretary gave "alternative facts."* https://www.nbcnews.com/meet-the-press/video/conway-press-secretary-gave-alternative-facts-860142147643

Meyer, J. H. F., & Land, R. (2003). Threshold concepts and troublesome knowledge: Linkages to ways of thinking and practising. In C. Rust (Ed.), *Improving student learning: Theory and practice ten years on* (pp. 412–424). OCSLD.

Milton, J. (1644). *Areopagitica.*

Mirra, N., Kelly, L. L., & Garcia, A. (2021). Beyond fake news: Culturally relevant media literacies for a fractured civic landscape. *Theory into Practice, 60*(4), 340–349. https://doi.org/10.1080/00405841.2021.1983316

Mitchell, A., Gottfried, J., Stocking, G., Walker, M., & Fedeli, S. (2019, June 5). *Many Americans say made-up news is a critical problem that needs to be fixed.* Pew Research Center. https://www.pewresearch.org/journalism/2019/06/05/many-americans-say-made-up-news-is-a-critical-problem-that-needs-to-be-fixed/

Mitchell, A., Jurkowitz, M., Oliphant, J. B., & Shearer, E. (2020, July 30). *Americans who mainly get their news on social media are less engaged, less knowledgeable.* Pew Research Center. https://www.pewresearch.org/journalism/2020/07/30/americans-who-mainly-get-their-news-on-social-media-are-less-engaged-less-knowledgeable/

Mueke, D. C. (1969). *The compass of irony.* Routledge.

National Public Radio. (2019, March 26). *What does "Born in the U.S.A" really mean?* NPR Music. https://www.npr.org/2019/03/26/706566556/bruce-springsteen-born-in-the-usa-american-anthem

Nguyễn, A. T., & Pendleton, M. (2020). Recognizing race in language: Why we capitalize "Black" and "White." *Center for the Study of Social Policy.* https://cssp.org/2020/03/recognizing-race-in-language-why-we-capitalize-black-and-white/

Nokes, J. D., & De La Paz, S. (2018). Writing and argumentation in history education. In S. A. Metzger & L. M. Harris (Eds.), *The Wiley international handbook of history teaching and learning* (pp. 551–578). Wiley Blackwell.

Nolevanko, J. (2022, June 8). Having impossible conversations. A teaching demonstration provided to the Boise state writing project's DBI squared: Democracy Building Instruction Institute.

Nyhan, B., & Reiflet, J. (2010, June). When corrections fail: The persistence of political misperceptions. *Political Behavior, 32*(2), 303–330.

Oliver, J., & Wood, T. (2014, October). Conspiracy theories and the paranoid style(s) of mass opinion. *American Journal of Political Science, 58*(4), 952–966.

Peck, T. C., Sockol, L. E., & Hancock, S. M. (2020). Mind the gap: The underrepresentation of female participants and authors in virtual reality research. *IEEE Transactions on Visualization and Computer Graphics, 26,* 1945–1954. https://doi.org/10.1109/TVCG.2020.2973498

Pennycook, G., & Rand, D. (2019, January 19). Why do people fall for fake news? *New York Times.* https://www.nytimes.com/2019/01/19/opinion/sunday/fake-news.html

Perkins, D., & Salomon, G. (1988). Teaching for transfer. *Educational Leadership, 46*(1), 22–32.

Perkins, D., & Salomon, G. (2012). Knowledge to go: A motivational and dispositional view of transfer. *Educational Psychologist, 47*(3), 248–258.

Perry, W. G., Jr. (1970). *Forms of intellectual and ethical development in the college years: A scheme.* Holt, Rinehart and Winston.

Rabinowitz, P. J. (1987). *Before reading: Narrative conventions and the politics of interpretation.* Cornell University Press.

Rabinowitz, P. J., & Smith, M. (1997). *Authorizing readers: Resistance and respect in the teaching of literature.* Teachers College Press.

Rainie, L., & Anderson, J. (2017, February 8). *Theme 5: Algorithmic categorizations deepen divides.* Pew Research Center, Internet, Science & Tech. https://www.pewresearch.org/internet/2017/02/08/theme-5-algorithmic-categorizations-deepen-divides

Rauch, J. (2021). *The constitution of knowledge.* The Brookings Institute.

Reed, P. (2020). Anxiety and social media use. *Psychology Today Online.* https://www.psychologytoday

.com/us/blog/digital-world-real-world/202002/anxiety-and-social-media-use

Reynolds, D. (n.d.). What is the message of "The Road Not Taken"? *eNotes.* https://www.enotes.com/homework-help/what-is-the-message-of-the-road-not-taken-340951

Reynolds, J. (2019). *Look both ways: A tale told in ten blocks.* Simon & Schuster.

Robb, M., & Wronski, L. (2019, August 13). *Majority of teens get news from social media and YouTube.* https://edsource.org/reports/majority-of-teens-get-news-from-social-media-and-youtube

Robb, M. B. (2017). *News and America's kids: How young people perceive and are impacted by the news.* Common Sense.

Rosenblatt, L. M. (1938). *Literature as exploration.* Modern.

Rosenblatt, L. M. (1978). *The reader, the text, the poem: The transactional theory of the literary work.* Southern Illinois University Press.

Rosling, H. (2018). *Factfulness: Ten reasons we're wrong about the world—and why things are better than you think.* Flatiron Books.

Rouan, R. (2020). Fact check: Ohio doctor who joked about shots didn't die from COVID-19 vaccine. *USA Today.* https://www.usatoday.com/story/news/factcheck/2021/05/20/fact-check-ohio-doctor-I-die-covid-19-vaccine/5167752001/

Rukeyser, M. (1968, February). *Poetry and the unverifiable fact: The Clark lectures.* Tuesday, February 13, 1968 [and] Thursday, February 15, 1968.

Scholes, R. (2001). *The crafty reader.* Yale University Press.

Shoemaker, P., & Reese, S. (2013). *Mediating the message in the 21st century: A media sociology perspective* (3rd ed.). Routledge.

Siegel, D. (2022). *Mindsight.* https://drdansiegel.com/mindsight/

Sims Bishop, R. (1990). Mirrors, windows, and sliding glass doors. *Perspectives, 1*(3), ix–xi.

Sinatra, G. M., & Lombardi, D. (2020). Evaluating sources of scientific evidence and claims in the post-truth era may require reappraising plausibility judgments. *Educational Psychologist, 55*(3), 120–131.

Smith, M. W. (1992). The effects of direct instruction in understanding unreliable narrators. *Journal of Educational Research, 85,* 339–347.

Smith, M. W., & Imbrenda, J. (2018). *Developing writers of argument: Tools & rules that sharpen students' reasoning.* Corwin.

Smith, M. W., & Wilhelm, J. (2006). *Going with the flow: How to engage boys (and girls) in their literacy learning.* Heinemann.

Smith, M. W., & Wilhelm, J. D. (2010). *Fresh takes on teaching literary elements: How to teach what really matters about character, setting, point of view, and theme.* Scholastic.

Smith, M. W., Wilhelm, J. D., & Fredrickson, J. (2012). *Oh, yeah?!: Putting argument to work both in school and out.* Heinemann.

Snow, C. (2002). *Reading for understanding: Toward an R&D program in reading comprehension.* RAND.

Snyder, T. (2017). *On tyranny.* Tim Duggan Books.

Style, E. (1988). *Curriculum as a window and mirror.* The National Seed Project. https://www.national-seedproject.org/Key-SEED-Texts/curriculum-as-window-and-mirror

Taylor-Jackson, J., & Moustafa, A. A. (2021). The relationships between social media use and factors relating to depression. *The Nature of Depression,* 171–182. https://doi.org/10.1016/B978-0-12-817676-4.00010-9

Thomas, A. (2017). *The hate u give.* HarperCollins.

Thomson, J. (1993). Helping students control texts: Contemporary literary theory into classroom practice. In S. Straw & D. Bogdan (Eds.), *Constructive reading: Teaching beyond communication* (pp. 130–154). Boynton/Cook.

Toulmin, S. (1958). *The uses of argument.* Cambridge University Press.

Tufecki, Z. (2018). YouTube, the great radicalizer. *The New York Times.* https://www.nytimes.com/2018/03/10/opinion/sunday/youtube-politics-radical.html

Turner, K. H., & Hicks, T. (2015). *Connected reading: Teaching adolescent readers in a digital world.* National Council of Teachers of English.

Turner, K. H., & Hicks, T. (2017). *Argument in the real world.* Heinemann.

Walton, D., & Koszowy, M. (2014). Two kinds of arguments from authority in the *ad verecundiam* fallacy. https://scholar.uwindsor.ca/crrarpub/17

Wardle, C. (2017, February 16). Fake news. It's complicated. *firstdraftnews.org.* https://firstdraftnews.org/articles/fake-news-complicated/

Weigel, B. (2016). Someone revived the Baltimore Gazette to spread fake news. *Baltimoresun.com.* https://www.baltimoresun.com/citypaper/bcpnews-someone-revived-the-baltimore-gazette-to-spread-fake-bullshit-20160923-story.html

Whitson, J. A., & Galinsky, A. D. (2008, October). Lacking control increases illusory pattern perception. *Science, 322*(5898), 115–117.

Wilhelm, J. D. (2013a). *Deepening comprehension with action strategies* (2nd ed.). Scholastic.

Wilhelm, J. D. (2013b). *Improving comprehension with think alouds* (2nd ed.). Scholastic.

Wilhelm, J. D., Bear, R., & Fachler, A. (2020). *Planning powerful instruction: 7 steps to transform how we teach—and how students learn. A practical guide to using the EMPOWER framework to help you engage every learner, grades 6–12.* Corwin.

Wilhelm, J. D., Miller, J., & Butts, C. (2020). *Planning powerful instruction: 7 steps to transform how we teach—and how students learn. A practical guide to using the EMPOWER framework to help you engage every learner, grades 2--5.* Corwin.

Wilhelm, J. D., & Smith, M. W. (2016). *Diving deep into nonfiction: Transferable tools for reading ANY nonfiction text.* Corwin.

Wineburg, S., McGrew, S., Breakstone, J., & Ortega, T. (2016). *Evaluating information: The cornerstone of civic online reasoning.* Stanford Digital Repository. https://purl.stanford.edu/fv751yt5934

Wood, T., & Porter, E. (2019, March). The elusive backfire effect: Mass attitudes' steadfast factual adherence. *Political Behavior, 41,* 135–163. https://doi.org/10.1007/s11109-018-9443-y

Zeichner, K. M., & Tabachnick, B. R. (1981). Are the effects of university teacher education "washed out" by school experience? *Journal of Teacher Education, 32*(3), 7–11.

Zeitchik, S. (2022, August, 30). Ready or not, mass video deepfakes are coming. *The Washington Post.* https://www.washingtonpost.com/technology/2022/08/30/deep-fake-video-on-agt/

Zhang, S., & Duke, N. K. (2008). Strategies for internet reading with different reading purposes: A descriptive study of twelve good internet readers. *Journal of Literacy Research, 40*(1), 128–162.

Index

Other Titles to Consider

Diving Deep Into Nonfiction, Grades 6–12
ISBN: 9781483386058

Planning Powerful Instruction, Grades 2–5
ISBN: 9781544342818

Planning Powerful Instruction, Grades 6–12
ISBN: 9781544342863

CORWIN

A SAGE Publishing Company

CORWIN HAS ONE MISSION: to enhance education through intentional professional learning.

We build long-term relationships with our authors, educators, clients, and associations who partner with us to develop and continuously improve the best evidence-based practices that establish and support lifelong learning.